EVERYMAN HIS OWN HISTORIAN

Carl L. Becker was born in Blackhawk County, Iowa, and studied at Cornell College (Iowa) and the University of Wisconsin. His many books included *Eve of the Revolution, The Declaration of Independence,* and *The Heavenly City of the Eighteenth Century Philosophers.* He taught for many years at Cornell University, Ithaca, before his death in 1945.

EVERYMAN HIS OWN HISTORIAN

Essays on History and Politics

By CARL L. BECKER

QUADRANGLE PAPERBACKS
Quadrangle Books / Chicago

DEDICATED with gratitude and affection
to the young people, some not so young now,
who have assisted the author in clarifying
his ideas: partly by listening with
unfailing amiability to his expoundings,
chiefly by avoiding the error of HWAY, a
pupil of CONFUCIUS: *Hway*, said CONFUCIUS,
*is of no assistance to me; there is nothing
that I say in which he does not delight.*

Preface

ALL of the essays in this volume, except the one on the Marxian philosophy, have been previously published. However well they may have served the immediate purpose for which they were written, it did not seem to me that there was any adequate reason for resurrecting them from the periodicals and other resting places in which they were so decently interred. Some of my former pupils were of a different opinion. Always too generous in their estimate of my writings, and convinced that many people would be glad to have the best of my casual essays and reviews conveniently at hand in a single volume, they offered to make the necessary arrangements for publication. To this I consented. My share in the enterprise has been confined to selecting the essays to be included and preparing them for the press. None but verbal changes have been made in any of the essays, except those entitled "Labelling the Historians" and "Freedom of Speech": these, for purposes of clarification, have been somewhat expanded. I take this opportunity to say (for the benefit of any too literally-minded readers) that the "manuscript" mentioned in "The Spirit of '76" is, except for one or two quotations, pure fiction.

The essays reprinted and the journals or books in which they first appeared are here given for purposes of acknowledgment: "Kansas" in *Essays in American History*, "Frederick Jackson Turner" in *Masters of the Social Sciences*,

Henry Holt and Company; "Lord Bryce and Modern Democracies" in *The Political Science Quarterly;* "The Spirit of '76" in *The Spirit of '76 and Other Essays*, The Brookings Institute; "The Modern Leviathan," "Liberalism—A Way Station," "Henry Adams Once More" in *The Saturday Review of Literature;* "Freedom of Speech" in *The Nation;* "Labelling the Historians," "Juliet Drouet and Victor Hugo" in *The Dial;* "The Education of Henry Adams," "Mr. Wells and the New History," "Everyman His Own Historian," "The Memoirs and The Letters of Madame Roland" in *The American Historical Review;* "The Dilemma of Diderot" in *The Philosophical Review;* "John Jay and Peter Van Schaack" in *The Quarterly Journal of the New York State Historical Association*.

To the editors and publishers who have kindly consented to the reprinting of the essays, and to Mr. F. S. Crofts who has been willing to undertake the venture, I wish to express my appreciation, and the appreciation of those former pupils who are so largely responsible for the appearance of the present volume.

Carl L. Becker

CONTENTS

I
LIBERTY AND EQUALITY

II
HISTORY AND HISTORIANS

III
INTERPRETATIONS

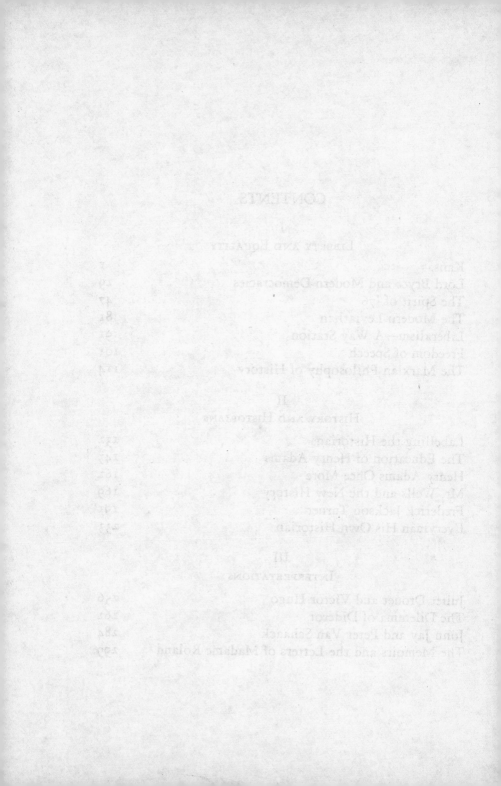

CONTENTS

I

LIBERTY AND EQUALITY

II

HISTORY AND HISTORIANS

III

INTERPRETATIONS

Kansas

SOME years ago, in a New England college town, when
I informed one of my New England friends that I was
preparing to go to Kansas, he replied rather blankly,
"Kansas?! Oh." The amenities of casual intercourse demanded a reply, certainly, but from the point of view of my
New England friend I suppose there was really nothing more
to say; and, in fact, standing there under the peaceful New
England elms, Kansas did seem tolerably remote. Some
months later I rode out of Kansas City and entered for the
first time what I had always pictured as the land of grass-
hoppers, of arid drought, and barren social experimentation.
In the seat just ahead were two young women, girls rather,
whom I afterwards saw at the university. As we left the
dreary yards behind, and entered the half-open country
along the Kansas River, one of the pair, breaking abruptly
away from the ceaseless chatter that had hitherto engrossed
them both, began looking out of the car window. Her attention seemed fixed, for perhaps a quarter of an hour, upon
something in the scene outside—the fields of corn, or it may
have been the sunflowers that lined the track; but at last,
turning to her companion with the contented sigh of a returning exile, she said, *"Dear old Kansas!"* The expression
somehow recalled my New England friend. I wondered
vaguely, as I was sure he would have done, why any one
should feel moved to say "Dear old Kansas!" I had supposed

that Kansas, even more than Italy, was only a geographical expression. But not so. Not infrequently, since then, I have heard the same expression—not always from emotional young girls. To understand why people say "Dear old Kansas!" is to understand that Kansas is no mere geographical expression, but a "state of mind," a religion, and a philosophy in one.

The difference between the expression of my staid New England friend and that of the enthusiastic young Kansan, is perhaps symbolical, in certain respects, of the difference between those who remain at home and those who, in successive generations, venture into the unknown "West,"— New England or Kansas,—wherever it may be. In the seventeenth century there was doubtless no lack of Englishmen—prelates for example, in lawn sleeves, comfortably buttressed about by tithes and the Thirty-nine Articles— who might have indicated their point of view quite fully by remarking, "New England?! Oh." Whether any New Englander of that day ever went so far as to say "Dear old New England," I do not know. But that the sentiment was there, furnishing fuel for the inner light, is past question. Now-a-days the superiority of New England is taken for granted, I believe, by the people who live there; but in the seventeenth century, when its inhabitants were mere frontiersmen, they were given, much as Kansans are said to be now, to boasting,—alas! even of the climate. In 1629, Mr. Higginson, a reverend gentleman, informed his friends back in England that "The temper of the aire of New England is one special thing that commends this place. Experience doth manifest that there is hardly a more healthfull place to be found in the world that agreeth better with our English bodyes. Many that have been weake and sickly in old England, by coming hither have been thoroughly healed

and growne healthfull strong. For here is a most extra-
ordinarie cleere and dry aire that is of a most healing nature
to all such as are of a cold, melancholy, flegmatick, rheu-
matick temper of body. . . . And therefore I think it a wise
course for all cold complections to come to take physic in
New England; for a sup of New England aire is better than
a whole draft of Old England's ale." Now, we who live in
Kansas know well that its climate is superior to any other
in the world, and that it enables one, more readily than any
other, to dispense with the use of ale.

There are those who will tell us, and have indeed often
told us, with a formidable array of statistics, that Kansas
is inhabited only in small part by New Englanders, and
that it is therefore fanciful in the extreme to think of it as
representing Puritanism transplanted. It is true, the people
of Kansas came mainly from "the Middle West"—from
Illinois, Indiana, Ohio, Iowa, Kentucky, and Missouri. But
for our purpose the fact is of little importance, for it is the
ideals of a people rather than the geography they have out-
grown that determine their destiny; and in Kansas, as has
been well said, "it is the ideas of the Pilgrims, not their
descendants, that have had dominion in the young commonwealth." Ideas, sometimes, as well as the star of empire, move westward, and so it happens that Kansas is more
Puritan than New England of to-day. It is akin to New
England of early days. It is what New England, old England itself, once was—the frontier, an ever changing spot
where dwell the courageous who defy fate and conquer
circumstance.

For the frontier is more than a matter of location, and
Puritanism is itself a kind of frontier. There is an intellectual "West" as well as a territorial "West". Both are
heresies, the one as much subject to the scorn of the judi-

cious as the other. Broad classifications of people are easily
made and are usually inaccurate; but they are convenient
for taking a large view, and it may be worth while to
think, for the moment, of two kinds of people—those who
like the sheltered life, and those who cannot endure it,
those who think the world as they know it is well enough,
and those who dream of something better, or, at any rate,
something different. From age to age society builds its
shelters of various sorts—accumulated traditions, religious
creeds, political institutions, and intellectual conceptions,
cultivated and well-kept farms, well-built and orderly cities
—providing a monotonous and comfortable life that tends
always to harden into conventional forms resisting change.
With all this the home-keeping and timid are well content.
They sit in accustomed corners, disturbed by no fortuitous
circumstance. But there are those others who are forever
tugging at the leashes of ordered life, eager to venture into
the unknown. Forsaking beaten paths, they plunge into the
wilderness. They must be always on the frontier of human
endeavor, submitting what is old and accepted to conditions
that are new and untried. The frontier is thus the seed plot
where new forms of life, whether of institutions or types of
thought, are germinated, the condition of all progress being
in a sense a return to the primitive.

Now, generally speaking, the men who make the world's
frontiers, whether in religion or politics, science, or geographical exploration and territorial settlement, have certain essential and distinguishing qualities. They are
primarily men of faith. Having faith in themselves, they
are individualists. They are idealists because they have
faith in the universe, being confident that somehow everything is right at the center of things; they give hostage to
the future, are ever inventing God anew, and must be al-

ways transforming the world into their ideal of it. They have faith in humanity and in the perfectibility of man, are likely, therefore, to be believers in equality, reformers, intolerant, aiming always to level others up to their own high vantage. These qualities are not only Puritan, they are American; and Kansas is not only Puritanism transplanted, but Americanism transplanted. In the individualism, the idealism, the belief in equality that prevail in Kansas, we shall therefore see nothing strangely new, but simply a new graft of familiar American traits. But as Kansas is a community with a peculiar and distinctive experience, there is something peculiar and distinctive about the individualism, the idealism, and the belief in equality of its people. If we can get at this something peculiar and distinctive, it will be possible to understand why the sight of sunflowers growing beside a railroad track may call forth the fervid expression, "Dear old Kansas."

I

Individualism is everywhere characteristic of the frontier, and in America, where the geographical frontier has hitherto played so predominant a part, a peculiarly marked type of individualism is one of the most obvious traits of the people. "To the frontier," Professor Turner has said, "the American intellect owes its striking characteristics. That coarseness and strength combined with acuteness and inquisitiveness; that practical, inventive turn of mind, quick to find expedients; that masterful grasp of material things, lacking in the artistic but powerful to effect great ends; that restless nervous energy; that dominant individualism, working for good and for evil, and withal that buoyancy and exuberance that comes from freedom." On the frontier, where everything is done by the individual and nothing by organized society, initiative, resourcefulness, quick, confident, and sure judgment are the essential qualities for success. But as the problems of the frontier are rather restricted and definite, those who succeed there have necessarily much the same kind of initiative and resourcefulness, and their judgment will be sure only in respect to the problems that are familiar to all. It thus happens that the type of individualism produced on the frontier and predominant in America, has this peculiarity, that while the sense of freedom is strong, there is nevertheless a certain uniformity in respect to ability, habit, and point of view. The frontier develops strong individuals, but it develops individuals of a particular type, all being after much the same pattern. The individualism of the frontier is one of achievement, not of eccentricity, an individualism of fact rising from a sense of power to overcome obstacles, rather than one of theory growing out of weakness in the face of oppression. It is not because he fears governmental activity, but because he has so often had to dispense with it, that the American is an individualist. Altogether averse to hesitancy, doubt, speculative or introspective tendencies, the frontiersman is a man of faith: of faith, not so much in some external power, as in himself, in his luck, his destiny; faith in the possibility of achieving whatever is necessary or he desires. It is this marked self-reliance that gives to Americans their tremendous power of initiative; but the absence of deep-seated differences gives to them an equally tremendous power of concerted social action.

The confident individualism of those who achieve through endurance is a striking trait of the people of Kansas. There, indeed, the trait has in it an element of exaggeration, arising from the fact that whatever has been achieved in Kansas has been achieved under great difficulties. Kansans have been subjected, not only to the ordinary hardships of the frontier, but to a succession of reverses and disasters that could be survived only by those for whom defeat is worse than death, who cannot fail because they cannot surrender. To the border wars succeeded hot winds, droughts, grass-hoppers; and to the disasters of nature succeeded in turn the scourge of man, in the form of "mortgage fiends" and a con-tracting currency. Until 1895 the whole history of the state was a series of disasters, and always something new, ex-treme, bizarre, until the name Kansas became a byword, a synonym for the impossible and the ridiculous, inviting laughter, furnishing occasion for jest and hilarity. "In God we trusted, in Kansas we busted," became a favorite motto of emigrants, worn out with the struggle, returning to more hospitable climes; and for many years it expressed well enough the popular opinion of that fated land.

Yet there were some who never gave up. They stuck it out. They endured all that even Kansas could inflict. They kept the faith, and they are to be pardoned perhaps if they therefore feel that henceforth there is laid up for them a crown of glory. Those who remained in Kansas from 1875 to 1895 must have originally possessed staying qualities of no ordinary sort, qualities which the experience of those years could only accentuate. And as success has at last rewarded their efforts, there has come, too, a certain pride, an exuber-ance, a feeling of superiority that accompany a victory long delayed and hardly won. The result has been to give a peculiar flavor to the Kansas spirit of individualism. With Kansas history back of him, the true Kansan feels that noth-ing is *too much* for him. How shall he be afraid of any danger, or hesitate at any obstacle, having succeeded where failure was not only human, but almost honorable? Having con-quered Kansas, he knows well that there are no worse worlds to conquer. The Kansas spirit is therefore one that finds something exhilarating in the challenge of an extreme difficulty. "No one," says St. Augustine, "loves what he endures, though he may love to endure." With Kansans, it is particularly a point of pride to suffer easily the stings of fortune, and if they find no pleasure in the stings themselves, the ready endurance of them gives a consciousness of merit that is its own reward. Yet it is with no solemn martyr's air that the true Kansan endures the worst that can happen. His instinct is rather to pass it off as a minor annoyance, furnishing occasion for a pleasantry, for it is the mark of a Kansan to take a reverse as a joke rather than too seriously. Indeed, the endurance of extreme adversity has developed a keen appreciation for that type of humor, everywhere prevalent in the west, which consists in ignoring a difficulty, or transforming it into a difficulty of precisely the opposite kind. There is a tradition surviving from the grasshopper time that illustrates the point. It is said that in the midst of that overwhelming disaster, when the pests were six inches deep in the streets, the editor of a certain local paper fined his comment on the situation down to a single line, which appeared among the trivial happenings of the week: "A grasshopper was seen on the court-house steps this morning." This type of humor, appreciated anywhere west of the Alleghenies, is the type *par excellence* in Kansas. Perhaps it has rained for six weeks in the spring. The wheat is seemingly ruined; no corn has been planted. A farmer, who sees his profits for the year wiped out, looks at the murky sky, sniffs the damp air, and remarks seriously, "Well, it looks like rain. We may save that crop yet." "Yes," his neighbor replies with equal seriousness, "but it will have to come soon, or it won't do any good." When misfortunes beat down upon one in rapid succession, there comes a time when it is useless to strive against them, and in the end they engender a certain detached curiosity in the victim, who finds a mournful pleasure in observing with philosophical resignation the ultimate caprices of fate. Thus Kansans, "coiners of novel phrases to express their defiance of destiny," have employed humor itself as a refuge against misfortune. They have learned not only to endure adversity, but in a very literal sense to laugh at it as well.

I have already said that the type of individualism that is characteristic of America is one of achievement, not of eccentricity. The statement will bear repeating in this connection, for it is truer of Kansas than of most communities, notwithstanding there is a notion abroad that the state is peopled by freaks and eccentrics. It was once popularly supposed in Europe, and perhaps is so yet, that Americans are all eccentric. Now, Kansans are eccentric in the same sense that Americans are: they differ somewhat from other Americans, just as Americans are distinguishable from Europeans. But a fundamental characteristic of Kansas individualism is the tendency to conform; it is an individualism of conformity, not of revolt. Having learned to endure to the end, they have learned to conform, for endurance is itself a kind of conformity. It has not infrequently been the subject of wondering comment by foreigners that in America, where every one is supposed to do as he pleases, there should nevertheless be so little danger from violence and insurrection. Certainly one reason is that while the conditions of frontier life release the individual from many of the formal restraints of ordered society, they exact a most rigid adherence to lines of conduct inevitably fixed by the stern necessities of life in a primitive community. On the frontier men soon learn to conform to what is regarded as essential, for the penalty of resistance or neglect is extinction: there the law of survival works surely and swiftly. However eccentric frontiersmen may appear to the tenderfoot, among themselves there is little variation from type in any essential matter. In the new community, individualism means the ability of the individual to succeed, not by submitting to some external formal authority, still less by following the bent of an unschooled will, but by recognizing and voluntarily adapting himself to necessary conditions. Kansas, it is true, has produced its eccentrics, but there is a saying here that freaks are raised for export only. In one sense the saying is true enough, for what strikes one particularly is that, on the whole, native Kansans are all so much alike. It is a community of great solidarity, and to the native it is "the Easterner" who appears eccentric.

The conquest of the wilderness in Kansas has thus developed qualities of patience, of calm, stoical, good-humored endurance in the face of natural difficulties, of conformity to what is regarded as necessary. Yet the patience, the calmness, the disposition to conform is strictly confined to what is regarded as in the natural course. If the Kansan appears stolid, it is only on the surface that he is so. The peculiar conditions of origin and history have infused into the character of the people a certain romantic and sentimental element. Beneath the placid surface there is something fermenting which is best left alone—a latent energy which trivial events or a resounding phrase may unexpectedly release. In a recent commencement address, Mr. Henry King said that conditions in early Kansas were "*hair-triggered.*" Well, Kansans are themselves hair-triggered; slight pressure, if it be of the right sort, sets them off. "Every one is on the *qui vive*, alert, vigilant, like a sentinel at an outpost." This trait finds expression in the romantic devotion of the people to the state, in a certain alert sensitiveness to criticism from outside, above all in the contagious enthusiasm with which they will without warning espouse a cause, especially when symbolized by a striking phrase, and carry it to an issue. Insurgency is native in Kansas, and the political history of the state, like its climate, is replete with surprises that have made it "alternately the reproach and the marvel of mankind." But this apparent instability is only the natural complement of the extreme and confident individualism of the people: having succeeded in overcoming so many obstacles that were unavoidable, they do not doubt their ability to destroy quickly those that seem artificially constructed. It thus happens that while no people endure the reverses of nature with greater fortitude and good humor than the people of Kansas, misfortunes seemingly of man's making arouse in them a veritable passion of resistance; the mere suspicion of injustice, real or fancied exploitation by those who fare sumptuously, the pressure of laws not self-imposed touch something explosive in their nature that transforms a calm and practical people into excited revolutionists. Grasshoppers elicited only a witticism, but the "mortgage fiends" produced the Populist régime, a kind of religious crusade against the infidel Money Power. The same spirit was recently exhibited in the "Boss Busters" movement, which in one summer spread over the state like a prairie fire and overthrew an established machine supposed to be in control of the railroads. The "Higher Law" is still a force in Kansas. The spirit which refused to obey "bogus laws" is still easily stirred. A people which has endured the worst of nature's tyrannies, and cheerfully submits to tyrannies self-imposed, is in no mood to suffer hardships that seem remediable.

II

Idealism must always prevail on the frontier, for the frontier, whether geographical or intellectual, offers little hope to those who see things as they are. To venture into the wilderness, one must see it, not as it is, but as it will be. The frontier, being the possession of those only who see its future, is the promised land which cannot be entered save by those who have faith. America, having been such a promised land, is therefore inhabited by men of faith: idealism is ingrained in the character of its people. But as the frontier in America has hitherto been geographical and material, American idealism has necessarily a material basis, and Americans have often been mistakenly called materialists. True, they seem mainly interested in material things. Too often they represent values in terms of money: a man is "worth" so much money; a university is a great university, having the largest endowment of any; a fine building is a building that cost a million dollars, better still, ten millions. Value is extensive rather than intensive or intrinsic. America is the best country because it is the biggest, the wealthiest, the most powerful; its people are the best because they are the freest, the most energetic, the *most* educated. But to see a materialistic temper in all this is to mistake the form for the spirit. The American cares for material things because they represent the substance of things hoped for. He cares less for money than for making money: a fortune is valued, not because it represents ease, but because it represents struggle, achievement, progress. The first skyscraper in any town is nothing in itself, but much as an evidence of growth; it is a white stone on the road to the ultimate goal.

Idealism of this sort is an essential ingredient of the Kansas spirit. In few communities is the word progress more frequently used, or its meaning less frequently detached from a material basis. It symbolizes the *summmum bonum*, having become a kind of dogma. Mistakes are forgiven a man if he is progressive, but to be unprogressive is to be suspect; like Aristotle's non-political animal, the unprogressive is extra-human. This may explain why every Kansan wishes first of all to tell you that he comes from the town of X——, and then that it is the finest town in the state. He does not mean that it is strictly the finest town in the state, as will appear if you take the trouble to inquire a little about the country, its soil, its climate, its rainfall, and about the town itself. For it may chance that he is free to admit that it is hot there, that the soil is inclined to bake where there is no rain, that there is rarely any rain—all of which, however, is nothing to the point, because they are soon to have water by irrigation, which is, after all, much better than rainfall. And then he describes the town, which you have no difficulty in picturing vividly: a single street flanked by nondescript wooden shops; at one end a railroad station, at the other a post-office; side streets lined with frame houses, painted or not, as the case may be; a school house somewhere, and a church with a steeple. It is such a town, to all appearances, as you may see by the hundred anywhere in the west—a dreary place which, you think, the world would willingly let die. But your man is enthusiastic; he can talk of nothing but the town of X——. The secret of his enthusiasm you at last discover in the inevitable "but it will be a great country some day," and it dawns upon you that, after all, the man does not live in the dreary town of X——, but in the great country of *some day*. Such are Kansans. Like St. Augustine, they have their City of God, the idealized Kansas of some day: it is only necessary to have faith in order to possess it.

I cannot illustrate this aspect of Kansas idealism better than by quoting from Mrs. McCormick's little book of personal experience and observation. Having related the long years of struggle of a typical farmer, she imagines the Goddess of Justice revealing to him a picture of "the land as it shall be" when justice prevails.

John beheld a great plain four hundred miles long and two hundred miles wide—a great agricultural state covered with farmers tilling the soil and with here and there a city or village. On every farm stood a beautiful house handsomely painted outside and elegantly furnished inside, and equipped with all modern conveniences helpful to housekeeping. Brussels carpets covered the floors, upholstered furniture and pianos ornamented the parlors, and the cheerful dining-room had elegant table linen, cut glass, and silverware. Reservoirs carried the water into the houses in the country the same as in the cities. The farmers' wives and daughters, instead of working like slaves without proper utensils or house furnishings, now had everything necessary to lighten work and make home attractive. They had the summer-kitchen, the wash-house, houses for drying clothes, arbors, etc. The door-yards consisted of nicely fenced green lawns, wherein not a pig rooted nor mule browsed on the shrubbery nor hen wallowed in the flower-beds. Shade trees, hammocks, and rustic chairs were scattered about, and everything bespoke comfort. Great barns sheltered the stock. The farms were fenced and subdivided into fields of waving grain and pastures green.

This is what John is supposed to have seen on a summer's day when, at the close of a life of toil, he had just been sold up for debt. What John really saw had perhaps a less feminine coloring; but the picture represents the ideal, if not of an actual Kansas farmer, at least of an actual Kansas woman.

This aspect of American idealism is, however, not peculiar to Kansas: it is more or less characteristic of all western communities. But there is an element in Kansas idealism that marks it off as a state apart. The origin of Kansas must ever be associated with the struggle against slavery. Of this fact, Kansans are well aware. Kansas is not a community of which it can be said, "happy is the people without annals." It is a state with a past. It has a history of which its people are proud, and which they insist, as a matter of course, upon having taught in the public schools. There are Old Families in Kansas who know their place and keep it—sacred bearers of the traditions of the Kansas Struggle. The Kansas Struggle is for Kansas what the American Revolution is for New England; and while there is as yet no "Society of the Daughters of the Kansas Struggle," there doubtless will be some day. For the Kansas Struggle is regarded as the crucial point in the achievement of human liberty, very much as Macaulay is said to have regarded the Reform Bill as the end for which all history was only a preparation. For all true Kansans, the border wars of the early years have a perennial interest: they mark the spot where Jones shot Smith, direct the attention of the traveler to the little village of Lecompton, or point with pride to some venerable tree bearing honorable scars dating from the Quantrill raid. Whether John Brown was as assassin or a martyr is a question which only a native can safely venture to answer with confidence. Recently, in a list of questions prepared for the examination of teachers in the schools, there appeared the following: "*What was the Andover Band?*" It seems that very few teachers knew what the Andover Band was; some thought it was an iron band, and some a band of Indians. The newspapers took it up, and it was found that, aside from some of the old families, ignorance of the Andover Band was quite general. When it transpired that the Andover Band had to do with the Kansas Struggle, the humiliation of the people was profound.

The belief that Kansas was founded for a cause distinguishes it, in the eyes of its inhabitants, as pre-eminently the home of freedom. It lifts the history of the state out of the commonplace of ordinary westward migration, and gives to the temper of the people a certain elevated and martial quality. The people of Iowa or Nebraska are well enough, but their history has never brought them in touch with cosmic processes. The Pilgrims themselves are felt to have been actuated by less noble and altruistic motives. The Pilgrims, says Thayer, "fled from oppression, and sought in the new world 'freedom to worship God.' " But the Kansas emigrants migrated "to meet, to resist, and to destroy oppression, in vindication of their principles. These were self-sacrificing emigrants, the others were self-seeking. Justice, though tardy in its work, will yet load with the highest honors, the memory of the Kansas pioneers who gave themselves and all they had to the sacred cause of human rights."

This may smack of prejudice, but it is no heresy in Kansas. The trained and disinterested physiocratic historian will tell us that such statements are unsupported by the documents. The documents show, he will say, that the Kansas emigrants, like other emigrants, came for cheap land and in the hope of bettering their condition; the real motive was economic, as all historic motives are; the Kansas emigrant may have thought he was going to Kansas to resist oppression, but in reality he went to take up a farm. At least, that many emigrants thought they came to resist oppression is indisputable. Their descendants still think so. And, after all, perhaps it is important to distinguish those who seek better farms and know they seek nothing else, from those who seek better farms and imagine they are fighting a holy war. When the people of Newtown wished

to remove to Connecticut we are told that they advanced
three reasons: first, "their want of accommodation for
their cattle;" second, "the fruitfulness and commodious-
ness of Connecticut;" and finally, "*the strong bent of their
spirits to remove thither.*" In explaining human history perhaps something should be conceded to "the strong bent
their spirits." Unquestionably cattle must be accommo-
dated, but a belief, even if founded on error, is a fact that
may sometimes change the current of history. At all events,
the people of Kansas believe that their ancestors were engaged in a struggle for noble ends, and the belief, whether
true or false, has left its impress upon their character. In
Kansas the idealism of the geographical frontier has been
strongly flavored with the notion that liberty is something
more than a by-product of economic processes.

If Kansas idealism is colored by the humanitarian liberalism of the first half of the last century, it has nevertheless
been but slightly influenced by the vague, emotional, Jean
Paul romanticism of that time. Of all despondent and
mystic elements, the Kansas spirit is singularly free. There
are few Byrons in Kansas, and no Don Juans. There is
plenty of light there, but little of the "light that never was
on land or sea." Kansas idealism is not a force that expends
itself in academic contemplation of the unattainable. It is
an idealism that is immensely concrete and practical, requir-
ing always some definite object upon which to expend itself,
but once having such an object expending itself with a
restless, nervous energy that is appalling: whatever the
object, it is pursued with the enthusiasm, the profound conviction given only to those who have communed with the
Absolute. It would seem that preoccupation with the concrete and the practical should develop a keen appreciation
of relative values; but in new countries problems of material

transformation are so insistent that immediate means
acquire the value of ultimate ends. Kansas is a new state,
and its inhabitants are so preoccupied with the present, so
resolutely detached from the experience of the centuries,
that they can compare themselves of to-day only with
themselves of yesterday. The idea embodied in the phrase,
"Weltgeschichte ist das Weltgericht," has slight significance
in a community in which twenty years of rapid material
improvement has engendered an unquestioning faith in
indefinite progress towards perfectibility. In such a community, past and future appear foreshortened, and the latest
new mechanical device brings us an appreciable step nearer
the millennium, which seems always to be just over the
next hill. By some odd mental alchemy it thus happens that
the concrete and the practical have taken on the dignity
of the absolute, and the pursuit of a convenience assumes
the character of a crusade. Whether it be religion or paving,
education or the disposal of garbage that occupies for the
moment the focus of attention, the same stirring activity,
the same zeal and emotional glow are enlisted: all alike
are legitimate objects of conquest, to be measured in terms
of their visual and transferable assets, and won by concerted and organized attack. I recall reading in a local
Kansas newspaper some time ago a brief comment on the
neighboring village of X—— (in which was located a small
college mistakenly called a university), which ran somewhat as follows: "The University of X—— has established
a music festival on the same plan as the one at the State
University, and with most gratifying results. The first
festival was altogether a success. X—— is a fine town, one
of the best in the state. It has a fine university, and a fine
class of people, who have made it a center of culture. X——
lacks only one thing; it has no sewers." Perhaps there are

people who would find the juxtaposition of culture and sewers somewhat bizarre. But to us in Kansas it does not seem so. Culture and sewers are admittedly good things to possess. Well, then, let us pursue them actively and with absolute conviction. Thus may an idealized sewer become an object worthy to stir the moral depths of any right-minded community.

An insistent, practical idealism of this sort, always busily occupied with concrete problems, is likely to prefer ideas cast in formal mold, will be a little at a loss in the midst of flexible play of mind, and look with suspicion upon the emancipated, the critical, and the speculative spirit. It is too sure of itself to be at home with ideas of uncertain pressure. Knowing that it is right, it wishes only to go ahead. Satisfied with certain conventional premises, it hastens on to the obvious conclusion. It thus happens that Americans, for the most part, are complaisantly satisfied with a purely formal interpretation of those resounding words that symbolize for them the ideas upon which their institutions are supposed to rest. In this respect Kansas is truly American. Nowhere is there more loyal devotion to such words as liberty, democracy, equality, education. But preoccupation with the concrete fixes the attention upon the word itself, and upon what is traditionally associated with it. Democracy, for example, is traditionally associated with elections, and many of them. Should you maintain that democracy is not necessarily bound up with any particular institution, that it is in the way of being smothered by the complicated blanket ballot, you will not be understood, or, rather, you will be understood only too well as advocating something aristocratic. Democracy is somehow bound up with a concrete thing, and the move for the shorter ballot is therefore undemocratic and un-American.

Or, take the word socialism. Your avowed socialist is received politely, and allowed to depart silently and without regret. But if you tell us of the movement for the governmental control of corporate wealth, we grow enthusiastic. The word socialism has a bad odor in Kansas, but the thing itself, by some other name, smells sweet enough.

If one is interested in getting the essential features of socialism adopted in Kansas, or in America itself, the name to conjure with is indeed not socialism, but equality.

III

In a country like America, where there is such confident faith in the individual, one might naturally expect to find the completest toleration, and no disposition to use the government for the purpose of enforcing uniform conditions: logically, it would seem, so much emphasis on liberty should be incompatible with much emphasis on equality. Yet it is precisely in America, and nowhere in America more than in the west, that liberty and equality always go coupled and inseparable in popular speech; where the sense of liberty is especially strong, there also the devotion to equality is a cardinal doctrine. Throughout our history, the west has been a dominant factor in urging the extension of the powers of the national government, and western states have taken the lead in radical legislation of an equalizing character. This apparent inconsistency strikes one as especially pronounced in Kansas. The doctrine of equality is unquestioned there, and that governments exist for the purpose of securing it is the common belief. "A law against it" is the specific for every malady. The welfare of society is thought to be always superior to that of the individual, and yet no one doubts that perfect liberty is the birthright of every man.

Perhaps the truth is that real toleration is a sentiment foreign to the American temper. Toleration is for the skeptical, being the product of much thought or of great indifference, sometimes, to be sure, a mere *modus vivendi* forced upon a heterogeneous society. In America we imagine ourselves liberal-minded because we tolerate what we have ceased to regard as important. We tolerate religions but not irreligion, and diverse political opinion, but not unpolitical opinion, customs, but not the negation of custom. The Puritans fought for toleration—for themselves. But having won it for themselves, straightway denied it to others. No small part of American history has been a repetition of the Puritan struggle; it has been a fight, not for toleration as a general principle, but for recognition of a civilization resting upon particular principles: in exterior relations, a struggle for recognition of America by Europe; in interior relations, a struggle for recognition of "the West" by "the East." The principle of toleration is written in our constitutions, but not in our minds, for the motive back of the famous guarantees of individual liberty has been recognition of particular opinion rather than toleration of every opinion. And in the nature of the case it must be so. Those who create frontiers and establish new civilizations have too much faith to be tolerant, and are too thoroughgoing idealists to be indifferent. On the frontier conditions are too hazardous for the speculative and the academic to flourish readily: only those who are right and are sure of it can succeed. Certainly it is characteristic of Americans to know that they are right. Certainly they are conscious of having a mission in the world and of having been faithful to it. They have solved great problems hitherto unsolved, have realized utopias dreamed of but never realized by Europe. They are therefore in the van of civilization, quite sure of the direction, triumphantly leading the march towards the ultimate goal. That every one should do as he likes is part of the American creed only in a very limited sense. That it is possible to know what is right, and that what is right should be recognized and adhered to is the more vital belief.

That liberty and equality are compatible terms is, at all events, an unquestioned faith in Kansas. The belief in equality, however, is not so much the belief that all men are equal as the conviction that it is the business of society to establish conditions that will make them so. And this notion, so far from being inconsistent with the pronounced individualism that prevails there, is the natural result of it. In Kansas at least, no one holds to the right of the individual to do as he likes, irrespective of what it is that he likes. Faith in the individual is faith in the particular individual, the true Kansan, who has learned through adversity voluntarily to conform to what is necessary. Human nature, or, at all events, Kansas nature, is essentially good, and if the environment is right all men can measure up to that high level. That the right environment can be created is not doubted. It is not possible for men so aggressive and self-reliant, who have overcome so many obstacles, to doubt their ability to accomplish this also. Having conquered nature, they cheerfully confront the task of transforming human nature. It is precisely because Kansans are such thoroughgoing individualists, so resourceful, so profoundly confident in their own judgments, so emancipated from the past, so accustomed to devising expedients for every new difficulty, that they are unimpressed by the record of the world's failures. They have always thrived on the impossible, and the field of many failures offers a challenge not to be resisted.

To effect these beneficent ends, the people of Kansas turn naturally to the government because they have a very simple and practical idea of what the government is and what it is for. The government, in Kansas, is no abstract concept. It is nothing German, nothing metaphysical. In this frontier community no one has yet thought of the government as a power not ourselves that makes for evil. Kansans think of the government, as they think of everything else, in terms of the concrete. And why, indeed, should they not? Within the memory of man there was no government in Kansas. They, Kansans, made the government themselves for their own purposes. The government is therefore simply certain men employed by themselves to do certain things; it is the sum of the energy, the good judgment, the resourcefulness of the individuals who originally created it, and who periodically renew it. The government is the individual writ large; in it every Kansan sees himself drawn to larger scale. The passion for controlling all things by law is thus not the turning of the hopeless and discouraged individual to some power other and higher than himself for protection; it is only the instinct to use effectively one of the many resources always at his command for achieving desired ends. Of a government hostile to the individual, they cannot conceive; such a government is a bogus government, and its laws are bogus laws; to resist and overthrow such a government, all the initiative and resourcefulness is enlisted that is devoted to supporting one regarded as legitimate. There is a higher law than the statute book; the law of the state is no law if it does not represent the will of the individual.

To identify the will of the individual with the will of society in this easy fashion presupposes a certain solidarity in the community: an identity of race, custom, habits, needs; a consensus of opinion in respect to morals and politics. Kansas is such a community. Its people are principally American born, descended from settlers who came mainly from the middle west. It is an agricultural state, and the conditions of life are, or have been until recently, much the same for all. "Within these pastoral boundaries," says ex-Senator Ingalls, in his best Kansas manner, "there are no millionaires nor any paupers, except such as have been deprived by age, disease, and calamity of the ability to labor. No great fortunes have been brought to the state and none have been accumulated by commerce, manufacture or speculation. No sumptuous mansions nor glittering equipages nor ostentatious display exasperates or allures." And the feeling of solidarity resulting from identity of race and uniformity of custom has been accentuated by the peculiar history of the state. Kansans love each other for the dangers they have passed; a unique experience has created a strong *esprit de corps*—a feeling that while Kansans are different from others, one Kansan is not only as good as any other, but very like any other. The philosophy of numbers, the doctrine of the majority, is therefore ingrained, and little sympathy is wasted on minorities. Rousseau's notion that minorities are only mistaken finds ready acceptance, and the will of the individual is easily identified with the will of society.

And in a sense the doctrine is true enough, for there is little difference of opinion on fundamental questions. In religion there are many creeds and many churches, but the difference between them is regarded as unimportant. There is, however, a quite absolute dogmatism of morality. Baptism is for those who enjoy it, but the moral life is for all. And what constitutes the moral life is well understood: to be honest and pay your debts; to be friendly and

charitable, good-humored but not cynical, slow to take offense, but regarding life as profoundly serious; to respect
sentiments and harmless prejudices; to revere the conventional great ideas and traditions; to live a sober life and a
virtuous—to these they lay hold without questioning.
Likewise in politics. One may be democrat or republican,
stalwart or square-dealer, insurgent or stand-patter: it is
no vital matter. But no one dreams of denying democracy,
the will of the people, the greatest good to the greatest
number, equal justice and equal opportunity to all. Whether
in respect to politics or economics, education or morals,
the consensus of opinion is very nearly perfect: it is an
opinion that unites in the deification of the average, that
centers in the dogmatism of the general level.

It goes without saying that the general level in Kansas is
thought to be exceptionally high. Kansans do not regard
themselves as mere westerners, like Iowans or Nebraskans.
Having passed through a superior heat, they are westerners
seven times refined. "It is the quality of piety in Kansas,"
says Mr. E. H. Abbott, "to thank God that you are not as
other men are, beer-drinkers, shiftless, habitual lynchers,
or even as these Missourians." The pride is natural enough,
perhaps, in men whose judgment has been vindicated at
last in the face of general skepticism. Having for many
years contributed to the gaiety of nations, Kansas has
ceased to be the pariah of the states. Kansans have endured
Job's comforters too long not to feel a little complaisant
when their solemn predictions come to naught. "While
envious rivals were jeering, . . . pointing with scorn's slow
unmoving finger at the droughts, grasshoppers, hot winds,
crop failures, and other calamities of Kansas, the world
was suddenly startled and dazzled by her collective display
of . . . products at the Centennial at Philadelphia, which

received the highest awards." It is inevitable that those who think they have fashioned a cornerstone out of the stone rejected by the builders should regard themselves as superior workmen.

To test others by this high standard is an instinctive procedure. There is an alert attention to the quality of those who enter the state from outside. The crucial question is, are they "our kind of men?" Do they speak "the Kansas language?" Yet the Kansas language is less a form of speech or the expression of particular ideas, than a certain personal quality. Some time since a distinguished visitor from the east came to the state to deliver a public address. He was most hospitably received, as all visitors are, whether distinguished or otherwise, and his address—permeated with the idealistic liberalism of a half century ago—was attentively listened to and highly praised. But to no purpose all these fine ideas. The great man was found wanting, for there was discovered, among his other impedimenta, a valet. It was a fatal mischance. The poor valet was more commented upon than the address, more observed than his master. The circumstance stamped the misguided man as clearly not our kind of man. Obviously, no man who carries a valet can speak the Kansas language. Needless to say, there are no valets in Kansas.

The feeling of superiority, naturally attaching to a chosen people, equally inclines Kansans to dispense readily with the advice or experience of others. They feel that those who have worn the hair shirt cannot be instructed in asceticism by those who wear silk. In discussing the university and its problems with a member of the state legislature, I once hazarded some comparative statistics showing that a number of other states made rather more liberal appropriations for their universities than the state of Kansas did for hers. I thought the comparison might be enlightening, that the man's pride of state might be touched. Not at all. "I know all about that," he replied. "That argument is used by every man who is interested in larger appropriations for any of the state institutions. But it doesn't go with a Kansas legislature. In Kansas, we don't care much what other states are doing. Kansas always leads, but never follows." And, in fact, the disregard of precedent is almost an article of faith; that a thing has been done before is an indication that it is time to improve upon it. History may teach that men cannot be legislated into the kingdom of heaven. Kansans are not ignorant of the fact, but it is no concern of theirs. The experience of history is not for men with a mission and faith to perform it. Let the uncertain and the timid profit by history; those who have at all times the courage of their emotions will make history, not repeat it. Kansans set their own standards, and the state becomes, as it were, an experiment station in the field of social science.

The passion for equality in Kansas is thus the complement of the individualism and the idealism of its people. It has at the basis of it an altruistic motive, aiming not so much to level all men down as to level all men up. The Kansan's sense of individual worth enables him to believe that no one can be better than he is, while his confident idealism encourages him to hope that none need be worse.

IV

The Kansas spirit is the American spirit double distilled. It is a new grafted product of American individualism, American idealism, American intolerance. Kansas is America in microcosm: as America conceives itself in respect to Europe, so Kansas conceives itself in respect to America.

Within its borders, Americanism, pure and undefiled, has a new lease of life. It is the mission of this self-selected people to see to it that it does not perish from off the earth. The light on the altar, however neglected elsewhere, must ever be replenished in Kansas. If this is provincialism, it is the provincialism of faith rather than of the province. The devotion to the state is devotion to an ideal, not to a territory, and men can say "Dear old Kansas!" because the name symbolizes for them what the motto of the state so well expresses, *ad astra per aspera*.

1910.

Lord Bryce on Modern Democracies[1]

MANY years ago, at a time when schemes of political reform were being copiously discussed in England, mostly on general principles, but also with references, usually vague and disconnected, to history and to events happening in other countries, it occurred to me that something might be done to provide a solid basis for argument and judgment by examining a certain number of popular governments in their actual working, comparing them with one another, and setting forth the various merits and defects which belonged to each. As I could not find that any such comparative study had been undertaken, I formed the idea of attempting it, and besides visiting Switzerland and other parts of Europe, betook myself to the United States and Canada, to Spanish America and Australia and New Zealand, in search of materials, completing these journeys shortly before the war of 1914 broke out. The undertaking proved longer and more toilsome than had been expected; and frequent interruptions due to the War have delayed the publication of the book until now, when in some countries conditions are no longer what they were when I studied them eight or ten years ago. . . . (But) it is not current politics but democracy as a form of government that I seek to describe. Events that happened ten years ago may be for this particular purpose just as instructive as if they were happening to-day.

Such are the circumstances to which we owe the good fortune of possessing these two substantial volumes. It is a good fortune indeed! If Lord Bryce in his youth had resolved that in his old age he would write such a book as

[1] *Modern Democracies.* By VISCOUNT JAMES BRYCE. The Macmillan Company, 1921.—Two vols.: xv, 508; vi, 676 pp.

this one, he could scarcely have prepared himself for the
task better than he has in fact done. Familiar with the
ancient world as if the classics had been his daily compan-
ions, celebrated among German professors of history for
his brilliant interpretation of the Holy Roman Empire;
distinguished in his own country as a statesman; in the
United States honored as an ambassador, beloved as a
friend, appreciated as an expounder and critic of our institutions; traveler in many lands, associating with all sorts
and conditions of people, ceaselessly observing, insatiably
inquiring, storing up endless knowledge of facts from the
odor of intrigue in the Palais Bourbon to the exact elevation above sea-level of Lawrence, Kansas—who indeed
could give us a comparative study of modern democracies
"in their actual working" if not James Bryce, whose ripe
wisdom springs from a reflecting mind so fortified by contact with men and things, so richly stored with knowledge
of past and present events, so humanely liberalized by
familiar converse with the best that has been thought and
said in the world?

In dealing with words one cannot always be as masterful
as Humpty Dumpty, but democracy is one of the words
which can be made to mean, within reason, pretty much
what one wishes. The term democracy, says Lord Bryce,

has in recent years been loosely used to denote sometimes a state
of society, sometimes a state of mind, sometimes a quality in
manners. It has become encrusted with all sorts of associations
attractive or repulsive, ethical or poetical, or even religious. But
democracy really means nothing more or less than the rule of the
whole people expressing their sovereign will by their votes. (p. ix).

It might be questioned whether democracy "really means"
nothing more than this; but it is an author's privilege to
determine the limits of his subject, and Lord Bryce leaves

us in no doubt as to what democracy is to mean for the purposes of the present study.

In this book I use the word in its old and restricted sense, as denoting a government in which the will of the majority of qualified citizens rules, taking the qualified citizens to constitute the great bulk of the inhabitants, say, roughly, at least three-fourths, so that the physical force of the citizens coincides (broadly speaking) with the voting power. Using this test, we may apply the name to the United Kingdom and the British self-governing Dominions, to France, Italy, Portugal, Belgium, Holland, Denmark, Sweden, Norway, Greece, the United States, Argentina, and possibly Chile and Uruguay. (I, p. 22).

This definition excludes Germany, Austria-Hungary, and all of the Balkan states except Greece, as those states were before the war. "Of the newer European states it is too soon to speak, and whatever we may call the republics of Central America and the Carribbean Sea, they are not democracies."

Thus defined and limited, Lord Bryce has chosen to present his subject under three main divisions. Part I has to do with considerations applicable to democratic government in general, and serves as an introduction to Part II, which deals with certain actual modern democracies. In Part II "six countries have been selected for treatment: two old European States, France and Switzerland; two newer States in the Western hemisphere, the American Union and Canada; and two in the Southern hemisphere, Australia and New Zealand" (I, p. 7). Great Britain was deliberately omitted because no citizen of Great Britain "who has himself taken a part in politics as a member, during forty years, of legislatures and cabinets, can expect to be credited with impartiality" (*ibid.*). The danger of partial treatment involved in a description of the British government

by Lord Bryce we should have met with great equanimity;
but if the inclusion of Great Britain meant the omission
of Switzerland, we are not sorry to see Britain excluded,
since Switzerland best exhibits the characteristics of democ-
arcy in small states, just as the characteristics of democracy
on a grand scale are best exhibited in the United States.
Perhaps as it is the book is a little over-freighted with
English-speaking countries, but in general the selection is
wide and representative enough. Having dealt rather fully
with these six countries, the work closes with Part III—
twenty-three chapters of comment and criticism based upon
the foregoing study. As to the general character and merit
of the book, nothing more need be said than that it re-
sembles in both respects the *American Commonwealth*, doing
for modern democracies what the *American Commonwealth*
did for what Lord Bryce himself called the greatest of
modern democracies.

Toward the end of the eighteenth century, when the
spirit of reform was in the air, the best minds believed that
with Authority dethroned, Reason would reign instead.

Reason, accompanied and inspired by Justice, was expected to
usher in a better world, with the sister angel Fraternity following
in their train, because human nature itself would be renovated.
Inequality and repression had engendered one set of vices in rulers
and another in their subjects. . . . Under good government—and
in an age of reason little government would be needed—human
nature, no longer corrupted by examples of successful wickedness,
would return to the pristine virtues the Creator had meant to
implant. . . . These beliefs were the motive power which for a
time made faith in democracy almost a religion. (I, p. 46).

The bright glamor of this ideal has departed long since;
but many men still have faith in democracy as Lord Bryce
defines it, still treasure a vision of things as they might be.

Lord Bryce is evidently one of these; and this ideal democratic community he describes for us, "in terms of our own day."

In it the average citizen will give close and constant attention to public affairs, recognizing that this is his interest as well as his duty. He will try to comprehend the main issues of policy, bringing to them an independent and impartial mind, which thinks first not of his own but of the general interest. If, owing to inevitable difference of opinion as to what are the measures needed for the general welfare, parties become inevitable, he will join one, and will attend its meetings, but will repress the impulses of party spirit. Never failing to come to the polls, he will vote for his party candidate only if satisfied by his capacity and honesty. He will be ready to serve on a local Board or Council, and to be put forward as a candidate for the legislature (if satisfied of his own competence), because public service is recognized as a duty. With such citizens as electors, the legislature will be composed of upright and capable men, single-minded in their wish to serve the nation. Bribery in constituencies, corruption among public servants, will have disappeared. Leaders may not always be single-minded, nor assemblies always wise, nor administrators efficient, but all will at any rate be honest and zealous, so that an atmosphere of confidence and good will will prevail. Most of the causes that make for strife will be absent, for there will be no privileges, no advantages to excite jealousy. Office will be sought only because it gives opportunities for useful service. Power will be shared by all, and a career open to all alike. Even if the law does not—perhaps it cannot—prevent the accumulation of fortunes, these will be few and not inordinate, for public vigilance will close the illegitimate paths to wealth. All but the most depraved persons will obey and support the law, feeling it to be their own. There will be no excuse for violence, because the constitution will provide a remedy for every grievance. Equality will produce a sense of human solidarity, will refine manners, and increase brotherly kindness. (I, p. 48).

This is an admirable expression of that ideal of popular government which has won the allegiance of generous and disinterested minds for a century past; but in the light of democratic government as we know it, we feel that if Lord Bryce has designed to compose a masterpiece of irony he could not have done better. Such certainly was not his purpose. His purpose is just to make clear the sharp contrast between anticipation and realization. Without having lost faith in democracy, he is yet no sentimentalist looking at the world though colored glasses, but an imperturbable, clear-eyed realist who wishes to see everything in a white light and to describe it as it is. This he does without sparing us, or himself, anything; and the upshot of his two volumes is to demonstrate, by a wealth of concrete fact and penetrating comment, just how and why modern democracies, in their "actual working," fall so far short of what was expected of them and of what we wish they might be. In its unimpassioned but relentless exhibit of conditions as they exist, this book is more disillusioning than Lecky's two volumes of sustained denunciation; yet Lord Bryce, while giving us every reason for despairing, does not himself despair, but contrives, by virtue of some sane, robust, temperamental optimism, to gather encouragement, such as it is, for the future.

The more general reasons for the failure of democracy to measure up to the ideal of its first protagonists are not far to seek.

As a rule, that which the mass of any people desires is not to govern itself, but to be well governed. (II, p. 501.)

Popular government has been usually sought and won and valued *not as a good thing in itself, but as a means of getting rid of tangible grievances or securing tangible benefits*, and when those objects have been attained, the interest in it has generally tended to decline. (I, p. 41.)

It was easy to idealize democracy when the destruction of despotism and privilege was the first and necessary step to a better world. Nowadays any one can smile or sigh over the faith and hope that inspired the successive revolutions that convulsed the European Continent in and after 1789. Any one can point out that men *mistook the pernicious channels in which selfish propensities had been flowing for those propensities themselves, which were sure to find new channels when the old had been destroyed.* (I, p. 49.)

Any one can see that these things which have not been attained ought not to have been expected. No form of government, nothing less than a change in tendencies of human nature long known and recognized as permanent, could have accomplished what philosophies and religions and the spread of knowledge and progress in all the arts of life had failed to accomplish. (II, p. 534.)

All this is no doubt a counsel of disillusionment. If men never expected more than could be attained, they would probably never attain even the possible. But after the event it is easy to see that too much was expected of democracy. Now that we have popular government, it is easy to see that it is only one method of being indifferently governed, with some advantages and some disadvantages over other methods.

If one doubts this, one has only to read Lord Bryce's account of the actual working of government in the six countries which he has selected for special treatment. In every country the story is much the same. Everywhere we see the mass of the people indifferent to government except "as a means of getting rid of tangible grievances or securing tangible benefits;" everywhere we see human nature working for good or for ill much as it did under previous forms of government; everywhere we see the "new channels" which selfish propensities have found in place of the old ones which have been destroyed. Lord Bryce has an un-

erring eye for these new channels, and an unrivaled pen
for describing their devious ways. One wonders what the
optimists of 1792 would have thought could they have
foreseen this picture of the modern French Deputy.

The large majority . . . have begun their political career by
acquiring influence among their neighbours. They enter local
councils, and thus become known in the canton. . . . They serve
as *Maires* in their commune; they are active in local party work,
and alert in looking after local interests generally. An ambitious
doctor or lawyer may give gratuitous consultations or otherwise
ingratiate himself with a local clientèle. To belong to a Masonic
lodge, or even to an angling society or a gymnastic club—all these
things help. . . . One must not only cultivate an easy and genial
manner, but observe, at least in the provinces, a decent regularity
of life, avoiding, especially in the northern parts of France (for the
South is indulgent), whatever could shock the *âme rigide de la
province*. If one has money to spend on local purposes, so much the
better. (I, p. 249.)

Once in, the deputy's first care is to stay in. This must be
achieved . . . by a sedulous attention to the interests not merely
of the district but of the individual residents of the district,
especially of those to whom he owes his seat. Every kind of service
is expected of him. He must obtain decorations for his leading
supporters, and find a start in life for their sons and sons-in-law.
Minor posts under government and licences to sell tobacco have
to be secured for the rank and file. All sorts of commissions to be
performed in Paris are expected from him, down to the choice of a
wet nurse or the purchase of an umbrella. . . . He is the fountain
of honor, the dispenser of patronage, inspiring a lively sense of
favours to come. . . . If he is well off, his subscriptions to local
purposes help him; if poor, people feel it would be hard to turn
him out and send him to seek a new means of livelihood. Accordingly, provided he keeps on good terms with the local wire-
pullers, and is not involved in a scandal which would reach the
constituency, he is likely, at least in rural areas, to hold his seat,

and may in the fulness of time transfer himself to the calmer waters and longer term of the Senate. (I, pp. 250-251.)

What a picture! And yet how familiar it is! The American Congressman would have the intelligence to recognize its points. The umbrella and the wet nurse are perhaps a little out of his line, but the career in general is one for which he is eminently fitted. For the career of an American Congressman, as Lord Bryce sees it, is

also a career the entrance to which is in most places neither easy nor agreeable. Services are exacted, pledges are demanded, which a man of high spirit does not like to render or to give. The aspirant to a seat in Congress, unable to make his way alone with a constituency, must get the party nomination, which is generally obtainable only by the favour of a Boss. The path is sentinelled by the party machine, which values party loyalty more than ability, and usually selects in each district the man who either possesses local influence or his place by local party service. (II, p. 65.)

Little wonder, therefore, that Congress "does not receive the attention and enjoy the confidence which ought to belong to a central organ of national life."

It seldom "faces right up" to the great problems, not even always to the lesser problems of legislation. It fumbles with them, does not get to the root of the matter, seems to be moved rather by considerations of temporary expediency and the wish to catch every passing breeze of popular demand than by a settled purpose to meet the larger national needs. In the handling of national finance it is alternately narrow-minded in its parsimony and extravagant in its efforts to propitiate some class or locality. . . . Every year sees the distribution from what is called "the Pork Barrel" of grants of money to particular districts or cities for so-called "local public works"—it may be for making a harbour which is sure to be silted up, or improving the navigation of a stream where there is just enough water to float a canoe. These things bring money to the neighbourhood, and "make work," so a member earns merit with his constituency by procuring for them all he can. It is nobody's business to stop him; and others who wish to earn merit in a like way would resent the discourteous act. . . . Congress does not impress the nation by its intellectual power any more than by its moral dignity. Men who care for the welfare of the country as a whole—perhaps more numerous in the United States than in any other free country—do not look to it for guidance. The House scarcely ever enlightens them by its debates, and the Senate less now than formerly. Its proceedings, largely conducted in the dim recesses of committee rooms, do not greatly interest the educated classes, and still less the multitude. (II, p. 63.)

These are long passages, all bearing on a single point; yet in many ways they serve, as well as any selections could, to present the book. They reveal admirably, for example, the author's well-known and unexcelled power of penetrating through the external forms of government to the living forces that determine its "actual working." It might be objected that the actual working here laid bare exhibits democracy almost if not quite at its worst. But the elected legislative body is after all the most characteristic feature of democracy as Lord Bryce defines it; and if he finds the elected legislative body everywhere with little prestige or dignity, everywhere devoted to footless activities and platitudinous verbiage, everywhere exhaling a sordid atmosphere, why then the sordid note must be in some measure the typical note.

I do not mean that Lord Bryce finds nothing good to say about democracy. On the contrary, he finds many good things to say about it; but his enthusiasm is at best pitched low, and the prevailing impression which one gets from this masterly exhibit of modern governments is of something solid and substantial no doubt, yet without grace or beauty, something essentially humdrum and sordid, as men and women are humdrum and sordid. What Lord Bryce does for us essentially, and so effectively that seemingly it need never be done again, is to demonstrate that popular government is no more "ideal" than any other form of government, but just a human affair which responds indifferently to the virtues or the frailties of average human nature. Human nature has not changed under democracy; only the "channels" in which selfish propensities flow have changed. The modern courtier stands not in the antechamber holding the king's shirt, but he is quite ready to bend the compliant hinges of the knee to the dispenser of favors; he makes his obeisance to the great god Demos, and presents him with an umbrella or a wet nurse. Demos is not so particular about his shirts!

Lord Bryce is too wise not to see that this human institution, which came from the desire to get rid of tangible grievances and to attain tangible benefits, may disappear for the same reason.

Frenchmen, Englishmen, and Americans find it so natural a thing that men should be interested in politics, that they assume men will always be so interested. But is it really true—so students of history will ask—that this interest can be counted on to last? . . . Greek democracy had been destroyed by force . . . and little regret was expressed at its extinction. The last blows struck for republican freedom in Rome were struck not by the people, but by a knot of oligarchs. . . . No one thought of trying to revive free self-government in Italy or Greece or around the coasts of the Aegean, where hundreds of republics had bloomed and died. (II, p. 599.)

We can well imagine other conditions which might have a like effect. The thing did happen: and whatever has happened may

happen again. Peoples that had known and prized political freedom resigned it, did not much regret it, and forgot it. . . . Is it
possible that a nation, tired of politics and politicians, may be
glad to be saved the trouble of voting? (II, p. 601.)

One road only has in the past led into democracy, *viz.* the wish
to be rid of tangible evils, but the roads that have led or may lead
out of democracy are many. Some few of them may be mentioned.
(II, p. 602.)

Lord Bryce discusses with penetrating insight the various possibilities. (1) "If wars continue . . . it is possible
that the lust of conquest or the need of defence may lead to
a concentration of power in the Executive dangerous to the
people." (2) "Dangers may also arise from civil strife,
when it reaches a point at which one party becomes willing
to resign most of the people's rights for the sake of holding
down the other faction." (3) "The less educated part of a
nation might become indifferent to politics, the most educated class throwing their minds into other things, such as
poetry or art, . . . and gradually leaving the conduct of
State affairs to an intelligent bureaucracy *capable of giving
business men the sort of administration and legislation they desire, and keeping the multitude in good humour by providing comforts and amusements"* (II, pp. 602-603). The upshot of it all
is that "few are the free countries in which freedom seems
safe for a century or two ahead." (II, p. 603). But "Popular
Government will evidently take its colour from and will
flourish or decline according to the moral and intellectual
progress of mankind as a whole."

The possibilities of such progress are now more open to
question than

at any time in the hundred years preceding. That many millions of
men should perish in a strife which brought disasters to the victors
only less than those it brought to the vanquished is an event with-

out parallel in the annals of the race. . . . The *explanations of the facts are no more cheering than the facts themselves*. Human passions have been little softened by the veneer of civilization that covers them: human intelligence has not increased, and shows no sign of increasing, in proportion to the growing magnitude and complexity of human affairs. Knowledge has been accumulated, the methods and instruments of research have been improved, a wonderful mastery over the forces of nature has been obtained, the world has become a more comfortable place to live in and offers a greater variety of pleasures; but the mental powers of the individual man have remained stationary, no stronger, no wider in their range, than they were thousands of years ago, and the supremely great who are fit to grapple with the vast problems which the growth of population and the advances in science have created come no more frequently and may fail to appear just when they are most needed. (II, pp. 606-607.)

At best not a cheering prospect! Yet, as I said, Lord Bryce does not despair—not wholly. The quality of his optimism may be seen in his closing words.

Some gains there have been, but they have lain more in the way of destroying what was evil than in the creating of what was good; and the belief that the larger the number of those who share in governing the more will there be of wisdom, of self control, of a fraternal and peace-loving spirit has been rudely shattered. Yet the rule of the many is safer than the rule of One . . . and the rule of the multitude is gentler than the rule of a class. However grave the indictment that may be brought against democracy, its friends can answer, "What better alternative do you offer?" (II, p. 608.)

The experiment has not failed, for the world is after all a better place than it was under other kinds of government, and the faith that it may be made better still survives. . . . Hope, often disappointed but always renewed, is the anchor by which the ship that carries democracy and its fortunes will have to ride out this latest storm. . . . There is an Eastern story of a king with an uncertain temper who desired his astrologer to discover from the stars when his death would come. The astrologer, having cast the horoscope, replied that he could not find the date, but had ascertained only this that the king's death would follow immediately on his own. So may it be said that Democracy will never perish till Hope has expired. (II, p. 609.)

Friends of democracy will no doubt agree to this last sentiment; but many will perhaps think that Lord Bryce is too much inclined to identify democracy with the particular form in which it appears today. Many people will say that democracy really means something more than "the rule of the whole people expressing their sovereign will by their votes." They will say that democracy, or at least the thing which will disappear only when Hope has been extinguished, is rather an idea than a form of government— the idea or the ideal that men should have equal freedom and opportunity, and an equal voice in determining the social arrangements by which this ideal may be, so far as it can be, attained; and they will therefore conclude that "the rule of the whole people expressing their sovereign will by their votes" is not democracy, but only a method for securing democracy, a method moreover which, as it actually operates in most of the six countries described by Lord Bryce, seems in a fair way of defeating rather than of securing the desired end.

This may seem a quarrel about words; but one often feels that Lord Bryce does not adequately meet the vital question of whether the whole people, where it has a legal right to express its sovereign will by its votes, does or can, under modern conditions, really express its will. To assume that democracy, and not class rule, exists because it exists formally, is much like assuming that Great Britain is not a democracy but a monarchy because it has a king. After all, words are powerful things, with the mass of the people more powerful than ideas; and just now the world is filled with valiant and verbal defenders of "democracy" whose chief fear is precisely that the whole people might in fact some day express its sovereign will, either by its votes or otherwise. If the future of our ideals of democracy (very nearly the only ideals the world has left) is to depend upon a form of government about which half of Europe has grown cynical, then must our hope be faint indeed.

A critic looking for the most vulnerable point of attack would no doubt seize upon Lord Bryce's contention that democracy has nothing to do with economic equality.

With this controversy (as to whether economic equality is possible) we are not here concerned, for Democracy—which is merely a form of government, not a consideration of the purposes to which government may be turned—has nothing to do with Economic Equality, which might exist under any form of government, and might possibly work more smoothly under some other form. The people in the exercise of their sovereignty might try to establish community of property, as they might try to establish a particular form of religion or the use of a particular language, but their rule would in either case be neither more nor less a Democracy. Political Equality can exist either along with or apart from Equality in property.

This is no doubt formally correct. One willingly admits that "if all property were divided up on one New Year's day, the next would see some men rich and some poor." If Lord Bryce means only that political equality can exist apart from an absolute equality of material possessions, no one, I suppose, would dissent. That one man should be rich and another poor, is inevitable under a competitive régime, and one can easily imagine political equality surviving in a community in which diversity of fortunes was not too great or too permanent. But it makes a great deal of difference whether the rich become rich as a result of superior ability and industry or as a result of special privilege; it makes a great deal of difference whether the rich can or cannot, by means of their wealth, exercise economic power over other men; it makes a great deal of difference whether they can or cannot, by means of this economic power, exercise an undue influence in that political process by which the whole people expresses "its sovereign will by its votes." Political equality can undoubtedly exist along with or apart from economic equality; but if Lord Bryce wishes us to understand that the question of political democracy can be considered to any purpose, much less satisfactorily answered, apart from the question of the economic organization of society, then I confess that his contention sounds like some Rabelaisian pleasantry. On the contrary, I should say that most of our political troubles, both domestic and international, are due precisely to the fact that as a result of the progress of the Industrial Revolution of the nineteenth and twentieth centuries the political organization of the modern world is out of harmony with its economic organization.

In fact, Lord Bryce has admirably described the precise way in which, under present conditions, the question of political democracy *is* connected with the question of economic quality. Referring to the labor unions, such as the *Confédération Génréale du Travail*, the American Federation of Labor, and the Triple Alliance, he says:

These bodies, democracies within the national democracy, . . . possess a double power, that of their votes as citizens and that of bringing commerce and industry to a standstill by ceasing to work. Such an exercise of the right of each individual to give or withhold his labour creates a difficult situation, for if the Government happens to be the employer there is no independent authority to arbitrate between it and the strikers, and if the employers are private persons the cessation from work may affect so seriously the welfare of the nation that the *matter becomes a political one with which the Administration must deal*. But how? It is a passive insurrection directed against all the rest of the community which cannot meet it by physical force. It is a disintegration of democracy, for matters of the first importance to the whole community are discussed and decided by each of these bodies, or by their League, among themselves, while the rest of the population, which has no share in the decision, is faced by a threat operating in effect as a command. (II, p. 578.)

This describes the situation exactly. It is a "disintegration of democracy," if you like; but if so, it is a disintegration due to economic inequality, and how then shall we say that democracy has nothing to do with economic inequality? I should prefer to say that the situation so aptly described is a symptom, and an ominous one, that the political mechanism intended to secure democracy, intended to enable the whole people to express "its sovereign will by its votes," is proving inadequate to attain that end. Since the laborers have the vote why do they not rely upon the vote to express their will and secure their interests? Not from mere perversity surely, but primarily because of a profound distrust in the ability or the capacity of those legislative bodies, which Lord Bryce finds everywhere of such diminished prestige, and not among laborers only, to deal fairly or even intelligently with the vital questions at issue. Such distrust is certainly very largely justified; and it is so largely because in place of nations of individuals, all more or less alike in respect to conditions and ideas, the Industrial Revolution has given us nations differentiated into classes and corporate and occupational groups, more or less different and often sharply antagonistic, in which the lines of division have little or nothing to do with the territorial areas on which political representation is based. The government, nominally composed of persons chosen to represent the will of the people in certain territorial areas, finds that the crucial problems of the time, which are essentially economic, cannot be solved without taking into account the will of the people grouped in certain economic categories. Such is doubtless the real source of the diminished state of Deputies and Congressmen. What they too often legally represent is a group of people without any definite common will to be expressed; what they have to deal with are groups of people (and not labor groups only) who can get their will expressed only, or much better, by using their extra-legal economic power as a means of dictation.

But comment on so acceptable a book must not close on a note of dissent. In any case the dissent is slight, and scarcely touches the substance of the work. The primary purpose of Lord Bryce is neither to define nor to reform nor even to defend democracy. His primary purpose is to exhibit modern popular government just as it is. This he does with such a wealth of concrete information, with so much shrewd insight into human motives, with so much charity for human frailty and yet so resilient a faith in human virtue, with so sustained a desire to know that which is true and to hold fast to that which is good, that these two volumes will be one of the great and indispensable records of early twentieth-century civilization. Lord Bryce does these great things in so casual a way that we are becoming habituated to taking them as matters of course.

1921.

The Spirit of '76

L AST October Mr. Lyon asked me to come down to the Brookings School and tell you about the Spirit of '76. I suspected
   that he hadn't any clear notion of what was meant by the
phrase "Spirit of '76," and I was positive I hadn't. I was therefore about to decline the invitation when, rummaging among my
papers, I came upon an old and imperfect manuscript which seemed
providently designed to throw some light on this obscure subject.
The manuscript bore the date of 1792, but who may have written it I
was unable to determine. There are obviously some pages missing,
and the tale ends suddenly as if never quite finished. But such as it
is I have transcribed it, and I give it to you for what it may be
worth. The title of the manuscript is "Jeremiah Wynkoop."

JEREMIAH WYNKOOP

During the war of independence I not infrequently heard
zealous patriots say that Mr. Wynkoop was not as warm in
the cause as he should be. The charge has lately been revived by those who had no great liking for Mr. Wynkoop's
Federalist principles. Mr. Wynkoop was of course not alone
in being thus distinguished. It is now said of many men who
were never suspected of being Tory that they look back
with regret to the old days before the breach with Britain.
It is said of them, to employ a phrase now becoming current, that they were never really inspired by the true spirit
of '76. For my part, I suspect that, in recalling the desperate

days of the war, we are likely to invest the so-called spirit
of '76 with a glamor which it did not have at the time. Be
that as it may, I knew Jeremiah Wynkoop as an honest man
and a genuine patriot. I was his closest friend, intimate
enough to know better than most the difficulties that confronted him and the sentiments that determined his conduct. And so I think it worth while, now that the man is
dead, to set down a plain tale of his activities and opinions
from the beginning of the quarrel in 1763 to the final
breach in 1776. This I do, not only for old friendship's
sake and as a justification of Mr. Wynkoop, but as a contribution to the history of those troubled times; for Jeremiah
Wynkoop was fairly representative, both in his station
in life and in his opinions, of that considerable class of
substantial men who did as much as any other class, and I
think more than any other class, to enable these states to
maintain their liberties against British tyranny.

Born of rich middle class parents of genuine Dutch-
American stock, Jeremiah was educated at Kings College,
then recently established. In fact we both entered the College the year it was founded, and graduated with the first
class in 1758. Jeremiah then spent two years in the office of
William Moore reading law, a profession which he nevertheless abandoned for the trade. Taking over a profitable
business upon the sudden death of his father, he rapidly
achieved a notable success in commerce, chiefly in West
Indian ventures, and was already known, in 1765, as a leading merchant in New York, where he had offices near the
wharves, and a town house, inherited from his father, on
the Bowling Green. But Jeremiah, being much given to
study and the reading of books, preferred to live away from
the distractions of the city, and had in fact for some years
resided in the country, out Greenwich Village way, where

he possessed a fine estate which had come to him as part of the generous dowry of his wife, the daughter of old Nicholas Van Schoickendinck, a great landowner in the province.

Mr. Wynkoop was much given to the reading of books, as I have said; and it is necessary to dwell on this matter a little since it helps to explain his opinions and conduct. Of all books, histories of the ancient and the modern times were his favorite study. It was an interest which he acquired in college, and never afterward lost. In college of course we all read the standard Greek and Roman writers, and acquired the usual knowledge of classical history. To admire the classical poets and essayists was nothing out of the way for young men in college, but the ancient civilization fascinated Jeremiah more than most of us, and I recall that he devoured every book on that subject which the college afforded, and many others which he bought or borrowed. The Parallel Lives of Plutarch he knew almost by heart, and was never weary of discanting on the austere morality and virtuous republicanism of those heroic times. For Jeremiah a kind of golden age was pictured there, a lost world which forever disappeared when Caesar crossed the Rubicon. The later Roman times never interested him much— "five hundred years," he used to say, "in which the civilized world groaned under the heavy hand of tyrants, relieved only by the reigns of five good emperors." Still less was he interested in the Dark Ages, when the light of learning and the spirit of liberty were submerged by feudal anarchy and ecclesiastical superstition. But the story of modern times fascinated Jeremiah as much as the story of the ancient world because all its significance seemed to lie in the slow and painful emergence from that long mediaeval night, through the recovery of the wisdom of the ancients, the progress of natural philosophy, and the struggle for political liberty.

All these matters I recall we used to discuss at great
length, so that I was perfectly familiar with Jeremiah's reflections on history. At that time his ideas seemed to me
wonderfully novel and interesting, but I have since thought
them, in a vague general way at least, those of most cultivated Americans. Be that as it may, all the significance of
history appeared to Mr. Wynkoop to lie in the agelong conflict between Truth and Error, between Freedom and
Oppression. And for this reason he opined that the central
event of modern times was the struggle of the last century
between the English people and the Stuart kings. With the
history of that heroic time he was entirely familiar, and in
a less degree I was too. Our heroes were Pym and Eliot, and
John Hampden, imprisoned for refusing to pay a twenty
shilling tax. Cromwell we admired as the man of iron who
had forever laid the ghost of the Divine Right doctrine, and
whose mistakes were later corrected by the liberal Whigs
who called in Dutch William to replace the last of the
Stuarts. We knew the great charters of liberty—the Magna
Charta, the Petition of Right and the Bill of Rights. We
knew our Milton, the man who defended the authority of
elected magistrates, and erected an impregnable bulwark
against the denial of free speech. We knew our Grotius,
who had discovered in right reason the foundation of civil
and international society. Above all we knew our Locke,
and especially his second discourse on Civil Government, in
which he so eloquently defended the Revolution of '88 as
an act of reasonable men defending their natural rights
against the usurping king who had broken the original
compact.

Much as Jeremiah admired England as the home of
political liberty, he was thoroughly American, and it was
always his idea that America had played a most notable

part in the great modern struggle against the oppression of Church and State. He used to find great satisfaction in recalling that our ancestors, at the hazard of their lives and fortunes, had braved the terrors of the new world in pursuit of religious and political liberty; that they had persisted, often at the point of failure, in the desperate determination to transform the inhospitable wilderness into a land fit for human habitation; and he would point out that they had succeeded beyond any reasonable expectation, so much so that these thirteen colonies were now the most fortunate and the freest countries in the world—thirteen communities living in peace and content, happily without kings, neither burdened with an idle aristocracy nor menaced by a depraved populace, with a press uncensored, and many religious faiths deprived of the power of persecution and long habituated to the spirit of toleration. For my part I used to complain sometimes that after all we were only "provincials," remote from the center of things. I used to express the wish that fate had set us down in London, nearer Piccadilly and the Beefsteak Club. But Jeremiah would have none of such repining. Provincials we might be in a geographical sense, he would say, but spiritually we were at "the center of the world, in the direct line of those heroes and martyrs who since the beginning of time have done battle for the dignity and happiness of mankind against the leagued assailants of both."

(Here some pages are missing in the manuscript. It goes on as follows.)

. . . . are become so populous and wealthy that we are as indispensable to Britain as Britain is to us. The time is surely approaching when this vast country will be the center of the power and wealth of the Empire. We are now freed from the French menace. The peace will be an enduring one, and the two branches of the English race will continue in the future as in the past to exemplify to the world those incomparable blessings that are the prerogatives of free peoples."

Such was Jeremiah Wynkoop's conception of history in general and of the part which Britain and America had played in the story of human progress. With him it was a kind of philosophy, a religion indeed, the only religion really that he had. I don't mean that he was of the atheistical school of thought. He believed indeed in the existence of the Deity as the First Cause and Original Contriver of the universe; and this was in fact the very reason why he found so much delight in the study of history. History was God's revelation of the meaning of life and of human destiny on earth, making plain the gradual progress and the ultimate triumph of Truth and Freedom. And this I think was the secret of his profound loyalty to bòth Britain and America; these were in his view the promised lands, the homes of the chosen peoples whose mission it was to lead mankind toward the final goal.

Nothing at all events was farther from his thought in 1763 than that there could be any serious differences between the two peoples who were so bound together by ties of blood and affection, by mutual respect, and by the common tradition of . . . .

(Another break in the manuscript here.)

In the year 1765 Mr. Wynkoop shared the general feeling of apprehension which for two years had been steadily increasing on account of the measures, as unprecedented as they were unfortunate, of the king's minister, Mr. George Grenville. The chief of these measures were undoubtedly the Sugar Act of the last, and the Stamp Act of the then present year. On the nature and effects of these measures Mr. Wynkoop had read and reflected as much as a busy man well could do. The Sugar Act, obviously designed to placate the British West Indian sugar planters, was certain, as indeed it was intended, to put obstacles in the way of the island trade with New York and New England. In that trade Mr. Wynkoop was personally interested. It is true, as indeed he was careful to tell me, that his profits for the last year were much as usual; but it had been abundantly demonstrated in pamphlets that the Sugar duties were bound to have a disastrous effect on American trade in general; would, for example, undermine the New England Rum industry and thereby depress the fisheries and the African trade; would diminish the exports of lumber and grain from New York and Pennsylvania; would above all, since the new duties were to be paid in silver, drain the colonies of their small store of hard money and thereby make it difficult for American merchants to settle their balances due in London on account of imported British manufactures.

No one doubted, at least no one in America, that the Sugar Act was unwise in point of policy, calculated to defeat the very end intended. Yet there it was, an act of Parliament imposing duties for the regulation of trade, and we could not deny that Parliament had long exercised without opposition the right to regulate trade. But I recall Mr. Wynkoop's pointing out to me one novel feature of the act, which was the declared purpose, expressed in the preamble, of raising a revenue in "his Majesty's dominions in America, for defraying the expenses of defending, protecting, and securing the same." For some reason Mr. Wynkoop disliked the term "dominions," always prefer-

ring the term "colonies." But he disliked still more the term
"securing." For two years ministers had been prone to talk
of laying restrictions on his Majesty's dominions for their
better security. This idea Mr. Wynkoop disliked extremely.
I remember his saying that the term "free-born Englishmen" had always given him great satisfaction, that he had
always supposed that Americans were possessed of all the
rights of Englishmen born within the realm; and indeed I
knew him well enough to know that he harbored the firm
conviction that Americans were not only as free as Englishmen but even a little freer, a degree less subservient to
aristocrats and kings, a degree more emancipated from
custom and the dead hand of the past. I often heard him
compare the Assembly of New York, chosen by the free
suffrages of the people, with the British Parliament in
which so often the members were chosen by irresponsible
Peers and Boroughmongers—compare them of course to the
disadvantage of the latter. To suppose that Parliament was
now bent upon restricting the dearly bought and well deserved liberties of America was to Jeremiah, as indeed it
was to all of us, an alien and distressing thought.

We could scarcely therefore avoid asking the question:
"What constitutional right has the British Parliament to
legislate in restraint of American liberties?" We never
doubted that we were possessed of liberties, and no American, certainly no American as well informed as Mr. Wynkoop, needed to be told that there was a British Constitution which guaranteed the rights of Englishmen. Yet, as I
recall those early years, I must confess that we were somewhat perplexed, had a little the air of groping about in the
dark for the precise provisions of the British Constitution.
The spirit of the British Constitution we knew was to be
found in the Magna Charta and the Bill of Rights. Rights

were indeed of its very essence; and to Mr. Wnykoop at least it was incredible that there was not to be found in it an adequate guarantee of the rights which Americans ought to enjoy. I remember his reading to me certain passages from the pamphlets of Stephen Hopkins and Governor Hutchinson—pamphlets which he thought expressed the American view very adequately. "What motive," Mr. Hopkins asked, "can remain to induce the Parliament to hedge the principles and lessen the rights of the most dutiful and loyal subjects—subjects justly entitled to ample freedom, who have long enjoyed and not abused, their liberties?" This passage I think expressed Mr. Wynkoop's state of mind very well in the year of the Sugar Act. His state of mind was one of amazement, the state of mind of a man who is still at the point of asking questions—Why? For what reason?

Meantime the Stamp Act, presenting the question more clearly, did much to clarify our ideas on the matter of American taxation; and certainly Mr. Wynkoop was never in doubt as to the unconstitutionality of that famous measure. In those days I was much at Mr. Wynkoop's house, and I remember one day in November, 1765, sitting with him and his father-in-law, old Nicholas Van Schoickendinck, discussing the state of the nation. Even old Nicholas had been startled out of his customary complacency by the furious excitement occasioned by the Stamp Act.

"The Act is unconstitutional, sir," Mr. Wynkoop had just declared, somewhat dogmatically it must be confessed, and for perhaps the third time. "There can be no question about that I think. It is not only contrary to precedent, but is destructive of British liberty, the fundamental principle of which is that Englishmen may not be taxed without their own consent. We certainly never gave our assent to the Stamp Act."

"I won't say no to that," old Nicholas remarked. "And if we had done no more than to protest the measure I should be well content."

"Little good protests would have done, sir. We protested before the bill was passed, and without effect. Mr. Grenville would not hear our protests, and now he finds the act virtually nullified. I can't say I regret it."

"Nullified!" Old Nicholas exclaimed with some asperity. "A soft word for a nasty business. Mr. Grenville finds his law 'nullified,' you say. But in getting the law nullified we get half the windows of the Broad Way smashed too, and Governor Colden gets his chariot burned. For my part I don't know what Mr. Colden's chariot had to do with the devlish stamps—it wasn't designed to carry them."

"Very true, sir, I admit. And regrettable enough, all this parading and disturbance. But if Ministers will play with oppression the people will play with violence. Similar incidents occurred in England itself in the last century. Let Mr. Grenville beware of playing the rôle of Strafford. God knows I am no friend of rioting. I have windows too. But a little rioting may be necessary on occasion to warn ministers that legislative lawlessness is likely to be met by popular violence."

Mr. Wynkoop had perhaps a little the air of talking to convince himself rather than old Nicholas. Old Nicholas at least was not convinced.

"Tush!" he exclaimed irritably. "That's a new word, 'popular.' You young fellows have picked up a lot of precious democratical phrases, I must say. Who are 'the people' you talk so loosely about? Another word for 'populace' or I miss my guess. Don't delude yourself by supposing that it was hatred of the Stamps that made them break Mr. Livingston's windows and burn Mr. Colden's chariot.

They hate Mr. Livingston and Mr. Colden because they are men of substance and standing. It is not windows they aim at but class privileges, the privileges of my class and yours, the class that always has, and I trust always will, govern this province. The bald fact is that a mob of mechanics and ne'er-do-wells, led by obscure fellows like John Lamb and Issac Sears who have hitherto doffed their caps and known their places, are now aiming to control the city through their self-constituted committees. Sons of Liberty, they call themselves; sons of anarchy, in fact. I wish as much as you to preserve our liberties. But I warn you that liberty is a sword that cuts two ways, and if you can't defend your rights against ministerial oppression without stirring the 'people,' you will soon be confronted with the necessity of defending your privileges against the encroachments of the mob on the Bowling Green."

Old Nicholas stopped to light his pipe, and after a few puffs added:

"You don't associate with *Mr.* John Lamb, do you? You ain't one of the Liberty Boys who erect poles and break windows, I hope."

Mr. Wynkoop laughed off the sarcasm.

"Certainly not, sir. I don't know the fellow Lamb, never saw him in fact, although I am told, and believe, that he is an honest, worthy man. The danger you mention has of course occurred to me, but I think you probably exaggerate it. Let Britain repeal the Stamp Act, as she must do, and the populace will be quiet enough."

We sat until a late hour. I took but little part in the discussion, enjoying nothing better than to listen to the good-natured wrangling of these two friends. During the course of the evening each repeated, many times over, his former argument, all without rancor, but all equally without effect. Except in opinion, they were not divided; and at last, pledging one another courteously in a glass of stiff toddy, we separated for the night.

During the following months Mr. Wynkoop continued firm in the defense of American rights. He agreed, as all the substantial merchants did, not to use the stamps, which was indeed not possible since none were to be had. Yet he would do no business without them. Let the courts close, he said. Let his ships stand idle in harbor, a year, two years, let them rot there rather than submit to an unconstitutional measure. So I often heard him declare roundly, sitting at dinner sipping his madeira. . . .

(Again something missing from the manuscript.)

. . . secret misgivings, during the long cold winter, by the continued disturbances in the streets, and by the clamor of those, mostly of the common sort, who demanded that the courts should open and denounced the merchants for timidly refusing to do business without stamps. The Sons of Liberty were saying that the stopping of business was all very well for gentlemen of fortune, but that it was ruining the people who must starve unless business went on as usual. The Sons of Liberty had grown more hostile to the merchants than they were to ministers, and they even hinted that the better sort were by their timidity betraying the cause. Meantime Old Nicholas appeared to enjoy the situation, and never lost an opportunity of asking him, Jeremiah Wynkoop, whether he hadn't yet joined the Liberty Boys, and why after all he didn't send his ships out, clearance papers or no clearance papers.

Mr. Wynkoop was therefore immensely relieved when the British Parliament finally repealed the hateful measure, thus at once justifying his conduct and restoring his con-

fidence in the essential justice of Britain. He had now, I recall, rather the better of the argument with Old Nicholas
(the two were forever disputing) and pointed out to him
ever so often that a little firmness on America's part was all
that was needful to the preservation of her liberties. For
two years he went about his business and pleasure with
immense content. I dare say he easily forgot, as men will
do, the distasteful incidents of the Stamp Act struggle, and
allowed his mind to dwell chiefly on its satisfactions. He
often spoke of the principle, "No taxation without representation," as being now fully established; often expressed
his gratification that, by taking a firm and sensible stand,
he and his substantial friends had brought Britain to recognize this principle; so that by the mere passing of time as it
were these ideas acquired for Jeremiah a certain axiomatic
character. I was never so sure of all this, and sometimes
called his attention to the Declaratory Act as evidence that
Britain still claimed the right of binding the colonies in all
matters whatsoever. Needless to say, old Nicholas called
his attention to the Declaratory Act oftener than I did. But
Mr. Wynkoop would not take the Declaratory Act seriously. It was, he said, no more than a bravely flying banner
designed to cover a dignified retreat from an untenable
position; and he had no fear that Britain, having confessed
its error by repealing the Stamp Act, would ever again
repeat it.

It presently appeared that the British government could
commit errors without repeating itself. In 1767, following
the mysterious retirement and delphic silences of Mr. Pitt,
Mr. Charles Townshend had come forward, no one knew
on whose authority, and promised the House to obtain a
revenue from America without doing violence to her
alleged rights. The Americans, he said, had drawn a distinc-

tion between "internâl" and "external" taxes, denying the former but admitting the latter. This distinction Mr. Townshend thought "perfect nonsense," but was willing to humor Americans in it; which he would do by laying an external tax on the importation of glass, lead, paper, and tea. These duties, which would bring into the Exchequer about £40,000, the Americans must on their own principles, Mr. Townshend thought, admit to be constitutional.

It may strike my readers as odd that any one could have been surprised by anything Mr. Townshend took a notion to; but we were indeed not then as well aware of the man's essential frivolity as we have since become. I recall at all events that Mr. Wynkoop followed the proceedings in the House with amazement; and when we learned, one day in 1768, that Mr. Townshend had actually blarneyed the House into passing the Tea Act, the whole business struck Jeremiah as preposterous—"doubtless one of those deplorable jokes," I remember his saying, "which Mr. Townshend is fond of perpetrating when half drunk." I had some recollection that in the time of the Stamp Act troubles certain writers had hinted at a distinction between "internal" and "external" taxes; and Mr. Wynkoop admitted that some such distinction may have been made. But he said that for his part he thought little of such subtle distinctions, agreeing rather with Mr. Pitt that the real question was whether Parliament could "take money out of our pockets without our consent" by any tax whatsoever. There was, however, a difficulty in taking so advanced a position at that time, and as usual it was old Nicholas, always quick to perceive difficulties, who pointed it out.

"I fancy," old Nicholas had said, "that every act in regulation of trade takes money out of our pockets, but I don't imagine you have yet become so ardent a Son of

Liberty as to deny Parliament the right of regulating our trade.''

At that time we were all reading Mr. Dickison's *Letters of A Pennsylvania Farmer*, and Mr. Wynkoop, who read everything, was able to meet that objection.

''The essential question,'' he said, ''is whether an act of Parliament is laid primarily for the regulation of trade or for the raising of a revenue. If for the latter, it is a tax. The intention of the framers must decide, and there can be no question that the Tea Act is a tax since the framers expressly declare its purpose to be the raising of a revenue.''

''A fine distinction, that! But it would be easy for the framers of an act to levy duties on imports with the real intention of raising a revenue, all the while professing loudly their intention of regulating trade. What then?''

''Americans would not be so easily deceived, sir. The nature of the Act would reveal the real intention clearly enough.''

''Ha! You would determine the nature of an act by the intention of the framers, and the intention of the framers by the nature of the act. Excellent! That is the logic of your Pennsylvania Farmer. The New Englanders are still more advanced, I see. They are now saying that our rights are founded on a law of Nature, and God only knows what that is. God and Mr. Adams—it's the same thing, I dare say.''

''The New Englanders are likely to be a little rash, sir, I think,'' Mr. Wynkoop admitted. ''This argument of their Mr. Adams is complicated, and I fear too subtle to be easily followed. I'm not sure I understand it.''

''Well, never mind. You will all understand it soon enough. First you say that Britain has no right to lay internal taxes. Then that she has no right to levy taxes of any

sort. Next you will be saying that Parliament has no right
of legislation for the colonies on any matter whatsoever.
And as you can't derive that from precedent you will derive it from the law of nature."

Mr. Wynkoop smiled at this outburst.

"I have no fear of its coming to that," he said. "The
Tea Act is not really an act of Britain; it is Mr. Townshend's foolish hobby. A firm and sensible resistance on our
part will effect its repeal. But if one could conceive Britain
to be so blind as to push matters to extremes—well, I
don't know. If it were really a choice between admitting
that Parliament has a right of making all laws for us or
denying that she has a right of making any laws for us, it
would be a hard choice, but should we not be forced to
choose the latter alternative? What other answer could we
make?"

"You may well ask! What answer will you make when
your precious Adams comes out with a declaration of independency from Great Britain?"

"Independence!" Mr. Wynkoop exclaimed. "Good
God, sir, what an idea!"

And indeed, at that time, the idea of separation from
Great Britain struck us all as fantastic.

A firm and sensible resistance, Jeremiah had maintained,
would bring a repeal of the Townshend duties, as it had
formerly brought a repeal of the Stamp Act. When it was
learned that Lord North, on March 5, 1770, had moved the
repeal of all the Townshend duties save that on tea, Mr.
Wynkoop could with some reason say, and did say, that
events had proved the justice of his view. And Mr. Wynkoop felt, rightly enough, although he modestly refrained
from boasting of it, that he had contributed to this happy
result. With no more than the grudging consent of old

Nicholas, he had taken a leading part in organizing the Merchants' Association—an agreement not to import any goods from Great Britain so long as the Townshend duties should be in force. That Association had been faithfully kept by the New York merchants of substance and standing. Mr. Wynkoop had himself kept it to the letter, and had sacrificed much in doing so. He told me that his enlarged stock of goods, ordered in anticipation of the agreement, had soon been sold out—at high prices indeed, but not sufficiently high to recoup him for his subsequent losses. For four months last past business had been dull beyond all precedent—scarcely a ship moving; debts not to be collected; money hardly to be had at any price; and the poorer sort of people in dire need for want of employment.

There were indeed plenty of unscrupulous men who had done well enough, who had even profited while pretending to defend their country's rights. The Boston and Philadelphia merchants, as was definitely known in New York, had observed the Association none too well; and even in New York men of no standing had done a thriving business in the smuggling way, especially in Holland tea. Obviously the longer the Association was maintained by honest merchants, the more unscrupulous smugglers would profit by it. We were therefore somewhat surprised to learn that the Boston merchants were in favor of maintaining the Association in full vigor, in spite of Lord North's concessions, so long as the 3d duty on tea was retained. This policy was also advocated by the dishonest beneficiaries of the system in New York, who made use of agitators like Mr. MacDougall to stir up the Mechanics' Asociation and the populace generally against the merchants, their argument being that our liberties were as much endangered by the 3d duty on tea as they had been by all the Townshend duties.

I am not so sure now that they were wrong, but at that time all of the substantial merchants of New York were strong for a modification of the Association. Mr. Wynkoop, I recall, took a leading part in the affair. He was much irritated with the Boston merchants whom he described as being more active in "resolving what to do than in doing what they had resolved." His opinion was that the Association no longer served any "purpose other than to tie the hands of honest men to let rogues, smugglers, and men of no character plunder their country." Besides, he was much gratified, as all the merchants were, by the recent act of the British government permitting the issue in New York of a paper currency, which was so essential to business prosperity. And therefore, in view of the fact that Britain had taken the first step by repealing the major part of the Townshend duties, it seemed to him the part of wisdom for the colonies to make some concession on their part. The New York merchants of standing were I think generally of Mr. Wynkoop's opinion; and at all events, after taking a canvass of the city, they resolved to abandon the old Association, agreeing for the future to import all commodities, "except teas and other articles that are or may be subject to an importation duty." Some were apprehensive lest New York might find itself alone in this action, and thereby suffer the stigma of having deserted the cause. But in the event it proved otherwise, as Mr. Wynkoop had anticipated. In spite of protests from Boston and Philadelphia, the merchants of those cities followed the lead of New York. Demonstrations in the streets soon subsided, importation became general, business revived, and the controversy with Britain seemed definitely closed.

The years of '71 and '72 were quiet years—ominously so as it proved. But in those days we all nourished the conviction that the controversy with Britain was definitely closed. Nothing occurred to remind us of it even, unless it would be the annual celebrations of the repeal of the Stamp Act, or the faint reverberations, always to be heard in any case, of political squabbles in the Massachusetts Bay. Then, out of a clear sky as it seemed, the storm burst—the landing of the tea ships, the destruction of the tea in Boston harbor, and the subsequent meeting of the Philadelphia Congress. These events, all occurring in rapid succession, seemed to fall like so many blows on Mr. Wynkoop's head, and I recall his saying to me. . . .

(*Here the manuscript breaks off again, and there are evidently some pages missing.*)

. . . return from Philadelphia, I met him at his father's house where we were to take dinner, as often happened. Arriving early, we had a long talk while waiting for old Nicholas to come down. I found Mr. Wynkoop in low spirits, an unusual thing for him. It may have been no more than a natural weakness after the excitement of attending the Congress, but to my accustomed eyes his low spirits seemed rather due to the uncomfortable feeling that he had been elbowed by circumstances into a position which he never intended to occupy. I was eager for the details of the Congress, but he seemed unwilling to talk of that, preferring rather to dwell upon the events leading up to it— matters which we had threshed out many times before. It was as if Mr. Wynkoop wished to revive the events of the last year and his own part in them, as if, feeling that he might and perhaps should have followed a different line of conduct, his mind was eagerly engaged in finding some good reasons for the line of conduct which he had followed in fact. What first gave me this notion was his saying, *apropos* of nothing.

"I will confess to you, what I would not to another, that if I could twelve months ago have foreseen the present situation I should probably not have attended the Congress."

The remark alarmed me. Mr. Wynkoop's admiration for Britain and his faith in her essential justice were always stronger than mine. For my part I doubted not, from the moment of the passing of the Coercive Acts, that we were in for it, that Britain would not back down again, and that we must either break with her or submit to her demands. My decision was made. I would go with America when the time came for the final breach, I knew that; and above all things I wished Mr. Wynkoop, who was my closest friend, to throw the weight of his powerful interest on the side of my country. But I knew him well enough to be sure that if he now convinced himself that it would come to a breach with Britain he would probably wash his hands of the whole business. What I counted on was a certain capacity in the man, I won't say for deceiving himself, but for convincing himself that what he strongly desired would somehow come to pass. I therefore did what I could to convince him, or rather to help him convince himself, that his past and present conduct was that of a wise and prudent man.

"No man can foresee the future," I remarked, somewhat sententiously.

"That is true," he said. "And even could I have foreseen the future, I fail to see how I could have acted differently, at least not honorably and with any satisfaction to myself. It is past a doubt that Britain, in authorizing the India Company to sell its teas in America, deliberately sought to raise the issue with America once more. It was a challenge, and so insidiously contrived that America had no choice but submission or a resort to a certain amount of violence. Once landed the teas were bound to be sold, since even with the 3d duty they were offered at a less price than the Holland teas. The issue could not be met by commercial agreements, still less by argument. Well, we sent the teas back to London. The Massachusetts people threw theirs into the harbor. Violence, undoubtedly. I had no part in it, but what could be done? Who after all was responsible for the violence? Let ministers who revived an issue happily settled answer that."

"There is no doubt in my mind," I said, "that Britain welcomed the violence in Boston harbor as a pretext for strong measures."

"It seems incredible," Mr. Wynkoop resumed, "but what else can we think? Hitherto it might be said of ministers that they blundered, that they did not know the consequences of their acts. But not on this occasion. They knew perfectly the temper of America; and in any case the destruction of a little tea was surely a mild offense compared with the abrogation of the Massachusetts Charter and the closing of Boston harbor. To subject a loyal province to military despotism, and then deliberately to set about starving the people into submission reveals a vindictiveness foreign to the British character. I can't think the Coercive Acts represent the will of the English people, and I am confident, always have been, that the sober second thought of the nation will repudiate these acts of ministerial despotism."

It was not the first time I had heard Mr. Wynkoop express that sentiment.

"I trust it may prove so," I said. "At least we have done our part. No one can say that the Congress has countenanced rash measures. It has merely adopted a com-

mercial agreement, a measure which we have frequently re-
sorted to before. I don't see how it could have done less."

Mr. Wynkoop seemed a little uncertain of that.

"Yes," he said. "I suppose we could not have done less;
Heaven knows we have shown a proper restraint. And I
may say that what little influence I have had has always
been exerted to that end."

I knew well enough what he was thinking of. After
the tea episode there were rash spirits who talked of resort
to arms, and even hinted at independence. There were such
men even in New York. They had formed the Committee of
twenty-five, but fortunately the more moderate minded had
got the committee enlarged to 51; and Mr. Wynkoop,
together with Mr. Jay and Mr. Alsop and other men of substance, had consented to serve on the Committee of Fifty-
one in order to prevent the firebrands from carrying the
province into violent measures. Old Nicholas had advised
against it.

"Beware of meddling with treason," I recall hearing
him say to Mr. Wynkoop at that time.

"Precisely my idea," Mr. Wynkoop had replied with
the smile he always had for old Nicholas' penchant for
using stronger terms than the occasion warranted. "I wish
to steer clear of treason, or anything remotely approaching
it. But it is plain to be seen that New York will support
Boston in some fashion, plain to be seen that she will send
delegates to Philadelphia. Suppose I and all moderate men
follow your advice and wash our hands of the affair? What
then? Then the Mechanics will take the lead and send Mac-
Dougall and Sears and men of their kidney to Philadelphia,
with instructions for vigorous measures. Vigorous measures! God only knows what measures they may be for!"

It was to keep New York from violent measures of all sorts that Mr. Wynkoop had consented to serve on the Committee of Fifty-one; it was for that reason he had gone to Philadelphia. I knew that better than most, and I knew that that was what he was now thinking of.

"I am very glad you went to Philadelphia," I said.

"What else could I have done?" he exclaimed. "I have asked myself that a dozen times without finding any answer. But about the Association I don't know. You say it is a moderate measure, but after all it was the measure of the New Englanders, and among the moderates of Philadelphia it was commonly thought to be perhaps too vigorous. I was opposed to it. I voted against it. And having done so perhaps I was ill advised to sign it. I don't know."

I was about to make some reply, when old Nicholas came into the room, and I fancied I could see Mr. Wynkoop stiffen to defend his conduct against inevitable sarcasms.

"Fine doings!" Old Nicholas growled. "The New Englanders had their way, as I expected. I warned you against meddling with treason."

"Treason's a strong word, sir."

"The Association smells of it."

"I cannot think so, sir. The Association is a voluntary agreement not to do certain things; not to import or to export certain goods after a certain date. No law that I know of compels me to import or to export."

"No law requires you to import or to export, very true. But does any law require *me not* to import or export? Certainly no law of the British Parliament or of New York Province obliges me. But suppose I exercise my lawful privilege of importing after the date fixed? What then? Will not your Association compel me not to import, or try to do so? Are not your committees pledged to inspect the customs, to seize my goods, and to sell them at public auction for the benefit of the starving mechanics of Boston? I tell you your Association erects a government unknown to the law; a government which aims to exert compulsion on all citizens. When I am given a coat of tar for violating the Association, will you still say it is a *voluntary* Association?"

"I think little compulsion will be necessary," Mr. Wynkoop replied. "The continent is united as never before; and when the British people realize that, and when British merchants find markets wanting, ministers will be made to see reason."

"You signed the Association, I hear."

"I did sir. I was opposed to it as Mr. Jay was, but when it was finally carried we both signed it. Once adopted as expressing the policy of Congress, it seemed useless to advertise our divisions, and so weaken the effect of the measures taken. Congress has decided. The important thing now is not what policy Congress should have adopted; the important thing now is for all to unite in support of the policy which it has in fact adopted. If the Colonies present a united front to Britain, as they will do, Britain must yield."

"My advice," old Nicholas said as we went into dinner, "is to drop it. And don't say I didn't warn you."

Over our after dinner wine the matter was gone into at greater length. I said but little, no more than to throw in a remark now and then to keep the argument alive; for I felt that the opposition of old Nicholas would do more to keep Mr. Wynkoop in the right frame of mind than anything I could say. Be that as it may, I left the house well satisfied; for whether it was the dinner, or the wine, or the truculent arguments of old Nicholas, or all of these combined, I felt sure that the total effect of the evening had been to confirm Mr. Wynkoop in the conviction that the Association was a wise measure, well calculated to bring Britain to terms.

As Mr. Wynkoop had anticipated, little compulsion was necessary to secure the observance of the Association; the threat of confiscation, on the authority of the Committee of 60, of which Mr. Wynkoop was a member, was quite sufficient, save in the case of certain obstinate but negligible traders. And at first it seemed to many that the measures taken would produce the desired effect, for in February Lord North introduced his famous Resolution on Conciliation. I thought the Resolution signified little or nothing, and when in April the news came from Lexington I was not much surprised. It meant war to a certainty, and my first thought was to learn what Mr. Wynkoop would make of it. Curiously enough, with that faculty he had for moulding the world close to the heart's desire, Mr. Wynkoop found some satisfaction in this untoward event. War with Great Britain—no, he would not pronounce the word prematurely. He spoke of the Lexington affair as a repetition of the Boston Massacre, seemingly more serious only because America was now prepared to defend its liberties with arms in its hands. I was delighted that he could take it so; for it convinced me that we might still carry him along with us. The Assembly of New York was too lukewarm to be depended on, half the members or more being frankly Tory, so that we found it convenient to organize a Provincial Congress, composed of delegates elected under the supervision of the Committees, in order to take charge of affairs and keep New York in line with the continent. The most advanced party was already suspicious of Mr. Wynkoop's loyalty; but the moderate men saw the wisdom

of winning his support if possible. Mr. Jay and Mr. Alsop
were especially keen to have Mr. Wynkoop serve in the
Provincial Congress, and they asked me to do what I could
to obtain his consent to stand as a candidate.

I did what I could, and I flatter myself that my repre-
sentations had some influence with him. Knowing his admiration for Mr. Jay, I put it to him as a thing strongly
urged by that gentleman.

"Mr. Jay thinks it the more necessary," I said to Mr.
Wynkoop, "for men of your sound and moderate views to
serve, since the Mechanics are every day gaining headway,
and at the same time many men of standing are withdrawing altogether. There is a twofold danger to meet; we must
keep the province loyal to the cause, and we must prevent
the leveling ideas of the New Englanders from gaining the
ascendancy here. If men of your standing refuse to direct
the affairs of the colony in these crucial times we shall
surely succumb to one or the other of these evils."

"I understand that very well," Mr. Wynkoop replied,
"but the decision is not, as you know, an easy one for me."

"Your difficulties are appreciated, and by no one more
than by Mr. Jay and all his friends. But it is precisely for
that reason, as they point out, that we need your support.
Old Nicholas is known to be Tory, and it is much commented on that the Van Schoickendinck Interest is largely
lukewarm if not actually hostile. The family Interest is a
powerful one, and if you are cordially with us it will do
much to bring over many who are hesitating. Your responsibility is the greater, as Mr. Jay rightly says, because
of the fact that you will carry with you, one way or another, a great number."

"It is very flattering of Mr. Jay to say so."

Mr. Wynkoop had a great respect for Mr. Jay's judgment—had always had. He consented to stand, and was
elected. Throughout the summer of 1775 he attended the
sessions of the Provincial Congress faithfully, giving his
support to those who were endeavoring to hold the province to a sane middle course—enforcing the Association;
raising a militia for defense; keeping the door carefully
open for conciliation. Old Nicholas charged him with
being too much led about by Mr. Jay. Mr. Wynkoop
naturally replied that the notion was ridiculous. What
kept him to the mark I feel sure was the feeling that his
views and his conduct had been hitherto justified by events,
and were now justified by Lord North's Resolution on
Conciliation. On this he placed all his hopes. Unacceptable
Lord North's Resolution was, he told me on one occasion;
but he regretted that the Congress at Philadelphia had seen
fit to pronounce it "unseasonable and insidious." When
bargains are to be struck, Mr. Wynkoop said, politicians
do not offer everything at the first approach. The Resolution proved, he thought, that Lord North was preparing
to retreat, as gracefully as possible no doubt. Meantime
the policy adopted by the Philadelphia Congress Mr. Wynkoop thought eminently satisfactory; the Resolution on
Taking up Arms was admirably phrased to convince
Britain that America would defend her rights; the Petition
to the King admirably phrased to prove her loyalty.
Throughout the summer and autumn Mr. Wynkoop therefore held the same language to men of extreme views—to
the over timid and to the over zealous: the Petition's the
thing, he said; it will surely effect the end desired.

Hope delayed makes the heart sick, it has been said.
But I think this was not the effect on Mr. Wynkoop. On
the contrary, I am sure that for four months he found peace

of mind by looking forward to the happy day when the king would graciously make concessions. I had little expectation of any concessions, and it was no great shock to me when the news arrived in November that the king had not even deigned to receive the Petition, much less to answer it. But I knew it would be a heavy blow to Mr. Wynkoop; and when the British government, placing an embargo on American trade, proclaimed America to be in a state of rebellion, it is not too much to say that Mr. Wynkoop's little world of opinion and conduct, held together by recollection of the past and hope for the future, was completely shattered. For a month I saw him scarcely at all. He rarely went abroad, even to attend the Provincial Congress. He must have sat at home in seclusion, endeavoring to adjust his thought to the grim reality, gathering together as best he could the scattered fragments of a broken faith.

During the winter of '76 I saw him more frequently. We often discussed the situation at length. The time for discussion, for discussion of the past that is, seemed to me to be over. But Mr. Wynkoop was seemingly more interested in discussing what had happened than in discussing what ought now to be done. At first this puzzled me; but I soon found the explanation, which was that he knew very well what had to be done; or at least what he had to do, and was only engaged in convincing himself that it had been from the first inevitable, that the situation that now confronted him was not of his making. His one aim from the first, he said, and he said it many times, was to prevent the calamity now impending. I know not how many times he reviewed his past conduct. Short of tamely submitting to the domination of Parliament, he was forever asking, what other course could America have followed but the one she had followed? What other course could he have followed? If America had appealed, not to force but to reason, was this not due to the efforts of men of substance and standing, men of Mr. Wynkoop's class? If Mr. Wynkoop and all his kind had washed their hands of the affair, would not the populace and their hot headed leaders long since have rushed America into violence, and so have given Britain's measures the very justification which they now lacked?

In all this I quite agreed with Mr. Wynkoop. I assured him that his conduct had always been that of a wise and prudent man, and that if events had disappointed the expectations of prudent men, the fault was clearly not his. Responsibility lay with the British government, with those mad or unscrupulous ministers who, wittingly or unwittingly, were betraying the nation by doing the will of a stubborn king. Mr. Wynkoop found consolation in the thought that since ministers had appealed to the sword, the decision must be by the sword. Fight or submit, they had said. The alternative was not of America's choosing, nor of Mr. Wynkoop's choosing. Could America submit now? Could Mr. Wynkoop submit now? Whatever he might have done a year ago, two years ago, could he now tamely submit, bowing the head like a scared school boy, renouncing the convictions of a lifetime, advising the friends with whom he had been associated on committees and congresses to eat their words, to cry out for mercy, saying that they did not mean what they said, saying that it was only a game they were playing. "I have made commitments," Mr. Wynkoop often said to me. "I have given hostages." This was true, and this I think was the consideration of greatest weight with him; he could not deny his words and renounce his friends without losing his self respect.

War with Great Britain! Mr. Wynkoop was forced to pronounce the word at last. But independence! That was the hardest word of all. Yet the word was in the air, passing from mouth to mouth behind closed doors and in the open streets. I had long since accustomed myself to the idea, but Mr. Wynkoop hated the thought of it, said he had never desired it, did not now desire it—"unless," he admitted as a kind of after thought, "the Britain I have always been loyal to proves an illusion." It was this notion, I think, that enabled Mr. Wynkoop to reconcile himself to the policy of separation. The Britain of his dreams was an illusion. The Britain he had known did not exist. In those days we were all reading the fiery papers of Mr. Paine entitled *Common Sense*. I know that Mr. Wynkoop read them, and I fancy that they helped him to see Britain in her true colors.

"I like neither the imprudence of the man's manner nor the uncompromising harshness of his matter," Mr. Wynkoop once said to me. "Yet it seems that events give only too much foundation for his assertion that we have deluded ourselves in proclaiming the advantages of the connection with Britain. I can't agree with him that the loyal and respectful tone of our pamphlets and petitions is no more than mawkish sentiment; but I do wonder if the alleged benefits of the union with Britain are but figments of the imagination. It is hard to think so. And yet what now are those benefits? We must surely ask that."

Thus in the long winter of '76 Mr. Wynkoop repaired the illusions by which he lived, reconciling himself to the inevitable step. At this time he saw little of Mr. Van Schoickendinck—it was too painful for both of them, I dare say. At least their last conversation I know (it was by Jeremiah's express invitation that I was present) was a

trying one. It was on the 30th of May that we found old
Nicholas in the hall of his house, standing, leaning on his
cane, evidently much moved.

"I asked you to come," old Nicholas said after greeting
us a little stiffly, "because I must know what you purpose
to do. General Howe is about to take New York. The
Philadelphia Congress is about to declare a separation
from Great Britain. The so-called Provincial Congress of
New York will hesitate, but it will probably support the
measure. Am I to understand that you will burn your
bridges and side with the rebels?"

With great seriousness and gravity, Mr. Wynkoop
replied:

"I wish you to believe, sir, that I have given the matter
every consideration in my power; and it seems to me that
I can't do other than go with America. America is my country, and yours too, sir."

"America *is* my country." The voice of old Nicholas
was shrill. "I have no great love for Britishers, as you
know. Damn them all, I say! But I am too old to meddle
with treason. Especially when it can't come to any good.
Either we shall be crushed, in which case our last state
will be worse than our first; or we shall succeed, in which
case we shall be ruled by the mob. Which is better, God
knows. What I can't see is why you have allowed the
fanatics to run away with the cart. Fight if you must, but
why close the door to reconciliation by declaring an
independency?"

"We can't fight without it, sir. That's the whole truth
of the matter. I was much against it, and so were most.
But the necessity is clear. First we refused to trade, hoping
that Britain would make terms as she had formerly done.
Instead of making terms, Britain closed our ports and pre-

pared to make war. To fight we must have supplies and munitions. We must have money. We can get none of these things without reviving trade; and to revive trade we must have allies, we must have the support of France. But will France aid us so long as we profess our loyalty to Britain? France will give money and troops to disrupt the British empire, but none to consolidate it. The act of separation will be the price of a French alliance.''

"Am I to understand that the act of separation is not to be seriously made, except to buy French assistance? That you will let France go by the board as soon as Britain is willing to negotiate?''

Mr. Wynkoop did not at once reply. After a monent he said,

"No, I would not say that, sir. The act of separation is intended for Britain's benefit too. It will make it plain that we mean what we say—that we mean to defend our liberties to the last ditch if necessary. Yet I hope, and believe, in spite of all, that it will not come to that.''

For a long moment old Nicholas stood stiff and silent. Suddenly extending his hand, but turning his face away, he said,

"Well, good by. Our ways part then.''

"Don't say that, sir.''

"I must say it. I must remain as I began—a loyal British subject. You have ceased to be one. I am sorry to have seen this day. But I must submit to necessity, and you must too.''

Slowly old Nicholas ascended the stairs, tapping each tread with his cane. Half way up, he cried out, as if in anger,

"Good bye, I say!''

"God keep you, sir,'' was all Mr. Wynkoop could find to reply.

Mr. Wynkoop afterwards told me that he spent a sleepless night in his half-abandoned house. In anticipation of General Howe's arrival he had already begun to move his effects out of the city, into Westchester County, near White Plains, where the Provincial Congress was adjourned to meet on July 2. With the business of settling his personal affairs to the best advantage he was so fully occupied that he did not attend the Congress on the opening days. But on the afternoon of the 9th of July he took his place, a little late. Slipping quietly into a vacant chair just in front of me, he was handed a copy of "A Declaration by the Representatives of the United States of America, in Congress Assembled." The chairman of a committee, appointed to report on the validity of the reasons given for separation from Great Britain, was reading the document. We listened to the felicitous and now familiar phrases—"hold these truths to be self-evident"—"just powers from the consent of the governed"—"right of the people to alter or abolish it"—

"Who are the people?" I heard Mr. Wynkoop murmur to his neighbor.

His neighbor, not hearing or not understanding him, whispered behind his hand,

"This is not an easy time for you, I dare say. Mr. Van Schoickendinck can't be induced to join us." The last a statement rather than a question.

"No," Mr. Wynkoop said. "He will go Tory. He will not oppose us. His sympathies are with us really, I think. He is thoroughly American, with no great love for Britain. But he is old—he will go Tory."

"The Declaration will carry, I think."

"Yes."

"It seems well phrased. Jefferson's pen, I understand."

Presently the chairman, having finished the reading of the Declaration, read the report of the committee. "While we lament the cruel necessity which has made that measure unavoidable, we approve the same, and will, at the risk of our lives and fortunes, join with the other colonies in supporting it."

The report of the committee was carried, unanimously, a bare majority being present.

Whereupon a member begged leave, before proceeding to other routine business, to make a few remarks. Permission being granted, the member spoke of the decisive step which had just been taken; of the solemn crisis which confronted all America; of the duty of meeting that crisis with high courage, with the indomitable perseverance of freemen fighting for their liberties. "The time for discussion is over," he said. "The time for action has come. Once thoroughly united, we cannot fail, and if we triumph, as we shall, a grateful posterity will recall these days, and do honor to the patriotic men whose conduct was inspired by the spirit of freedom. God grant we may so act that the spirit of freedom will ever be synonymous with the spirit of '76!"

In the perfunctory applause which greeted these remarks, Mr. Wynkoop joined, as heartily I think, as . . . .

(*Here, most unfortunately, the manuscript ends. What the conclusion of the story may have been, if indeed it ever was concluded, will probably never be known.*)

1927

The Modern Leviathan

MOST books on government and history are well enough in their way, but I too often feel that almost anyone, with intelligence and industry, might have written them. They remind me of cold potatoes and vinegar, which as a boy I used to eat "between meals" when nothing better offered. Nourishing enough they were, but nothing about them to arouse interest in the cook. The books of Charles A. Beard are not like that. What their author contributes is far more interesting than the cold sliced facts they contain. They contain cold facts enough, heaven knows; but the facts are gathered there, not on their own account, but in elucidation of some central idea which the author wishes to present. I may not cotton to the idea; but there it is, something to think about, and always worth thinking about whether I agree with it or not.

The American Leviathan, which certainly gives one enough to think about, is perhaps the best book Mr. Beard has yet written. Its subject is the American Federal Government. Its substance is a thoroughly realistic description of the way that government actually functions. The central idea which coördinates this factual description is the sharp contrast between government as presented in legal fiction and government as actually conducted by living men. The book is a systematic exposition of the forces that have operated, and the devices that have been employed, to stretch and twist and manhandle an eighteenth-century constitution in order to adapt it to the complicated society created by the industrial and technological revolution of our time.

After pointing out the importance of modern technology in enhancing the difficulties of government, the author presents the central theme in general terms in the second chapter, which deals with the Constitution. The fiction is that the Constitution, a written document prepared by the fathers, sets definite limits to the powers of the Federal Government, and that the Supreme Court keeps the government within these limits by annulling laws that are "contrary to the Constitution." But the terms of the Constitution, not being always self-evident, have to be "interpreted" by the Court. What are the tests employed by the Court for determining the meaning of the Constitution? One test is the "intention of the framers." Unfortunately there were many framers, and their intentions were not always recorded, or else the intentions of some of the framers were different from the intentions of others. By this test the Constitution means what the judges of the Supreme Court guess the framers intended it to mean. Another test frequently used is "logic"—the terms of the Constitution being so and so, it logically follows that, etc. But logic is a treacherous guide at best. In one notable case logic led four judges to one conclusion, four others to a diametrically opposite conclusion, and the ninth judge to one of these conclusions until he changed his mind. In this case the logic of the Constitution depended on the unstable mind of one judge. In short, as Mr. Beard so conclusively shows, the "interpretation" of the Constitution has no other significance than this: at any time the Constitution means what any five out of nine judges, taking all the circumstances into account and God helping them, think it wise or expedient that it should mean.

The theory that the Constitution is a written document is a legal fiction. The idea that it can be understood by a study of its language and the history of its past development is equally mythical. It is what the Government and the people who count in public affairs recognize and respect as such, what they think it is. More than this. It is not merely what it has been, or what it is today. It is always becoming something else, and those who criticize it and the acts done under it, as well as those who praise, help to make it what it will be tomorrow.

The remaining chapters, dealing in turn with the various departments or special activities of the Federal Government, develop this theme in detail. A few examples must suffice. The fiction is that Congress makes the laws, the President executes them. The fact is that the President often determines legislative policy, the Congress often nullifies executive action. The fiction is that treaties can be made only by the President with the approval of the Senate. The fact is that the President can, and sometimes does, make "secret executive agreements" with foreign governments that are in effect binding. The fiction is that the Federal Government can do nothing not authorized by the Constitution. The fact is, to take one example only, that although the Constitution nowhere authorizes the Federal Government to do anything for the promotion of health and morals, the Federal Government does annually spend under these heads far more money than the entire Federal budget of Washington's first administration. The fiction is that the President is elected by a college of electors whose procedure is as deliberate and decorous as that of a board of trustees in electing a college president. The fact is that the election of a president is largely determined in self-constituted national nominating conventions which, for blare and blarney and bluster, for passion and pandemonium, reduce a World Series to the familiar measure of a church festival on the village green. Of course it is well known that the Constitution has in some respects been ignored and in others "liberally interpreted." I knew it myself; but until I read *The American Leviathan* I never quite realized that "liberal interpretation" is scarcely more than a euphemism, a verbal cloak charitably thrown over the naked fact that the Federal Government does somehow manage, under the pressure of social forces, to do whatever seems necessary or highly desirable.

It is in developing this theme that Mr. Beard gives us that thoroughly realistic description of the operation of the Federal Government, which is one of the chief merits of the book. Perhaps an even greater merit is that it disposes us to think more realistically about government in general. Long established tradition has accustomed us to think of government as something, not ourselves, that makes, or should make, for righteousness. We are apt to think of government as something "up there," over the heads of men, exercising in its own right "authority" over us, and exacting "obedience" from us, in virtue of some transcendent capacity to shape our ends rough hew them how we may. This paternalistic notion is no doubt largely a survivial from medieval Christian philosophy which conceived of Church and State as exercising, each in its own sphere, the delegated authority of God the father over his helpless and erring children. Having wrested authority from God and kings, men transferred it to the State which they invested with the quality of sovereignty.

Within my own memory political philosophers were still occupied with the problem of defining and locating sovereignty. In the United States a band of heretics maintained that the One Only Supreme and Irresistible Essence was divided—a logical absurdity to be surmounted only by the mystic doctrine of Trinity in Unity. This engaging occupation of "putting salt on the tail of sovereignty," as Reed Powell once defined it, has now been abandoned by most political philosophers: but politicians and people are still dominated, in their political thinking, by the abstract notions of Authority, Obedience, Duty. This is one of the unnoted reasons why so many people insist that the Volstead Act, even after it has been trampled in the dust and for ten years mirthfully kicked about, is being enforced, can be enforced, must be enforced. Otherwise the majesty of the One Only Sovereign Power would be impaired.

In other realms of thought and activity, human relations are regarded more sensibly—in terms of process, function, adjustment. Thus, to take a most vulgar example, when a director has produced, at great expense and travail of spirit, a picture which the movie fans ignore, he does not swell up with "righteous indignation" and shout "disloyalty," "lack of respect for Art," and so on. He says, "The thing's a flop. What the devil do the people want anyway!" Mr. Beard invites us to think of government in this realistic way, to regard it as a device fashioned by men for the purpose of effecting workable social adjustments. Instead of trying to locate sovereignty, he describes the way in which Roosevelt exerted power by gladhanding and outwitting congressmen.

This is all to the good. We might carry it a little farther. Regarding government as a device for effecting social adjustments, there is still the fiction that such adjustments are effected as the result of a disinterested "policy" formulated at the behest of the Will of the

People. This sometimes happens no doubt. But in the normal course governments, that is to say politicians, act under the pressure of individuals or groups intent on advancing their special interests. Such pressure we call "corrupt." "Almost all of us," says Walter Lippmann in a recent article, "feel that Tammany, for example, is a kind of disease which has affected the body politic. . . . We feel that it is not supposed to be there, and that if only we had a little more courage or sense or something we could cut away the diseased tissue and live happily ever after." The implications of this idea Mr. Lippmann thinks false. He prefers to think of Tammany and such like organizations as a species of "natural government" upon which our artificial constitutions have been superimposed. Very true. Such organizations may be a disease, but if so they are chronic— they have become, as it were, acquired characteristics.

Tammany is in fact no more corrupt than the Republican or the Democratic party machine. They all function in the same way and for the same purposes. They may not be provided for in the Constitution, but they are provided for in the nature of man. They are at all events a normal part of the mechanism of government, as normal as the House of Representatives. It may be "wrong" for interested groups to seek and obtain favors from government, but there it is; they do and always have done. In the eighteenth century there was government of the people, by the king, for the nobles and the rich. In the twentieth century there is government of the people, by the politicians, for whatever groups are strong enough to get what they want. The selfish propensities of men remain constant, as Lord Bryce says, it is only the channels through which these selfish propensities flow that change.

The reverse side of this fiction is that all loyal citizens, since they all derive the same benefits from government, take an active and intelligent interest in politics. The fact is that some citizens derive much greater benefits from government than others, and consequently take a far more lively and a far more intelligent interest in it. Many big business men retain high-priced attorneys to keep them inside the law; many bootleggers retain low-priced enforcement agents to keep them outside of it. Such citizens take an intelligent interest in politics because they are constantly in need of those social adjustments which can be effected only through the aid of government or by side-stepping its restraining hand. But there are many millions of loyal and intelligent citizens whose real concern with government is limited to paying taxes in return for reasonable protection to life and property. Their occupations are such that they neither need the special aid of government nor fear its intervention. I am one of these. Yet I am told that it is my duty to read daily all the news that's fit to print so that I may vote intelligently.

Well, I do read the *Times*, not every day but now and then. And I do vote, usually. But intelligently? That's a large order. In forty years I have voted eight times for a president of the United States. In each case, unless I wished to "throw away my vote," I had to choose between two candidates. To make a choice was not difficult, but to make an intelligent choice was impossible, since both candidates stood for the same things—progress and prosperity, higher wages and higher profits but lower taxes, the preservation of the inherent rights of the individual and at the same time the maintenance of equal opportunity for all. So I usually flipped a penny and voted. I am unfortunately one of those who have no special interests to be attended to.

Twice only, in forty years, I made what seemed at the time an intelligent choice. The first occasion was in 1896, when I helped to save the country (I was young then) by voting for "sound" money. The second was many years later, in 1920 I think, when Debs was running. It seemed to me that the position of Debs was distinctly different from that of any of the others. Therefore I voted for Debs, not because he was a Socialist, but because he was in jail. If one of the others had been in jail I should have had the same difficulty in making a choice that I usually have when all are free. But that was an exceptional case. Such opportunities to vote intelligently are unfortunately rare.

In all seriousness, looking back over this forty years after all the hurrah and hokum is past, I ask what difference it could have made to me which party won. Obviously it was of vital importance to many people that the Republicans should have the offices, to many others that the Democrats should have them. But to me, and to millions of others, it really made no difference at all.

I don't mean to say that government is of no importance. Government is undoubtedly the most important of all the associations of men that compete and bargain for power. But the elections did not decide whether there should be government or no government; they decided only whether the government should be directed by the Democratic or the Republican political machine. Our property, our lives, and our sacred honor would be as safe under one as under the other. The President, whether Democrat or Republican, would make false prophecies, and promises which he could not keep. Congress would in any case enact many statutes, some of which would be obviously necessary, some designed to solve the "agricultural problem" by lowering the tariff on commodities rarely imported,

others to raise the standard of living for American labor by
bolstering the cost of the things laboring men buy. Mr.
Wilson could not keep us out of war; Mr. Hughes would
not have tried to. Maybe the Democrats wouldn't have
busted the trusts or bludgeoned their way through the
Isthmus of Panama. Maybe the Republicans wouldn't have
established the Federal Reserve System. But this much is
certain: that marvelous and unanticipated development of
technology which so largely shapes the external conditions of life, which saves us so much time and leaves us so
little leisure, which so greatly increases the wealth produced and the number of men seeking jobs in vain, which
so multiplies our opportunities and diversifies our interests
and dulls our enthusiasms—this development would
neither have been accelerated nor retarded nor diverted by
a hair's breadth even if the Democrats had always won,
even if the Republicans had never lost.

The government is in fact not the omniscient power we
like to think. If we expected less of it we should the less
often be disappointed. Presidents would not need to make
such ridiculous promises, pessimistic radicals would not
need to so mournfully wail, or helpful liberals so often
venture to say that they had never been altogether convinced. With the best will in the world government can do
little to change the character or the working of the complex social mechanism. It can't do much because it is not
outside the mechanism, repairing and rebuilding it as a
mechanic repairs or rebuilds a motor car. It is itself a part
of the machine, intermeshed through and through it, conditioned by the very forces it professes to master and to
direct. The real Leviathan is not government, but society—
this amazing and vital and arresting and formidable

phenomenon we call American civilization. What can we do with it? Very little since we too are a part of it. It carries us along whether we will or not. We must accept it, as Margaret Fuller accepted the universe. We may accept it with fragile optimism, or with futile pessimism, with indifference or resignation or rebellion: no matter, it carries us along we know not whither. We can at best play our part, perform our function, cultivate our gardens. Some there will always be whose gardens are in the vicinity of Capitol Hill. Well, it's an indifferent soil, but there's plenty of manure. Something may grow even there.

Liberalism—A Way Station

ONE day, talking with a Cornell student from Brooklyn about the difficulty of getting jobs in this time of depression, I asked him, with ironical intent, what he thought of liberty. He replied: "I've never been through it; I don't drive a car." There may have been less irony in my question than in his answer. The answer, at all events, suggested that liberty is perhaps no more than a small station on the main traveled road of human history—a place which humanity passes rapidly through.

I am referring to that liberty which for the last century and a half has commonly been associated with democratic government. "It is evident," wrote DeTocqueville in 1835, "that a great democratic revolution is going on among us." From the vantage of 1932, we can see that this democratic revolution was the outstanding political event of the nineteenth century. During all that time the public issues which chiefly engaged statesmen were these. What is the best form of government? What are the proper functions of government? What are the rights properly reserved to the individual? How can the powers of government and the rights of the individual be definitely guaranteed in constitutional form? Between 1789 and 1871, the chief occupation of statesmen and publicists, one might almost say, was the manufacture of constitutions, the construction of locked-vaults and strong-rooms for safeguarding the rights of the individual. The emancipation of the individual from class or corporate or governmental restraint—this was the democratic revolution noted by DeTocqueville. To be a Conservative was to be, with whatever reservations, against such emancipation. To be a Liberal was to be, with whatever reservations, in favor of it.

Liberalism was the doctrine that rationalized this emancipation of the individual. In its most naive form it comes to us from the eighteenth century. In that optimistic age the middle-class man, conscious of his virtues and desiring to rise in a world in which he was repressed by royal tyranny and class privilege, naturally believed in liberty; and while the Revolution had as yet occurred only in men's minds, it seemed to him that liberty was achieved as soon as it was adequately defined: liberty—that is to say, "the right of every one to do whatever does not injure others." Meanwhile, slow-footed time brought its heavy baggage of experience. The great Revolution came, bequeathing to the nineteenth century its furious fanaticisms and hatreds, its partial achievements, its hopes deferred, its fears and disillusionments. Often checked, the Revolution was never quite suppressed; and the liberal creed lived on, toned down by the impact of many defeats, and reduced to classic form by John Stuart Mill in his famous book *On Liberty*.

In restating the liberal creed, the hard-headed if forward-looking utilitarians of the Victorian age adapted it realistically to the needs of the business men and bankers who rode to power on the swelling tide of the industrial revolution. Liberty was still defined as the "right to do whatever does not injure others." But of the things one could do that did not injure others, not the least important, since it benefited every one concerned, was to engage in any legitimate business and make a private profit by buying in

the cheapest and selling in the dearest market available.
Free competition—this also, as well as political and intellectual freedom, was one of the natural rights proclaimed
by the great Revolution, or at least one of the privileges so
clearly demonstrated by Bentham to be useful to society.
At a much later date Cecil Rhodes announced that "philanthropy is all very well, but philanthropy plus five per cent
is a good deal better." The impregnable strength of nineteenth century liberalism was chiefly in this, that it recognized the high value of philanthropy plus five per cent: it
united liberty and competition in the holy bonds of wed-
lock, made liberty useful by setting it up in business, and
sanctified competition by annointing it with the incense of
human freedom.

With this battery of principles, the middle and lower
classes gradually edged their way, through many an un-
guarded opening, into the "political country" hitherto
held chiefly by the aristocrats. If in the end the gates were
opened to the common man by those within rather than
forced by those without, it was not that the upper classes
wanted democracy, but that upper-class statesmen could do
with more votes. Yet with whatever concessions in theory
or compromises in practice the democratic revolution may
have been accomplished, all was still done in the name of
liberty; and never was the prestige of liberalism so high as
in that age of brass and iron when those shoddy substitutes
for the ideal (the Third Republic, the German Empire, the
Austro-Hungarian *Compromise*, a household suffrage thrown
as a sop to tenants on entailed estates) were complacently
exhibited as examples of "democracy triumphant."

This Indian Summer of liberal content was nevertheless
no more than a brief season. The moment of victory was in
truth the beginning of defeat, since with all the famous

"liberties" formally conferred on the individual the great rôle of nineteenth century liberalism was ended. When all statesmen loved the common man, sufficiently so at least to solicit his vote, and even the priests, as Georges Sorel said, "claim to be the best of democrats . . . and if a little persuasion is exerted . . . will have illuminations on the anniversary of August 10, 1792," where *then* was the enemy? The enemy appeared soon enough, but most disconcertingly: on two fronts, panoplied partly in conservative partly in liberal armor, and bearing banners strangely resembling both those which liberalism had carried to victory and those others which it had trampled in the dust.

The prophets of democracy had supposed that when political Liberty appeared economic Equality would come trailing affectionately along. *Laissez-faire*, free competition—what a wealth of subtle dialectic was employed to exhibit the social utility of these cleanly-kept but unfurnished concepts! The prophets of democracy could not forsee that the industrial revolution, superimposed on a régime of free competition, would give to the possessors of machines and the instruments of production powers and privileges which would have reduced dead and gone kings and nobles, could they have imagined them, to envious admiration. Before the end of the nineteenth century it was clear to the discerning that liberal democracy had belied the hopes of its prophets. Liberty, that liberty which was to have enlightened and emancipated the world, had ironically given birth to a brood of mean-faced tyrants, and so far from walking hand in hand with equality was to be found consorting chiefly, and secretly, with puffed and bedizened privilege.

The first to feel the new oppressions were the industrial workers. Sooner or later, therefore, in every country they organized political parties committed to the defence of their class interests. These new parties had all much the same practical program—to obtain for the masses a larger share of the social income. They had all much the same social philosophy: some brand of Marxian socialism, which proclaimed the coming social revolution and the end of the competitive system. Not *laissez-faire* but socialization, not a competitive but a regulated economy, not individual liberty for private profit but restraint of the individual for the welfare of all—such was the new gospel of socialism that arose to contend with the old gospel of liberalism.

Confronted with the rising power of socialism, the possessing classes closed their ranks. Landed aristocrats, recently dispossessed by the political revolution, united with the aristocracy of bonded bourgeois wealth created by the industrial revolution, to defend the régime of liberal democracy. They were now all good conservatives since they wished to conserve the existing régime, all good liberals since the régime they wished to conserve was the one liberals had so long heralded and fought for. With the issue thus reshaped, with conservative-liberals to the right of them and revolutionary socialists to the left of them, the old Liberal parties, not well knowing whether to be guided by their humanitarian impulses or by their individualist principles, could only stand irresolute, while their once loyal followers deserted to one camp or the other. This process of dissolution was well under way in continental countries before the war. In England it is more recently that the great Liberal party of Gladstone has dropped to third place. For some years now its chief function, as J. M. Keynes so aptly puts it, has been "to serve the State by supplying the Conservative party with leaders and the Laborites with ideas;" and we need not be surprised that it has at present so few of either, having in the last twenty years surrendered so many of both.

Of all the leaders thus lost to the Liberal party, the most notable is undoubtedly Ramsay MacDonald, whose career throws a brilliant light on the predicament from which all old-fashioned liberals now strive with indifferent success to extricate themselves. Aristocratic in his avocations and in his demeanor, he lives by preference the life of a gentleman and a scholar; inheriting the Scots' canny caution and thoroughly rooted in British tradition, he understands the high virtue of compromise and has always set his face against violence, not always with pleasant consequences to himself; nevertheless, being eminently humane, he has consistently preached social reform in behalf of the poor; being eminently reasonable and reasonably ambitious, he has called himself a socialist but has risen to power as a leader of the Labor party; and yet through all the vicissitudes of an exciting career he has managed to preserve the liberal point of view, watching his step both ways, often uncertain whether to be counselled by his conscience which bids him budge with the masses, or by the fiend who bids him budge not with the classes: the upshot of which is that he has been three times prime minister, and today, deprived of a party, stands in splendid isolation, discreetly holding a faded socialist flag and courageously leading a conservative House of Commons. All this is but an abstract and brief chronicle of Liberalism in our time.

Before the war this game could be played without fatalities. The liberals had so expertly socialized their program, the socialists had so expediently denatured their revolutionary doctrine, that there was not between them (for example, between the liberalism of Lloyd George and the socialism of Ramsay MacDonald) the difference of the twentieth part of one poor scruple. But the harsh implications of anti-liberal doctrine, now fast becoming real issues, have revealed to liberals and socialists alike the puerility of their playboy disputes. The Marxian, communist, anti-liberal revolution has actually occurred in Russia. The fascist, anti-liberal revolution has occurred in Italy. We have only to remove our heads from the sand to see, on the arena of western civilization, old fundamental issues clearly defined, old fundamental conflicts realistically staged: on the one side, a ruthlessly regulated economy as it appears in Soviet Russia or in Fascist Italy; on the other, a free competitive economy (made workable by whatever patchwork of socialistic devices) as it appears in Great Britain and the United States.

As the implications of these contrasted systems become more apparent, the predicament in which all liberals find themselves (and in the liberal camp all tepid, skimmed-milk socialists are now huddled for shelter) becomes more acute, becomes even, if we wish to do anything about it, really pathetic. Our predicament arises from the fact that, having been long enamored of both liberty and equality, we are now ever more insistently urged (by the gods that be, those wooden-faced *croupiers* at life's gaming table) to choose between them and the truth is we cannot with a clear conscience or a light heart choose either without the other. So we stand irresolute, pulled one way by our humane sympathies, another by our traditional ideals. As we are humane, we look with compassion on the "looped and windowed raggedness" of the poor, invoke on their behalf the sacred principle of equality, and perhaps secretly admire, at the safe distance of three thousand miles, the high Russian endeavor to realize it in practice. Yet we shudder at the thought of blood, and assure the bolsheviks that the Great Society cannot be created by cutting off heads or suppressing freedom of speech (for which, in the distant past, so much blood was ruthlessly shed!) Although humane lovers of the masses, we are, on the other hand, highly differentiated individuals who prize our liberties, including the liberty of not belonging to the masses whom we love; and having been long unaccustomed to authority arbitrarily exercised, we hate Mussolini for the professors he has silenced, and write letters to *The Nation* protesting, in the name of liberty, against his brusk tyrannies. Yet we find it impossible not to denounce, in our own country where we are still free to denounce them, those oppressions that have emerged under the aegis of the very liberty we invoke. Choose? Oh me, that word choose! We cannot choose liberty without denouncing the drastic methods now being taken to obtain equality, or choose equality so obtained without betraying liberty.

Choose as we will or can; the event is less likely to be decided by our choices than by the dumb pressure of common men and machines. The intellectual liberty we so highly prize is of little moment to the average man, since he rarely uses it, while the liberties he can make use of are just now of diminishing value to him. Of the many liberties which, in our free democratic society, the average man now enjoys (if that is the word), I will mention the one which concerns him most. He is free to take any job that offers, if any offers; if none offers, free to look for one that will pay a bare living wage, or less: if none is found, free to stand in line begging a crust from charity, or from the government that makes him a free man. What the average man wants, more than he wants this kind of liberty, is security; and when the pressure of adverse circumstances becomes adequate he will support those who can and will give it to him. The average man likes of course to do what he pleases, but he is averse to being made responsible for what it is that he pleases to do. Instinctively suspicious of eccentricity, he is nowise irked by conformity. The equality of mediocrity gives him all the liberty he cares for really, since he is not measurably different from the great majority of people, and does not wish to be. Give him security, and within security the liberty to do and to think what most people do and think—give him bread and motor cars—and he will never know, or soon forget, that liberty has departed.

And the machines, unfortunately for us perhaps, appear to be on the side of the average man. Having invented the machines, we must make the best of them. Master them we will, no doubt. Master them we do. But a prime condition of our mastering them is that we should adapt our conduct to their necessities. To make the best use of the machines we must meet them more than halfway, since they care nothing for us while we care greatly for them. It is the machines that make life complicated, at the same time that they impose on it a high tempo; and what the machines demand of the individual living in a closely inter-meshed society running at top speed is not eccentricity, however cultivated and engaging, but conformity. The idle curiosity, the mental vagabondage of the brooding, reflective mind, the machines will indeed accept, but at high discount rates only; they put a premium on the immediately realizable virtues—on promptness, regularity, precision, effortless adaptability to the accelerated movement and rhythm of modern life.

Liberty is one of those magic words that have, on the world's stage, their entrances and their exits, playing

meanwhile their brief parts. One wonders whether the rôle
of liberty, in its modern mask, is nearly played out. Is
liberalism as we have understood it for a hundred years
past no more than rationalization, an intellectual by-
product of democracy? Is democracy itself but a passing
phase, a loose and extravagant method of government,
practicable only in relatively simple agricultural societies
suddenly dowered with unaccustomed wealth by the
industrial revolution? If so, then is equality not, as we
have fondly supposed, the blood brother and indispensable accomplice of liberty? Will equalitarianism, in its
turn, prove to be a new rationalization, an intellectual
by-product of complex, economically interdependent industrial societies working inevitably, and no doubt impersonally, towards stability and equilibrium? These are
questions which, in this time of disturbance and failing
confidence, the reflecting mind cannot put lightly aside.

1932

Freedom of Speech

The worth of men consists in their liability to persuasion.

WHITEHEAD.

THE *Nation* has recently reaffirmed its faith in freedom of speech. I suppose there has rarely been a time since the foundation of that distinguished journal when such a statement would not have been true. What is notable in the present instance is that the unashamed affirmation of the old doctrine called forth an unusual number of protests —all from persons who presumably accept the doctrine of free speech in principle. They protest, not against the principle, but against an unlimited application of it. Free speech, they seem to say, is a wholesome diet under normal conditions, but it should be taken in moderation when the community, being subject to unusual strain, is not feeling so good. A re-examination of the liberal doctrine is always in order, and never more so than now. The times are such that every liberal may well ask himself, not so much how far he is willing to carry the principle of free speech, but rather how far the principle is capable of carrying him.

It seems necessary to ask what we mean by freedom of speech, since people often have disconcerting ideas about it. A woman once asked me what all the pother was about. Weren't people always free to say what they thought? Of course one must be prepared to face the consequences. I didn't know the answer to that one. Last summer a Col-

umbia University student explained to me that all governments, being based on force, were dictatorships, and that
there was no more freedom of speech in the U. S. A. than
in the U. S. S. R., the only difference being in the things one
was permitted to say. I suggested that, supposing freedom
of speech to be a good thing, a poor way of getting more of
it than we already had would be to adopt a philosophy
which denied that it was worth having. The editors of
The Nation do not say that the laws guaranteeing freedom
of speech are always effective. They say that freedom of
speech, as defined in our fundamental law, is the foundation of free government, and should therefore never be
denied to anyone—''even to the Nazis.''

The fundamental law guaranteeing freedom of speech
was well formulated in the Virginia constitution of 1780:
''Any person may speak, write, and publish his sentiments
on any subject, being responsible for the abuse [as defined
by law] of that liberty.'' As thus defined, freedom of speech
was the principal tenet of the eighteenth-century doctrine
of liberal democracy. Its validity, for those who formulated it, rested upon presuppositions which may be put in
the form of a syllogism. *Major premise:* The sole method of
arriving at truth is the application of human reason to the
problems presented by the universe and the life of men in
it. *Minor premise:* Men are rational creatures who can easily
grasp and will gladly accept the truth once it is disclosed
to them. *Conclusion:* By allowing men freedom of speech
and the press, relevant knowledge will be made accessible,
untrammeled discussion will reconcile divergent interests
and opinions, and laws acceptable to all will be enacted.

Accepting this syllogism at its face value, the prophets
of democratic government knew very well how people
would behave once they were granted political privileges.

This ideal and purely imaginary behavior has been described for us by Lord Bryce. In the ideal democratic government,

the average citizen will give close and constant attention to public affairs, recognizing that this is his interest as well as his duty. He will try to comprehend the main issues of policy, bringing to them an . . . impartial mind, which thinks first not of his own but of the general interest. . . . Never failing to come to the polls, he will vote for his party candidate only if satisfied by his capacity and honesty. . . . With such citizens as electors, the legislature will be composed of upright men. . . . Bribery in constituencies, corruption among public servants, will have disappeared. Most of the causes that make for strife will be absent, for there will be no privileges . . . to excite jealousy. Office will be sought only because it gives opportunities for useful service. . . . Even if the law does not—perhaps it cannot—prevent the accumulation of fortunes, these will be few and not inordinate, for public vigilance will close the illegitimate paths to wealth. All but the most depraved persons will obey and support the law, feeling it to be their own. There will be no excuse for violence, because the constitution will provide a remedy for every grievance. Equality will produce a sense of human solidarity, will refine manners, and increase brotherly kindness. (*Modern Democracies*, I, 48.)

Evidently there is something wrong with the eighteenth century syllogism from which this ideal of human conduct was derived. In the light of liberal democracy as we know it, the minor premise is obviously false, the conclusion untenable. There remains the major premise. What can we do with it?

II

The major premise, with reservations as to "human reason," we can accept—must do so in fact, since there is nothing else to cling to. Even if reason be not always Reason, even if, like Hitler, we have nothing better than our blood to think with, we must make the most of whatever thinking we can muster. "All our dignity," said Pascal, "consists in thought. Endeavor then to think well: that is the essence of morality." It was by taking thought that man first differentiated himself from the beasts; by taking more thought that he achieved whatever men have, by taking thought, judged worthy. What more he may achieve can be achieved, and whether it is worthy can be determined, only by taking still more thought. Since men must in any case think, and do what they think of doing, it seems axiomatic to say that they should be free to think and to express their thoughts as well as they can.

Nevertheless, the statement is not axiomatic—obviously not, since, if it were, *The Nation* would not bother to print articles about it. There is a catch somewhere. Perhaps we are too prone to think of freedom of speech in terms of Man and Speech. This was the way in which eighteenth-century liberals thought of it. Confronted with a social régime which hedged in the individual at every point, they found the obvious solution in the maximum of liberty for the individual—political liberty, economic liberty, liberty of speech and the press. Knowing little of these liberties in the concrete, they visualized them as ideal abstractions, so that all the spacious but unfurnished chambers in the Temple of Freedom could be brilliantly illuminated by turning on certain phrases—as, for example, Voltaire's epigram: "I disagree absolutely with what you say, but I will defend to the death your right to say it." Liberals still think of liberty somewhat too much in the eighteenth-century manner. Give us, in a mental test, the words:"free speech," and we are apt to recall Voltaire's epigram, which then fades into a picture of two amiable, elderly gentlemen engaged in a rational discussion of the existence of the Deity.

Voltaire's epigram expresses a profound truth in the ideal world of knowledge. It would be equally relevant to the world of practical activities if society were a debating club of well-intentioned and reasonable men in which speech, being the only form of action, issued in nothing more dangerous than abstract propositions about reality. Since the activities of men are diverse, the ideal of a debating club is sometimes nearly realized. Mathematical physicists, discussing the nature of the atom, enjoy (at least in this country) the utmost freedom of speech without having (as yet) to call upon *The Nation* for first aid. Economists, historians, even biologists are more likely to encounter obstacles, since their activities have a more direct bearing on practical affairs. Where the principle of free speech has to fight for its life is in the realm of concrete political activities. Since the eighteenth century we have learned at least this much, that society is something more than a debating club of reasonable men in search of the truth. We know what use men actually make of their liberties. We are therefore in a position to estimate the principle of free speech in terms, not of Man and Speech, but of men and speeches—in terms of the best that has been thought and said by the Honorable Members we have elected, the Attorney-Generals we have known, the Insulls we have suffered, the fruity-throated announcers who, every day, for a profit, avail themselves of the Liberty of Lying.

Estimated in terms of its concrete manifestations, the principle of free speech is resolved into a diversity of oral and printed utterances, some of which need to be suppressed. No one has ever thought otherwise. Even the editors of *The Nation* do not approve of the freedom of speech that issues in slander and libel. Do they approve of the freedom

of speech that issues in the lynching of Negroes? In the sale
of poisoned cosmetics? The sale of worthless stock to honest
but gullible people? They would say that of course there
are, as the Virginia constitution recognizes, "abuses" to
be defined by law; but that unless the law is careful, the
definition may be a greater abuse than the speech it sup-
presses. True enough: the law is always in danger of being
"a ass." But as soon as abuses appear, the principle of free
speech is merged in another and broader principle: "Liberty is the right of everyone to do whatever does not injure
others;" and we are at once confronted with the fundamental practical problem of all government: What individual acts, including the act that is speech, do here and now
injure others?

By no formulation of principles beforehand can answers
to this question be provided for concrete situations. The
answers must wait on experience. Experience has taught us,
or surely will teach us, that the eighteenth-century solution
for social ills will no longer serve. Economic liberty, which
was to have brought in equality of conditions, has contrived, with the aid of machines, to bring about a monstrous inequality of conditions. That there are rich and
poor is nothing new, nor even disastrous. What is disastrous is that a great part of social wealth is owned by the
many who do not control it, and controlled by the few
who do not own it. Having well learned this, liberals find
the obvious solution for social ills not in extending but in
restricting the economic liberty of the individual. What
we have not learned, or not sufficiently, is that the economic liberty of the individual is intimately associated with
his political liberty, and that both are associated with his
liberty of speech and the press. It will prove extremely
difficult to restrict the one without restricting the others.

The speech that is socially vicious, to the point of endangering all our liberties, functions chiefly as an instrument of the competitive "business" economy. Such an instrument it has always been, no doubt; but never before so important an instrument, for the reason that modern methods of communicating thought are more subtle and effective than any ever before known, while the verification of the truth or relevance of the thought so communicated is far more difficult. The result is that there issues daily from the press and the radio a deluge of statements that are false in fact or misleading in implication, that are made for no other purpose than to fool most of the people most of the time for the economic advantage of a few of the people all of the time. This steady stream of falsification is called by various names which smell, if not too sweet, at least not foul—"advertising," "propaganda," "selling the public." Selling the public is an exact description of what is essential to the "successful" conduct of "business" —so essential that it is itself a business; and not the least of its evil consequences is that it is creating a state of mind disposed to regard anything as O. K. if you can get by with it. This manifestation of free speech is a far greater menace to liberal democracy than the freest dissemination of an alien political philosophy by Nazis or Communists is ever likely to be; and the only defense for it is that to restrict it would endanger the principle of free speech.

III

The danger is chiefly verbal, since the practical problem carries us beyond the speech we condemn to the practical activities that occasion it. The evil cannot of course be cured by creating a board of censors pledged to exclude lies from oral discourse and printed matter. But neither can it be cured by waiting while truth crushed to earth pulls itself up and assembles its battered armor. In the competitive business economy, as it now operates, those who largely control and extensively use the avenues of expression are not seeking truth but profits; and freedom of speech will not cease to be used for purposes that are socially vicious until it ceases to be profitable so to use it. It would seem, then, that the essential thing is either to abolish the profit motive or divert it into socially useful channels. Communists and Fascists confidently assert that neither of these objects can be attained through the liberal democratic political mechanism. They may be right. Liberals who think otherwise must at least take account of a disturbing fact: the liberal democratic political mechanism functions by enacting into law the common will that emerges from free discussion. Thus the circle seems completed: for curing the evil effects of free speech we must rely upon a public opinion formed in large part by the speech that is evil.

The editors of *The Nation* admit that the situation is full of "uncomfortable possibilities," but they hold to the traditional liberal method of meeting them—the promotion, by appealing from free speech drunk to free speech sober, of a "healthy movement to the left." The uncomfortable possibilities, as seen by *The Nation*, are that "continued economic decline," and the "demand of a despairing people for drastic action," may enable a "well-directed [Nazi] propaganda" [free speech] to bring about the "triumph of fascism . . . with all its attendant horrors." Another uncomfortable possibility, as I see it, is that the "healthy" movement to the left may become "unhealthy," and end in the triumph of communism with all its attendant horrors. Among the attendant horrors, in either case, *The Nation* would no doubt include, as one of the drastic actions demanded by a despairing people, the drastic suppression of free speech as a political method. The logical dilemma involved in free speech for political objects is therefore this: if social ills cannot be alleviated by the democratic method of free speech, this very freedom of speech will be used by those whose avowed aim is the abolition of the democratic method, and free speech as a part of it. Am I expected to be loyal to the principle of free speech to the point of standing by while, writhing in pain among its worshipers, it commits suicide? It is asking a lot.

It is asking too much only so long as we remain in the realm of logical discourse. In demanding the privilege of free speech from a liberal government in order to convince its citizens that free speech is a present evil, neither Nazis nor Communists have any standing in logic. Their programs, so far as the preliminaries of social reform are concerned at least, are based on an appeal to force rather than to persuasion. Very well, since that is their program, let us cease talking, resort to force, and see which is the stronger. Their own principles teach us that it is logical for them to resist oppression but merely impudent to resent it. Nevertheless, the logic of events is not very logical, and I see no practical virtue in a syllogistic solution of the problem presented by Nazi and Communist propaganda. The freedom of speech which by their own logic I deny them, I am therefore quite willing to concede them in fact.

I concede it because, for one thing, there is a bare chance that the Nazis, or the Communists, or both of them may be, as they seem to claim, true prophets whom the world would not willingly have stoned—agents of the God Woden or the Dialectic duly accredited and predestined to establish truth and justice by a ruthless suppression of oppressors. I should dislike very much to put myself in opposi-

tion to the forces, not of persuasion, that make for righteousness, apart from the fact that it would be futile to do
so if they are in any case to triumph. But perhaps a better
reason for conceding freedom of speech to Nazis and Communists is that freedom of speech can neither be suppressed
by argument nor maintained by suppressing argument. The
principle of free speech must justify itself or go under. The
real danger, from the liberal point of view, is not that
Nazis and Communists will destroy liberal democracy by
free speaking, but that liberal democracy, through its own
failure to cure social ills, will destroy itself by breeding
Nazis and Communists. If liberal democracy can sufficiently
alleviate social ills, freedom of speech will have sufficiently
justified itself; if not, freedom of speech will in any case
be lost in the shuffle.

Whatever may be the virtues of freedom of speech in the
abstract world of ideas, as a rule of political action it is like
any other law—it works well only if the conditions are
favorable. It works not too badly in a society in which the
material conditions of life, being relatively easy, create no
radical conflicts of interest, and in which there exists a
common tradition of moral and social ideas, one of which
is that just government rests upon the consent, freely expressed and freely given, of the governed. A long-time view
of human civilization discloses the fact that such favorable
conditions have existed only in a few places or for short
times. Experience gives us slight ground for supposing that
nineteenth-century liberal democracy is a permanent conquest of intelligence. It may very well be but a passing
phase, a cumbersome and extravagant form of government,
practicable only in relatively simple agricultural societies
suddenly dowered with unaccustomed wealth by the dis-

covery of new instruments of power and the invention of new machines.

Present events do little to discredit this view. Certain European countries have already abandoned liberal democracy—gladly by all accounts—for one or another form of dictatorship. Even in this Land of the Free there are developing, under the pressure of continued economic distress, significant movements to the left and to the right. These movements can surely not be checked by declaring a quarantine—by pronouncing them "unhealthy," and closing the mouths of Nazis and Communists in order to prevent the spread of verbal infection. They can be checked only by removing the economic confusion and distress on which they thrive. Perhaps this can be done by the methods of liberal democracy. Perhaps not. If not, it needs no prophet to tell us that sooner or later a "despairing people" will demand "drastic action." The demand may assume the voice of communism, or of fascism, or of both. It may conceivably lead to another "irreconcilable conflict," similar to that of 1861. Outmoded liberals would not then need, any more than they did in 1861, to ask whether they should abandon the principle of free speech, since the principle of free speech would already have abandoned them. The logic of events would present them—perhaps is already, without their knowing it, presenting them—with nothing better than that choice of evils which liberals always have to face in times when arms speak and laws are silent, the choice of joining one uncongenial armed camp or the other.

There would, it is true, be another way out for any liberal who wished to take it. Any man might in desperation cry, "A plague on both your houses!" Withdrawing from the world of affairs, he might, as a non-resistant pacifist, still exercise the right of private judgment, having deliberately fortified himself to face, as the woman said, "the consequences." In short, he might, as a last refuge from imbecility, turn Christian and practice the precept that it is better to suffer evil than to do it. In that elevated spiritual retreat he would have leisure to meditate the bitter truth of Pascal's profound commonplace: "It is *right* to follow that which is just, it is *necessary* to follow that which is stronger."

1934

The Marxian Philosophy of History

I SOMETIMES find myself discussing communism with those who profess that faith; and not infrequently I note an implicit assumption on their part that I, as an intelligent person with some knowledge of history, ought either, (1) to refute the Marxian philosophy of history, or (2) in all honesty to support the communist cause. In such discussions I have maintained, (1) that an intelligent person may regard the Marxian philosophy of history as an illuminating interpretation of the past without subscribing to it as a law of history, and, (2) that even if convinced that the Marxian doctrine is a valid law of history, one might still with excellent reasons refuse to support the communist cause. Such discussions, developed more fully and presented more formally, may for convenience be put in the form of a discussion between a communist and a liberal.

Communist: Don't you think, Professor, that history proves that social progress, or change if you prefer, is the result of an inevitable class-conflict?

Liberal: Put in that precise way, no. I can't see that history proves anything except that what happened did happen, or that anything is inevitable except what happened; but what happened is precisely the question at issue. In using the words "prove" and "inevitable" you are, as the logicians say, begging the question.

Communist: I don't insist on those precise words.

Liberal: Very well. I agree then that history does support, or can easily be made to support, the Marxian doctrine in a general way. For example, in the middle ages the chief source of wealth was certainly land; and it is obvious that at that time the land-owning aristocracy was the ruling class. No great ingenuity is required to show that political, social, and religious customs and ideas of that time were suited to maintaining the political and economic ascendancy of the aristocracy. Likewise, it is obvious that during the last three centuries land has gradually been replaced by capital as the chief source of wealth; and the history of this time may easily be regarded as a conflict between the middle-class capitalist and the land-owning aristocracy, as a result of which the former have replaced the latter as the ruling class and have substituted, in their interest, a new set of institutions and ideas (representative government, individual liberty, popular sovereignty, free competition) for the old. Yes, as an interpretation of the last thousand years of European history, the Marxian theory is most illuminating.

Communist: Isn't it a bit more than merely illuminating? Can you deny that it is a more convincing and realistic interpretation than any other?

Liberal: I could very easily deny it, but I have no wish to do so. Let us admit that it is the most convincing interpretation. I will go farther. For purposes of argument I will admit that it is the only valid interpretation.

Communist: Very well then. If you admit that Marx has correctly interpreted the past, why not admit that he has correctly interpreted the future? Why not admit that just as the bourgeois-capitalist class displaced the land-owning aristocracy as the ruling class, so the proletariat will in its turn replace the bourgeois-capitalist class? And if they do so, isn't it reasonable to suppose that the characteristic ideas of the present society (representative government, freedom of speech, *laissez-faire*) will in turn give way to others suited to the interests of the proletariat?

Liberal: If I accept Marx's interpretation of the past it is because I know what it is, and can test it. If I hesitate to accept his interpretation of the future it is partly because I do not know precisely what it is, and partly because, even if I know what it is, I cannot test it. I willingly admit that the future will, in some way that can after the event be rationalized, resemble the past. Certainly change is the law of life, and it is obvious that the institutions and ideas of the nineteenth century, which were so well suited to the interests of the capitalist class, will not suffice without modification for the needs of the complex mechanized society of the twentieth. I willingly admit also that the ideas and institutions of today will be changed in such a was as to conform more closely with the economic interests of the workers, the mass of the people, the proletariat. But that is not to say that the change will come about in the way predicted by Marx, or that the result will be the the sort of utopia predicted by him.

Communist: Utopia! I am not aware that Marx predicted any utopia.

Liberal: Well, let us say that he didn't. What then did he predict?

Communist: He predicted that the capitalist régime would by its own nature destroy itself. Its nature is to be ruthlessly competitive, so that in any industrial society the tendency is for wealth to be more highly concentrated in the hands of a few, while the mass of the people tend to fall to the condition of wage slaves. When this process reaches a certain point, the system breaks down, as it is now breaking down because it has deprived the people of the means of buying the commodities which it is the sole aim of the capitalist class to make and sell for a profit. When the system ceases to work the people will necessarily take control, and, since it is their interest to do so, they will establish a classless society based upon the common ownership of instruments of production, and a more equitable distribution of the product. This is the social revolution that Marx predicted, and it has already begun—in Russia.

Liberal: In Russia, yes. In Russia, that is to say not the most highly industrialized society but the least highly industrialized society. That is surely not according to Marx.

Communist: No, it is not. But you cannot maintain that because Marx's prediction is not verified in every detail it is not therefore valid in its general outline. The Great War created a special set of circumstances which were peculiarly favorable to the social revolution in Russia.

Liberal: Very true. The social revolution clearly occurred before its time in Russia. Providence, or Dialectic Materialism, or whatever it is that regulates social changes, certainly did a very curious thing in bringing the social revolution to Russia before it brought it to more highly industrialized countries, such as England. For my part I don't think the Russian revolution does anything to verify the predictions of Marx; to me it indicates only that in a country in which the people were accustomed to being ruled by a dictatorship, a country moreover in which the prevailing form of dictatorship was especially corrupt and incompetent, it was very easy to establish a dictatorship of a different sort. But let that pass. My reluctance to accept the Marxian doctrine arises from something far more fundamental than the Russian accident. There are two difficulties which have always troubled me. Perhaps you can solve them. One is that it is extremely difficult to predict the future on the basis of past experience; or rather it is extremely easy to find in the past support for diverse predictions of the future. The other difficulty is to understand why a persistent economic class conflict in the past justifies us in predicting a classless society in the future.

As to the first difficulty. What little I know of history makes me chary of any prediction as to the form which social institutions will take in the future. Especially so when such predictions, based upon a realistic view of the past, take an idealistic view of the future. During the last two thousand years all the saints and sages of the world, deploring greed and strife, poverty and injustice, have looked forward to the time when a more just society would be established. They have many times predicted the coming of a classless society in which everyone would have enough; but the course of events has never yet verified their hopes. This generalization is as solidly based on historical fact as any that Marx has made, and it is more widely based; and if I am to judge the future by the past, I see no reason for discarding this generalization for that which Marx offers me. The less so, since Marx's interpretation of the past, if projected into the future, seems to refute his own prediction.

Communist: I don't understand that.

Liberal: Perhaps it will become clear if I elaborate the second difficulty I just mentioned. Marx's interpretation of the past is explicit and realistic; his forecast of the future seems to me vague and idealistic. I have called it utopian, but you object to that word. I do not insist on it. I will even surrender the word "idealistic." But the point is this. Marx finds that in the past the effective force that has determined social change is the economic class conflict. He

points out that this economic class conflict explains the
rise of the present capitalistic society. He shows, or at
least his disciples show, how this economic class conflict
is working to undermine our capitalistic society. Very
well. If then I project this explanation of social changes
into the future, what does it tell me? It seems to tell me that
there will be in the future what there has been in the past
—an endless economic class conflict, an endless replacement
of one dominant class by another, an endless transformation
of institutions and ideas in accordance with the changes
effected by the class conflict. But this is not what Marx predicts. What he predicts is the end of the economic class
conflict, the establishment of a classless society. What you
and he are asking me to accept is an explanation of history
that will explain it only up to a certain point. Marx criti-
cised Hegel for that very weakness. Hegel explained past
history as a transformation effected by the Transcendent
Idea realizing itself in the actual events of history; according to him the great objective of history was the complete
realization of the Idea in the form of Freedom, and this
great objective had already been in some sense attained in
the Prussian state. Marx wanted to know what the Transcendent Idea would find to do in the future, now that it was
entirely realized. That is a sound criticism. Now, my
difficulty is to know how Marx has improved on Hegel. To
be sure Marx does not say that the great objective of history
has already been attained. He says the economic class conflict will bring about another social revolution. But after
the social revolution, what then? What becomes of the
economic class conflict after the revolution has established
a classless society? I can't find that it will have anything
more to do than Hegel's Transcendent Idea. A law of history which, at some determinate moment, ceases to explain

history, a law of history which is required, at the appropriate moment, to commit hari-kari on the doorstep of the ideal, surely leaves something to be desired.

Communist: Well, that's a point. But really, Professor, you know very well that this objection has been noted before, and that there is a good answer to it. Marx was not so blind as to overlook it. How could he have done so, since he pointed out that very weakness in Hegel's philosophy of history?

Liberal: I should be glad to learn how Marx avoids that difficulty.

Communist: I am not sure that Marx himself does altogether avoid it. But you must allow Marxian philosophy to be elaborated and interpreted by his followers in the light of later experience. You have no objection to that?

Liberal: None at all. We must by all means discuss Marxianism at its best, as it is now interpreted by the most expert exegesis available.

Communist: Very well. According to a recent interpreter of Marxianism, history is explainable in terms of a dialectic of transformation, in which conflicts appear only to be resolved in a higher synthesis. This conflict is not necessarily always an economic class conflict. After the classless society is established the conflict will continue, but on a different level. According to Professor Sidney Hook, a recent interpreter of Marx, the dialectic in a communist, classless society, will not be "historically conditioned in the same sense" as in earlier times. "It finds expression . . . on a more elevated plane. Although in advance no one can describe the detailed forms it will take, it is clear that its general locus is individual and personal." In other words, having solved the economic problem by establishing a classless society, men will be occupied with the higher, spiritual problems of human development.

Liberal: Well, I must confess that this greatly surprises me. A while back you would not allow me to apply the term "utopian" to the future society predicted by Marx; and yet this sounds to me very similar to all the utopian societies I ever heard of. Throughout the past men have engaged in brutal conflict for material gain; but this brutal conflict is somehow to bring about a classless society in which men will suddenly change their natures and devote themselves to the nobler things of life. A dialectic materialism will be replaced by what we may call a dialectic spiritualism; or to put it in simple English, conflict will cease on the economic plane, and continue only on the moral plane.

Well, it may be so: and if it should turn out so, it would be grand. I point out merely that this is what all the idealistic prophets of the world have always hoped would happen. It is what the early prophets of democracy predicted. It is what all humane liberals may hope for. But what I don't understand is how the Marxian philosophy permits us to hope for it. I suppose it to be a fundamental tenet of Marxian philosophy that the conduct of men is strictly conditioned; and if their conduct in the past has been strictly conditioned by the economic class conflict, how can it cease to be so conditioned in the future?

Communist: Your difficulty arises from a false assumption—an assumption that is made by many of the hostile critics of Marx. The assumption is that Marx accepted the nineteenth-century doctrine of mechanistic determinism. That is not so. Marx always insisted that "man makes his own history." He contributes something novel to the conditions that determine his own conduct. Marx says explicitly: "By acting on the external world man changes his own nature." This means that man can, by acquiring knowledge, modify his environment, and so modify also his own ways of submitting to the environment. Therefore it is quite possible that men might for a very long time submit blindly to the influence of the economic class conflict; for a long time, but not necessarily forever; since, having become aware that they had been in the past submitting to the economic class conflict, they would, in the future, even if they submitted to it, not be submitting to it blindly. This awareness that their conduct has been determined by the economic class conflict becomes a new element in the conditions, and so changes the conditions that will determine men's conduct in the future. One might say that the great object of Marx was just this: to make men aware of the conditions that made social revolutions in the past, so that in the coming social revolution, being aware of what was happening, they could consciously direct it. To quote once more from Professor Sidney Hook: "Once man acquires control of the conditions of social life, he can consciously make over his own nature in accordance with a morally free will, in contradistinction to men in the past, whose nature has been unconsciously made over by the economically determined will of economic classes."

Liberal: I see; at least I think so, in spite of Professor Hook's somewhat obscure academic phraseology. But what it comes to, I suppose, is this. In the physical world a law operates forever in the same way because the physical object is not aware of, and is indifferent to, what happens. A billiard ball (to use the classic example) has no desire to make over its nature. But man is aware of, and is not indifferent to, what happens. His acts are indeed strictly conditioned, but as soon as he becomes aware of what it is that conditions them, his awareness enables him to react differently; his acts are then not less strictly conditioned than formerly, but his own awareness becomes a new element that changes and complicates the conditions. For a long time men may worship the sun; when they become aware of the influences that make them worship the sun, this awareness may become an influence that will make them cease to worship the sun. Freedom of the will, as Engels said, is no more than man's knowledge that his acts are conditioned.

Very well, Marx then (or perhaps his disciples) applies this principle of freedom to the social changes or revolutions that occur in history. In the past, social revolutions have been conditioned by the economic class conflict. As long as men are not aware of this fact, social revolutions will continue to be conditioned by the economic class conflict. But when men become fully aware, through the great discovery of Marx, that social revolutions in the past have been conditioned by the class conflict, this knowledge will enable them to react differently—to react in such a way as to abolish the class conflict. This, I take it, is how you interpret Marx.

Communist: Yes, that is right.

Liberal: Well, I agree with this idea of free will. It seems to me obvious that as men acquire knowledge of the influences that determine their acts, this knowledge becomes a new influence that enables them to act differently. But if we accept this principle it seems odd to me that men shouldn't have acquired, before the time of Marx, some knowledge of the fact that their conduct was determined by the economic class conflict. I should have supposed that this element of awareness would have been steadily modifying the conditions that determine social changes from the time of the Neanderthal man down to the present. How does it happen that this element of awareness has had no appreciable influence up to the time of Marx? Marx must have been a much greater man than I have always thought —a veritable Messiah, who at a single stroke has given mankind this epoch-making revelation that is to transform so radically the conditions that determine human history. I find it difficult to believe that.It seems more reasonable to believe that knowledge has been steadily modifying the economic influences that have determined social changes in the past, and that in the future further knowledge, knowledge unknown to Marx, will continue to modify those influences in ways not dreamed of by Marx.

But that is a minor point. Let us assume that up to the time of Marx men have been submitting blindly to the economic class conflict, and that now, thanks to Marx, they are in the way of becoming aware of that fact, and that being aware of it they are in a position to modify profoundly the conditions that will determine social changes. What then? Well, it seems to me that this great revelation made by Marx is precisely what makes it impossible for him to predict the character of the coming social revolution. If we did not know that social changes had been conditioned by the economic class conflict, the coming social revolution would presumably follow the course of previous ones, in which case no classless society would emerge from it. But since we do know that social revolutions in the past were conditioned by the class conflict, this very knowledge, according to Marx, will make the coming social revolution follow some different course, in which case we may hope, but cannot be sure, that a classless society will emerge from it. In short, in so far as Marx has made men aware of the influence of the economic class conflict in the past, he has destroyed the very conditions that would have enabled him to predict the nature of the social revolution in the future. If Marx wished to predict correctly the nature of the coming social revolution, he should not have told us what it is that makes social revolutions: since he has told us, the secret is out, and hence no one can predict it. The great secret is out, thanks to Marx, and this knowledge will enable us to make of the coming social revolution something different than it otherwise would have been. Marxian philosophy presents his disciples with a dilemma which they either do not see or refuse to meet. It is this. Either social changes are always determined by the same conditions, in which case we may be sure that the coming social revolution will be similar to those in the past—it will transform the present class conflict only to create the conditions that will issue in a new one. Or else knowledge of the conditions that have determined social revolutions in the past introduces a novel influence in the conditions that will determine social revolutions in the future, in which case we cannot predict with any certainty the nature of those revolutions. The profound conviction of Communists that the proletariat is destined to establish a classless society on the ruins of the present capitalist régime is not justified by Marxian philosophy: if you interpret Marx in terms of mechanistic determinism, this profound communist conviction is a pure delusion; on the other hand, if you interpret Marx in terms of free will, this conviction is no more than a splendid hope. That is why I cannot accept the Marxian philosophy as a law of history.

Communist: Very well. Suppose, for purposes of argument, that the communist conviction is only a splendid hope. You yourself have said that the present capitalist régime must be changed in such a way as to harmonize better with the interests of the mass of the people, the proletariat. That is just what the Communists want. Since you sympathize with their object, and believe that it will in some measure be realized, why not join the Communists and help to realize this splendid hope?

Liberal: I refuse to join the Communists because, while I sympathize with their desire to make a better world for the mass of the people, I have no faith in the methods which they propose for obtaining this object. If I understand them, they claim that nothing really worth while can be done until conditions are ripe for the application of the revolutionary technique. When that time comes, they propose, following the example of the Bolsheviks in Russia, to seize control of the government, forcibly expropriate the bourgeois class, and ruthlessly suppress the expression of all opinion that a dictatorial government judges to be hostile to the welfare of the community of workers.

Now I have no faith in force and repression as the *primary* means of achieving the good life. I am not as yet a non-resistance pacifist. Any government is probably better than none, and all government rests at last on force. But I believe that the essential test of civilized society is the extent to which law and public authority rest on free discussion and voluntary consent. A resort to force as a means of obtaining consent may be sometimes necessary to prevent a society from falling into virtual anarchy; but the resort to force in place of persuasion is so far a confession of failure. I have no faith in the possibility of abolishing oppression by oppressing oppressors. I have no faith in the infallibility of any man, or of any group of men, or of the doctrines or dogmas of any man or group of men, except in so far as they can stand the test of free criticism and analysis. I agree with Pascal that "thought makes the dignity of man"; and I believe therefore that all the great and permanently valuable achievements of civilization have been won by the free play of intelligence in opposition to, or in spite of, the pressure of mass emotion and the effort of organized authority to enforce conformity in conduct and opinion. I do not believe that there has been, or that there will be, a high civilization in any country in which the mind of man is limited to the expression of ideas authorized by public authority. Dictatorship is as old as European society; and whether it be the dictatorship of a Stalin, a Mussolini, or a Hitler, it does not become something new and admirable by being dressed up in a new and mystical idealogy. I recognize it as a possibility that our modern, complex, machine civilization may so far fall into confusion that a dictatorship will in fact replace the present régime; but I refuse to recognize this outcome as inherently desirable, and I refuse to join in any effort to make it inevitable.

This is why I do not join the Communists. I believe that profound changes in our economic and industrial system are necessary; but I believe that they can and I hope that they will be made, in this country, without resorting to violent revolution, without resorting to dictatorship, without abandoning our traditional reliance on free discussion and criticism of public authority and of the measures it proposes for the solution of social ills. And there is nothing in the Marxian philosophy, as you expound it, that makes it illogical for me to take this position. According to you, now that Marx has made us aware of the influence of the economic class conflict in the past, this very awareness will enable us to master and modify the class conflict in the future. I agree. But why is it necessary to assume that this knowledge which Marx has revealed to us is the exclusive possession of the proletariat? After all the bourgeoisie have a certain amount of intelligence. They can read Marx, or at least Sidney Hook. They can observe what has occurred in Russia, in Italy, in Germany. It is possible for them, too, to understand that the capitalist competitive system is in a fair way of destroying itself. Marxian doctrine tells me that capitalists, like proletarians, are motivated by their economic class interest; it does not tell me that they, any more than the proletarians, must forever be motivated by a blind illusion as to what that interest is. At the present moment it obviously is not to the interest of the capitalist class that the mass of the people should be without the means of buying the goods which the capitalist class produces in order to sell. It is still possible that the capitalist system in this country, subjected to the pressure of economic necessity and the force of public discontent, may by reasonably peaceful procedure be sufficiently transformed into a coördinated and planned economic system to make it, not a utopia indeed, but at least a decently workable system. And a decently workable system which preserves our traditional liberty of discussion and criticism will, in my opinion, be superior in the long run to any system that can be established by the repressive measures now employed by the Communists of Russia, the Fascists of Italy, or the Nazis of Germany.

Communist: A decently workable system. That's certainly vague enough—as vague as Marx's idealistic society of the future which you derided. No doubt a decently workable system is one which you would prefer to something which you don't like, such as the Russian communist state.

Liberal: It is. But you must permit me to prefer a decently workable system which I like to a decently workable system which I don't like. You can hardly expect me to become a Communist until I am convinced that communism would be preferable to the system under which I live.

Communist: No. But you have already admitted that the "decently workable system" which you hope will be established may fail to be established—that the present system may end in a dictatorship. That I think is the more probable outcome. It is likely that in the long run the capitalist class, confronted by the rising power of the proletariat, will resort to force, as it has done in Italy and Germany. If then you are faced with the alternative of supporting a dictatorship of the proletariat or a dictatorship of the bourgeoisie, what will you do? What then will become of freedom of speech and the appeal to persuasion? Since you sympathize with the objectives of the Communists, will you not then be forced to join them? Why wait till then? Why not join now the side which is bound to win in the long run because it is in harmony with the dominant trend of social forces?

Liberal: I do not admit that communism is necessarily in harmony with the dominant trend of social forces. I see that when it suits your argument you, like most Communists, fall back on the doctrine of a fatalistic determinism which makes the communist revolution inevitable whatever men do about it; but when your argument requires another doctrine you admit that the social revolution may be mastered and directed by the conscious purposes of men. You ought really to accept one doctrine or the other, and stick to it. But no matter. Accept one doctrine or both, as you like. In either case I see no good reason for joining the Communists. If the communist revolution is inevitable, whatever men do about it, why do anything? Why join either side, if you know beforehand that one side is bound to win anyway? But if the communist revolution is not inevitable, then the proletariat can indeed do something to hasten it, and by the same token the bourgeoisie can do something to retard it. And in that case why should I join the Communists? I am a professor; and the Communists are never weary of telling me that professors as a class support the capitalist régime because it is their economic interest to do so. Very well, I will be a sufficiently good Marxian to accept the doctrine that men's actions are motivated by their economic class interest. If then my economic interests are bound up with the capitalist régime, and I can do something to retard the communist revolution, I should be, according to Marx himself, a poor humanitarian fool to desert my class and work for a revolution which, if successful, would ruthlessly suppress me. As a liberal humanitarian, or a Christian mystic, I might logically sacrifice myself and my class for the welfare of the masses; but as a Marxian that would be to adopt the very "utopian" attitude which Marx never ceased to ridicule. You really ask too much. The Marxian philosophy teaches me either that the communist revolution is inevitable, in which case I merely resign myself to it: or else it teaches me that the communist revolution can be hastened or retarded by the conscious efforts of men, in which case I stick to my class and do what I can to retard it. In either case I have the profound consolation of knowing that my conduct is based on the solid foundation of the Marxian philosophy of history.

These, you are to understand, are choices logically open to me on the assumption that I accept the Marxian philosophy of history. But life is less simple than logic. In logic you can present me with clear-cut alternatives. You can ask me whether I will "choose" to support the dictatorship of the proletariat or the dictatorship of the bourgeoisie, quite as if some day, the two contending parties being lined up in battle array on a *champs de mars*, I should be asked to step out and join one side or the other. In actual life it does not seem to me that I am ever confronted with choices as simple or as dramatically staged as that. When I voted for Mr. Roosevelt (if I *did* vote for him—I can't be sure now) I made a choice, without being certain (any more than Mr. Roosevelt himself was) what would come of it. I am now "supporting" (so far as I am supporting anything) the Roosevelt administration, and it is possible that in 1936 I shall vote for the reëlection of Mr. Roosevelt. Does this mean that I am "choosing" to support a fascist rather than a communist régime? Thoroughgoing Communists appear to know that I am: the New Deal, they say, is obviously an American species of fascist technique. But I am sufficiently naïve not to be aware of having made any choice between communism and fascism. And very glad I am that it is so. I should dislike very much to be confronted with a clear-cut choice between a dictatorship of the proletariat and a dictatorship of the bourgeoisie. I should be inclined to say, "A plague on both your houses!" I find Mussolini as offensive as Stalin, and Hitler more offensive than either.

Communist: That is all very well, but a real revolution is not impossible. There are plenty of Russians who could assure you that the alternative you so much dislike has been presented to them in a quite sufficiently clear-cut and dramatic manner. If it should be similarly presented in this country, it seems to me that you would, however much you might dislike it, have to choose one side or the other.

Liberal: Not necessarily. There would still be another possibility.

Communist: What would that be?

Liberal: I might still refuse to join either side. I might persist in the futility of expressing my faith in the superior virtues of persuasion.

Communist: That would have serious consequences for you. You would be suppressed.

Liberal: True enough. But I might accept the consequences. I might choose to be suppressed rather than to support what I object to. In short, I might, as a last refuge from imbecility, become a Christian and practise the precept that it is better to suffer evil than to do it.

Communist: That would be to fall back upon a far more mystical type of idealism than Marx ever contemplated, and I fail to see that it would get you anywhere.

Liberal: I dare say it wouldn't. But, as I said before, I am a professor, and a professor, as the German proverb has it, is "a man who thinks otherwise": if he is not permitted to talk freely he cannot get anywhere anyway.

Labelling the Historians[1]

BY THE middle group of American historians, we are to understand those whose work was done within the period from "let us say about 1826, when Sparks began to give himself to history," to a certain not precisely determined date (sometime after the Civil War it was) when "the scientific spirit secures domination over the patriotic school that had ruled for several decades." Professor Bassett does not bring into the story all who wrote history during this period, but has preferred to deal rather fully with the most eminent men, letting them serve as representative of the group as a whole. Therefore, apart from a preliminary chapter on historical writing in colonial and revolutionary times, in which one regrets to note that Cotton Mather is not mentioned, the volume takes the form of four biographical essays—three rather long ones devoted to Sparks, Bancroft, and Peter Force, and one rather short one devoted to the "two literary historians," Prescott and Motley.

A distinguishing characteristic of the work is that it has to do with historians rather than with history: the author is far more interested in the men themselves and in their activities than he is in the books they wrote. Of the seventy-three pages given to Bancroft, a very few would include all that could be called an analysis or a criticism of

[1] *The Middle Group of American Historians.* By John Spencer Bassett. (Macmillan Co.)

his history. Prescott and Motley, whose lives were relatively uneventful, who at least did little for history except to write histories, are dispatched in short space; whereas the chapter devoted to Peter Force falls only three pages short of being the longest in the book. And, on the whole, I should say the chapter on Peter Force is the best one of all, and next to that, the one on Sparks; the reason being that these men were primarily collectors of documents, and their work appeals to Professor Bassett (who has no high opinion of the literary or patriotic histories) as having a higher value than the works of such men as Bancroft and Motley, as being, in fact, a kind of "permanent contribution to knowledge," such as *The Rise of the Dutch Republic* can lay no claim to being. Professor Bassett is therefore at his best—and his best is very good—in relating, for example, the efforts of Sparks to obtain possession of the Washington letters, or in untangling for us the somewhat intricate history of the enterprise which resulted in the publication of the *American Archives*. The book is itself a piece of careful research rather than a contribution to historical criticism or the history of ideas; and taken for what it is, it will be found, by professional historians at least, and I should think by a rather wide reading public as well, a very useful book and an extremely interesting one.

If Professor Bassett had been primarily interested in criticism or the history of ideas, his selection of eminent men would necessarily have been different. It would be difficult to find a principle of classification which would include under one category men so different as Prescott and Peter Force. Prescott might be described as a literary, but hardly as a patriotic historian, since he was not concerned with the history of his own country; but Peter Force, certainly not literary and scarcely a historian, does not easily come under either category. Bancroft, of course, is the one representative who meets both requirements: he was both literary and patriotic. Professor Bassett does not indeed stress these principles of classification, his middle group being mainly a chronological affair. But at least the implication is that the middle group may be more or less conveniently labelled with either one or both of these tags, and that the middle period, in this sense, closes when "the scientific spirit secures domination over the patriotic school that had ruled for several decades."

Perhaps it is this latter distinction which enables the author to dispense with any special attention to criticism, since it is clearly a distinction which reduces the business of estimating earlier writers to relatively small proportions. The scientific method and its accompanying attitude of detachment having been at last discovered and applied, criticism becomes mainly a question of how far, and in what respects, any historian of the old school, whether literary or patriotic, falls short of measuring up to the modern ideal. With these simple fundamentals in hand, Bancroft, for example, can be readily dismissed by saying that, while he was an industrious student of the sources and is generally accurate so far as the facts go, he too often sacrificed exact statement for literary effect, and, on account of his militant patriotism and enthusiasm for democracy, interpreted the facts in a glaringly prejudiced way. When this is said, what else is there to say? Nothing really, except that Bancroft is now read only for his style.

Style, even in historical writing, is something for which modern scientific historians profess admiration. To possess literary excellence is certainly a merit; and while it would be "retrogressing," as Professor Bassett says, to go back to the literary school in other respects, it would be a good thing if we "could bring forward their best qualities into our own group of scholarly and conscientious workers." Excellent in general and in the abstract, in particular cases style seems nevertheless to impress Professor Bassett as something likely to cover hidden sins. "Men who write with the hastening fingers of imagination," he says, "sometimes drop into obscurity details which more literal minded persons would consider very important, or they use expressions meaning more or less than they intend them to mean." In theory Professor Bassett is far from maintaining any irreconcilable antithesis between the scientific and the literary *genres*, but in practice his scientific conscience makes it difficult for him to admit a literary historian to all the privileges of the modern guild. Thus it happens that Parkman, on account of his excellent writing, barely escapes being put with the middle group. "*While* he wrote with that full appreciation of style which was characteristic of Bancroft and the literary historians, his industry, his research among documents, and especially his detachment *seem* to place him among the men of to-day." If Parkman had only written badly, no one could question his scientific standing.

All these conventional labels, having little to do with ideas or the quality of a man's work, seem to me quite useless for purposes of historical criticism. To say of any historian, ancient or modern, that he is scientific, or literary, or patriotic, tells me little that I care to know; and, particularly, to regard the term "scientific" as an adequate characterization of any group of historians is but to dispense with distinctions, and with that discrimination which is essential to genuine criticism. Many accurate, unprejudiced, and dull histories were written before the Civil War. H. A. L. Fisher writes better than Bancroft, and so do George Otto and George Macaulay Trevelyan; and I should think them all scientific, although I speak with some misgiving, not knowing very well what is meant by scientific. Meanwhile, if I understand what others mean by the term, Germany is full of scientific historians—all patriotic, a few, perhaps, literary.

The inadequacy of such conventional labels for purposes of criticism is nowhere better illustrated than in the case of Bancroft, who has suffered rather more than he has gained in the process. What one should say about Bancroft seems well understood among present-day professional historians. It is that his history is interesting to read, but unsafe to follow; he was a literary, but a prejudiced, historian. The case is one which calls for a little, not after all so very subtle, discrimination. If "style" is anything more than a kind of metaphorical embroidery, it should be clear that the chief merit of Bancroft is not his style but his scholarship, that careful investigation and exceptional accuracy which make his book, in the editions which contain his footnotes, still a useful one for the student—at least for the student of the American Revolution. On the other hand, his chief defect is not his bias. Gibbon had bias, and so had Henry Adams, and, although the bias of Adams was in part patriotic, that of Gibbon was not. All historians, even the most scientific, have bias, if in no other sense than the determination not to have any. The chief defect of Bancroft is his lack of ideas, the lack at all events of fresh and novel general ideas, and of any subtle discrimination in handling such ideas as he had. It is for this reason that his patriotism is so obtrusive and so irritating; and it is for this reason that his style, since he was bound by convention to have a style, is extremely bad.

I very much doubt whether anyone now reads Bancroft for his style. To do so would be wasted effort. Reading any writer "for his style" is indeed largely wasted effort—an occupation that in any event should cease with adolescence, except perhaps for the pseudo-literary who must be allowed to retain some sustaining illusion. It is wasted effort for the reason that any style worth attention cannot be separated from the matter of which it is, in the measure of its excellence, merely the most appropriate form. The very word "style" does incredible harm, since it brings with it, from common usage, connotations that are inapplicable to literary discourse. Style? Stylish dress, stylish woman. Every one knows what a stylish woman is—a woman attractively dressed, a woman with an air, a manner. How then can a writer "have style" unless he has a manner, unless his writing is, in some sense, stylish? Writers who know their business instinctively shudder when the undiscriminating speak of style as if it were something external, something to be put on or taken off at will—a kind of rich, bespangled cloak in which any, even the most emaciated and unprepossessing, body of thought can readily be dressed up and made presentable. One thing only concerns the writer, and that is to find an arrangement of words that will fully and exactly convey the thought or feeling which he wishes to convey. In so far as the form (arrangement of words) is determined by some conventional notion of good writing, rather than by the nature of the thought and feeling to be expressed, it is bad form, bad style—in short, it is "style."

This is why Bancroft's style is bad. It is not determined primarily by the subject he wishes to render. It is a borrowed, and therefore an artificial, style, a form of writing imposed on historians as such by the current literary convention. In Bancroft's time the Muse of History still lived.

Surviving from the days of great epic poetry, she still had her place (a less prominent place than formerly) in the literary pantheon, and was still offered by the faithful a conventional if somewhat perfunctory worship. Since the subjects of epic poetry had always been the great events and heroic deeds of history, it seemed fitting to those whose minds were tuned to the rhythm of Vergil and Homer that history, however little heroic, should be related in the epic manner. As a matter of course, therefore, Bancroft invoked the Muse—"O Muse, inspire my pen to the end that these heroic deeds may be related in a manner worthy of thee!" In reading his history, one feels that he never forgets either the facts which are in his head, or the Muse who is at his elbow. He is at once aware of his subject and of his obligation as a writer to adapt his subject to the literary *style* appropriate to it. The result is a persistent discord, at best a dissonance never quite resolved, at worst a hollow verbal eloquence drumming the ear and distracting the attention from the essence of the thing said. The reader forgets what has happened in the United States, being so much more interested in what is happening in Bancroft's history. What is happening is clear enough. Bancroft is making a composition, a long one, in which he seems always striving consciously, not indeed always successfully, to impose on the multifarious and commonplace facts that measured, stately rhythm which was supposed to be suited to the march of great events.

Open the famous history—almost anywhere. One cannot read five pages without being a little oppressed by the heroic effort to sustain the grand manner. Unfortunately for the grand manner, as honest and informed a historian as Bancroft is constantly reduced to the hard necessity of conveying matter-of-fact information. Bancroft must have known (and Gibbon too) that the best way to convey such information is by direct statement. The best way to convey, for example, the fact that the Roman government declined Aleric's request to be made commander of the Roman armies, is just to say, "The Roman government declined Aleric's request to be made commander of the Roman armies." But it was almost impossible for Gibbon to fall into this right way of stating a fact. He had invoked the Muse, and the Muse had pronounced that sort of thing not in keeping with the dignity of history. And so, with the Muse at his elbow, Gibbon was constrained to write: "Aleric . . . had solicited the command of the Roman armies; and the Imperial court provoked him to demonstrate the folly of their refusal and the importance of their loss." Bancroft is rarely so good (that is, so bad) as Gibbon at his worst, but he knows what the Muse expects. Having occasion to say that in the reign of Henry IV the French civil wars of religion were ended, he lifts the simple fact to the epic level, thus: "At length, under the mild and tolerant reign of Henry IV, the star of France emerged from the clouds of blood . . . and civil war, which had so long eclipsed her glory." To be sure, every age has its conventions, and Bancroft need not be condemned for having learned from Gibbon that emperors are never crowned, but always "assume the purple." Still, one wonders a little why a Harvard man with sufficient independence to become a Jacksonian democrat, should not have realized that a "style" suitable for telling the story of the Trojan War or the Fall of Lucifer is not the best for relating the history of the United States.

It is not quite fair, it is indeed a little cruel, to test Bancroft's style (or Gibbon's either) by asking him to make a simple statement of fact. Accepting the grand man-

ner as given by the Muse, let us see what he can do with it
in elucidating a less concrete, a more subtle and impalpable
matter—for example, the character of James I. Disliking
kings in general, and this particular king for having dissolved the Virginia Company, Bancroft wished to leave
with the reader a vivid and exact impression of the man's
less admirable qualities. In describing James, he is obviously
doing his best, writing at the top of his "style." This is
the result.

Dissimulation is the vice of those who have neither true judgment
nor courage. King James, from his imbecility, was false, and
sometimes vindicated his falsehood, as though deception and
cunning had been worthy of a king. But he was an awkward liar,
rather than a crafty dissembler. He could, before Parliament, call
God to witness his sincerity, when he was already resolved on
being insincere. His cowardice was such, that he feigned a fond-
ness for Carr, whose arrest for murder he had already ordered. He
was afraid of his wife; could be governed by being overawed; and
was easily intimidated by the vulgar insolence of Buckingham.
In Scotland, he solemnly declared his attachment to the Puritan
discipline and doctrines; but it was from fear of open resistance.
The pusillanimous man assents from cowardice, and recovers
boldness with the assurance of impunity. (*History of the United
States*. 15th Edition, Boston, 1856. I, 293.)

I suspect that the Muse, while dictating this passage,
may have winked an eye. It is unlikely that she could have
had much sympathy with the notion that history, although
calling for the epic manner, must of necessity be written in
prose. Certainly she must have known, what Bancroft perhaps never suspected, that the "prose" of the passage just
quoted was in imminent danger of rising to the level of
blank verse. I feel sure, therefore, that the Muse would have
much preferred the following version.

> Dissimulation is the vice of those
> Who have not judgment or true courage.
> King James, from imbecility, was false,
> And sometimes did his falsehood vindicate
> As though deception had been worthy of a king.
> He was an awkward liar, rather than crafty
> In dissembling. He could, before the Parliament,
> Call God to witness his sincerity, the while
> He was resolved to be wholly insincere.
> He feigned, such cowardice was his,
> A fondness for that Robert Carr,
> Whose arrest, for murder, he had secretely decreed.
> He was afrighted of his wife, could be governed
> By being overawed, or with ease intimidated
> By the vulgar insolence of Buckingham.
> In Scotland, he solemnly declared attachment
> To Puritan practice and belief; but 'twas for fear
> Of open resistance. The pusillanimous man
> Assents from cowardice, and recovers boldness
> With the assurance of impunity.

This, to be sure, is not good verse, but neither is the original good prose.

Let no one suppose that I am "attacking" Bancroft. On the contrary, I am defending him. I wish to dispel the notion, often encountered, that he was a "good writer" but an unreliable historian. The reverse of this is nearer the truth. I therefore repeat, what I have already said: the chief merit of Bancroft is his scholarship. He learned from Heeren that the first duty of the historian is to be sure of his facts, and he spared neither time nor money in the faithful performance of this duty. Many years ago I found ample evidence of the fact in his notebooks, in many volumes, then preserved in the old Lenox library. In them were innumerable extracts copied from sources (some of them unprinted) which were not then, and some of which I dare say are not now available elsewhere in this country. I remember reading somewhere that the footnotes to his history were omitted from the last edition because so many lesser men used the quotations in them without giving him credit. There are, I should guess, as few errors of fact in Bancroft's history as in any historical work of equal length. Perhaps it is unfortunate that he did not live and write at a later time. If he had written his history sometime after the Civil War, when the convention required historians to "state the facts and let them speak for themselves," he would undoubtedly have been acclaimed as a "scientific" historian of the first rank. But in that event, of course, his history would not have run to ten volumes, or to anything like fifteen editions. If then it is desirable that histories should be read, we need not regret the fact that Bancroft lived at a time when the convention required historians to write badly.

1917.

The Education of Henry Adams[1]

IN 1771, Thomas Hutchinson wrote to one of his friends, "We have not been so quiet here these five years . . . if it were not for two or three Adamses, we should do well enough." From that day to this many people have agreed with the fastidious governor. But so far, an Adams or two we have always had with us; and on the whole, although they have sometimes been exasperating, they have always been salutary. During four generations the men of this family have loved and served America as much as they have scolded her. More cannot be said, except that they have commonly given, on both counts, more than they have received. Theirs is therefore the blessing, and ours the benefit.

Among other things, we have to thank them for some diaries and autobiographies which have been notable for frank self-revelation. Henry Adams would of course have stoutly denied that any such impertinence as self-revelation was either intended or achieved in the *Education*. There is no evidence that he ever kept a diary (all things considered, the burden of proof is not on us!); but it is not to be supposed that he would have published it in any case. A man who regarded himself as of no more significance than a chance deposit on the surface of the world might indeed

[1] *The Education of Henry Adams: an Autobiography* (Boston and New York, Houghton Mifflin Company, 1918, pp. 519).

write down an intimate record of his soul's doings as an exercise in cosmic irony; but the idea of publishing it could hardly have lived for a moment in the lambent flame of his own sardonic humor. He could be perverse, but perversity could not well go the length of perpetrating so pointless a joke as that would come to.

No, Henry Adams would not reveal himself to the curious inspection of an unsympathetic world; but he would write a book for the purpose of exposing a dynamic theory of history, than which nothing could well be more impersonal or unrevealing. With a philosophy of history the Puritan has always been preoccupied; and it was the major interest of Henry Adams throughout the better part of his life. He never gained more than a faint idea of any intelligible philosophy, as he would himself have readily admitted; but after a lifetime of hard study and close thinking, the matter struck him thus:

Between the dynamo in the gallery of machines and the engine-house outside, the break of continuity amounted to abysmal fracture for a historian's objects. No more relation could he discover between the steam and the electric current than between the Cross and the cathedral. The forces were interchangeable if not reversible, but he could see only an absolute *fiat* in electricity as in faith.

In these two forces the secret must lie, since for centuries faith had ruled inexorably, only to be replaced by electricity which promised to rule quite as inexorably. To find the secret was difficult enough; but

any schoolboy could see that man as a force must be measured by motion, from a fixed point. Psychology helped here by suggesting a unit—the point of history when man held the highest idea of himself as a unit in a unified universe. Eight or ten years of study had led Adams to think he might use the century 1150-1250, expressed in Amiens Cathedral and the Works of Thomas Aquinas, as the unit from which he might measure motion down to his own time, without assuming anything as true or untrue except relation. . . . Setting himself to the task, he began a volume which he mentally knew as "Mont-Saint-Michel and Chartres: a Study in Thirteenth-Century Unity." From that point he proposed to fix a position for himself, which he could label: "The Education of Henry Adams: a Study in Twentieth-Century Multiplicity." With the help of these two points of relation, he hoped to project his lines forward and backward indefinitely, subject to correction from any one who should know better. Thereupon, he sailed for home.

You are to understand, therefore, that the *Education of Henry Adams* has nothing to do really with the person Henry Adams. Since the time of Rousseau,

the Ego has steadily tended to efface itself, and, for purposes of model, to become a manikin, on which the toilet of education is to be draped in order to show the fit or misfit of the clothes. The object of study is the garment, not the figure. . . . The manikin, therefore, has the same value as any other geometrical figure of three or four dimensions, which is used for the study of relation. For that purpose it cannot be spared; it is the only measure of motion, of proportion, of human condition; it must have the air of reality; it must be taken for real; it must be treated as though it had life. Who knows? Perhaps it had.

Whether it had life or not is, however, of no importance. The manikin is to be treated impersonally; and will be indicated throughout in the third person, not as the author's ego, but as a kind of projected and animated geometrical point upon which cosmic lines of force impinge!

It turns out that the manikin had life after all—a good deal of it; with the effect that as you go on you become more concerned with the manikin than with the clothes, and at last find yourself wholly absorbed with an ego more subtle and complex, at times more exasperating, yet upon the whole more engaging, and above all more pervasive, than you are likely to come upon in any autobiography of modern times. It is really wonderful how the clothes fall away from the manikin, how with the best effort at draping they in fact refuse to be put on at all. The reason is simple; for the constant refrain of the study is that no clothes were ever found. The manikin is therefore always in evidence for lack of covering, and ends by having to apologize for its very existence. "To the tired student, the idea that he must give it up (the search for philosophy-clothes) seemed sheer senility. As long as he could whisper, he would go on as he had begun, bluntly refusing to meet his creator with the admission that the creation had taught him nothing except that the square of the hypothenuse of a right-angled triangle might for convenience be taken as equal to something else." On his own premises, the assumption that the manikin would ever meet his creator (if he indeed had one), or that his creator would be concerned with his opinion of the creation, is gratuitous. On his own premises, there is something too much of the ego here. The *Education of Henry Adams*, conceived as a study in the philosophy of history, turns out in fact to be an *Apologia pro vita sua*, one of the most self-centred and self-revealing books in the language.

The revelation is not indeed of the direct sort that springs from frank and insouciant spontaneity. Since the revelation was not intended, the process is tortuous in the extreme. It is a revelation that comes by the way, made manifest in the effort to conceal it, overlaid by all sorts of cryptic sentences and self-deprecatory phrases, half hidden by the protective coloring taken on by a sensitive mind commonly employing paradox and delighting in perverse and teasing mystification. One can never be sure what the book means; but taken at its face value the *Education* seems to be the story of a man who regarded life from the outside, as a spectator at the play, a play in which his own part as spectator was taken by a minor character. The play was amusing in its absurdity, but it touched not the spectator, Henry Adams, who was content to sit in his protected stall and laugh in his sleeve at the play and the players—and most of all at himself for laughing. Such is the implication; but I think it was not so. In the *Mont-Saint-Michel*[2] Adams speaks of those young people who rarely like the Romanesque. "They prefer the Gothic. . . . No doubt they are right, since they are young: but men and women who have lived long and are tired—who want rest—who have done with aspirations and ambitions—*whose life has been a broken arch*—feel this repose and self-restraint as they feel nothing else." The *Education* is in fact the record, tragic and pathetic underneath its genial irony, of the defeat of fine aspirations and laudable ambitions. It is the story of a life which the man himself, in his old age, looked back upon as a broken arch.

One is not surprised that a man of Henry Adams's antecedents should take life seriously; but no sane man, looking upon his career from the outside, would call it a failure. Born into a family whose traditions were in themselves a liberal education, Henry Adams enjoyed advantages in youth such as few boys have. It was at least an unusual experience to be able, as a lad, to sit every Sunday "behind a President grandfather, and to read over his head the tablet in memory of a President great-grandfather, who had 'pledged his life, his fortune, and his sacred honor' to secure the independence of his country." This to be sure might not have been an advantage if it led the lad to regard the presidency as a heritable office in the family; but it was certainly

2 *Mont-Saint-Michel and Chartres*, p. 7.

a great deal to be able to listen daily, at his father's table, to talk as good as he was "ever likely to hear again." This was doubtless one of the reasons why he got (or was it only that it seemed so to him in his old age?) so little from Harvard College; but at any rate he graduated with honors, and afterwards enjoyed the blessed boon of two carefree years of idling and study in Germany and Italy. For six years, as private secretary to his father on one of the most difficult and successful diplomatic missions in the history of his country, he watched history in the making, and gained an inside knowledge of English politics and society such as comes to one young man in ten thousand. Returning to America, he served for a time as editor of the *North American*, and was for seven years a professor of history in Harvard College. During the last thirty-five years of his life, he lived alternately in Washington and Paris. Relieved of official or other responsibility, he traveled all over the world, met the most interesting people of his generation, devoted himself at leisure to the study of art and literature, philosophy and science, and wrote, as an incident in a long life of serious endeavor, twelve or fifteen volumes of history which by common consent rank with the best work done in that field by American scholars.

By no common standard does such a record measure failure. Most men would have been satisfied with the life he lived apart from the books he wrote, or with the books he wrote apart from the life he lived. Henry Adams is commonly counted with the historians; but he scarcely thought of himself as one, except in so far as he sought and failed to find a philosophy of history. It is characteristic that in the *Education* he barely mentions the *History of the United States*. The enterprise, which he undertook for lack of something better, he always regarded as negligible—an episode in his life to be chronicled like any other. But it is safe to say that most of us who call ourselves historians, with far less justification, would be well content if we could count, as the result of a lifetime of effort, such a shelf full of volumes to our credit. The average professor of history might well expect, on less showing, to be chosen president of the Historical Association; in which case the prospect of having to deliver a presidential address might lead him to speculate idly in idle moments upon the meaning of history; but the riddle of existence would not greatly trouble his sleep, nor could it be said of him, as Henry Adams said of himself, that "a historical formula that should satisfy the conditions of the stellar universe weighed heavily upon his mind." He would live out the remnant of his days, an admired and a fêted leader in the scholar's world, wholly unaware that his life had been a cosmic failure.

The chief question which the *Education* presents to the critic is therefore this: why did Henry Adams look back upon his life, which to other men was so enviable in itself and so notable in its achievements, as a failure? Why should he have thought of it as a broken arch? The answer may possibly be found by inquiring what he had in mind when he spoke of "education." That he did not use the term in the narrow sense of formal education may be taken as a matter of course. He disposes of his formal education by saying that he hated it, and that it never did him any good.[3] But everything, as he often says, had value for education, if one could only find out what that value was; and the reader is inclined to dismiss the question by saying that for Henry Adams education and life were identical. In a sense this is true. The careful reader will nevertheless

[3] He says that no professor in Harvard ever mentioned Karl Marx's *Das Kapital* in his time; which was very likely true since Adams graduated in 1858 and *Das Kapital* was not published till 1867!

discover that one of two rather definite, quite different, yet fundamentally related conceptions was present in Adams's mind when he used the term education: sometimes he conceives of education as that training and knowledge which would enable a man deliberately to identify himself and his work with the main "stream of tendency" of his time; at other times he conceives of education in a wider sense, as essentially identical with a scientific explanation of the social process, so that to be educated is to possess a philosophy which will solve the mystery of life.

It is the first of these conceptions which Adams has in mind when he says,

> Pernaps Henry Adams was not worth educating; most keen judges incline to think that barely one man in a hundred owns a mind capable of reacting to any purpose on the forces that surround him, and fully half of these react wrongly. The object of education for that mind should be the teaching itself how to react with vigor and economy. No doubt the world at large will always lag so far behind the active mind as to make a soft cushion of inertia to drop upon, as it did for Henry Adams; but education should try to lessen the obstacles, diminish the friction, invigorate the energy, *and should train the minds to react, not at haphazard, but by choice, on the lines of force that attract their world.*

This sort of education Adams felt that he never attained. He appeared to himself to have drifted through life, to have been shunted about, by circumstances which he could neither foresee nor control, from one track to another, with the result of arriving at stations which, however attractive they may have been, it was never his intention to reach. He went to Germany to study the civil law, without any good reason for so doing; he attended one lecture (one was enough!), and idled away two years in Germany and Italy, for no reason except that he did not know what he could do if he came home. He became his father's secretary in London because his father asked him to do so and nothing better offered. He returned after six years fully determined to enter journalism as the best road to the career of a political reformer. The prospect looked good, for like every one else he had great faith in Grant; but the announcement of Grant's cabinet, "within five minutes, changed his intended future into an absurdity so laughable as to make him ashamed of it. . . . He had made another total misconception of life—another inconceivable false start." He became a professor of history, without possessing any qualifications for the position, because his family and friends urged him to accept an offer that came out of a clear sky; and afterwards wrote history because that was the thing professors of history were supposed to do. Whatever he did or accomplished in life, he did by accident and not as the result of reasoned purpose.

Not only did Adams fail of that education which would have enabled him to react "by choice, on the lines of force" that attracted his world; he was never able to determine what sort of education would have given him this power. He observed attentively the careers of his friends and of the notable men of his generation; but the reasons for their failures or successes were not to be found; why some men, such as W. C. Whitney, should have won all the prizes the age had to offer, while others, such as his friend King, should have failed, remained a mystery to the end.

Society had failed to discover what sort of education suited it best. Wealth valued social position and classical education as highly as either of these valued wealth, and the women still tended to keep the scales even. For anything Adams could see he was himself as contented as though he had been educated; while Clarence King, whose education was exactly suited to theory, had failed; and Whitney, who was no better educated than Adams, had achieved phenomenal success.

This was one aspect of the failure, that he had never been able to do anything which he deliberately set out to do. But the chief aspect of the failure was that, having done only those things which the accident of circumstances imposed upon him, the things he had done were in no way identified with the "lines of force" that attracted his age, and were therefore of negligible importance. Henry Adams's chief reason of discontent was that he had never been able to impress himself powerfully upon his time. He knew that he had as good ability, and better ability, than most men—he was well within the "one in a hundred" who were worth educating. He knew that he had written as good history as any one was likely to write; but he was quite sincere in saying that he "worked in the dark," and that he never could see that his history was worth the doing. One reason for this was that histories as commonly written, and as he had himself written them, led nowhere and explained nothing.

Historians undertake to arrange sequences—called stories, or histories—assuming in silence a relation of cause and effect. These assumptions, hidden in the depths of dusty libraries, have been astounding, but commonly unconscious and childlike; so much so, that if the captious critic were to drag them to light, historians would probably reply, with one voice, that they had never supposed themselves required to know what they were talking about. Adams, for one, had toiled in vain to find out what he meant. He had even published a dozen volumes of American history for no other purpose than to satisfy himself whether, by the severest process of stating, with the least possible comment, such facts as seemed sure, in such order as seemed rigorously consequent, he could fix for a familiar moment a necessary sequence of human movement. The result had satisfied him as little as at Harvard College.

Later in life, when he had turned to science for an explanation which he could not find in history, it seemed to him that, supposing Kelvin's law to be rigorously true, the professor of American history should "begin his annual course by announcing to his class that their year's work would be devoted to showing in American history 'a universal tendency to the dissipation of energy' and degradation of thought, which would soon end in making America 'improper for the habitation of man as he is now constituted.' "[4] It must be admitted that professors of history do not commonly begin their courses in this way; but if this is indeed the proper way, Adams was quite right in supposing that his own histories were enterprises of no great significance.

But assuming that the method was good, Adams had another reason for being indifferent to his work as historian. He says that after having given ten or twelve years of serious labor to writing his history of Jefferson and Madison, he never had, so far as he could learn, more than three serious readers. No doubt this is not mathematically true; but from Adams's point of view, considering the population of the world, and the likelihood of his books ever having a decisive influence upon the course of civilization, the statement was relatively true. The point was that whether his histories were good or bad, the world, or even America, would have been precisely what it was if the *History of the United States* had never been written. The point was that America would have been precisely what it was if Henry Adams had never lived. And Henry Adams

[4] *A Letter to American Teachers of History*, p. 85.

was not content that it should be so. Henry Adams, son and grandson and great-grandson of men who had helped to shape the destiny of their country, precisely because he had had every advantage and was possessed of mental qualities that he knew to be first-rate, should have been able, in any well-ordered universe with a decent regard for its needs and for the economy of its available resources, to make an adequate contribution to the sum of human achievements. With such advantages and such abilities, he should have figured as an outstanding influence, in no matter what line of endeavor—in politics, in finance, in art, in ideas. To have been merely the writer of books that gathered dust on the shelves, of books that, even if they had run to the thousandth edition, would not have made a dent on the shell of destiny—this was to be a failure, whatever the gild of professors might say. Such a man, having "shed his life-blood for the sublime truths of Sac and Soc," might well be forgotten under the epitaph: Hic Jacet Homunculus Scriptor Doctor Barbaricus Henricus Adams Adae Filius Et Evae Primo Explicuit Socnam.

Another grandson of John Quincy Adams closed his life with much the same sense of futility; and he too was much concerned, in his *Autobiography*, with the failure to obtain the education which he needed. But while Charles Francis Adams lays this failure to his father, Henry Adams places the responsibility upon the cosmos. Charles Francis knew precisely the education he should have had; he ought to have done those things which his father did not require him to do, and he ought not to have done those things which his father required him to do; he ought to have learned to play games; he ought to have gone to the public school; he ought—but the list is long. Henry

Adams blamed no one, not even himself. He did not know what education he should have had, and no one could have told him. To the last day of his life he did not know. The whole thing was a cosmic riddle. How indeed could men be trained "to react, not at haphazard, but by choice, on the lines of force that attract their world," if no one knew what those lines of force were? But to determine the lines of force that attract the world is the problem of all history; and so the question of education, in the last analysis, was identified in Henry Adams's mind with an intelligible philosophy of history, a scientific explanation of the universe.

With this problem he was occupied from an early date, and during the later years it absorbed all his energies. His study of science, into which he delved as deeply as his knowledge of mathematics enabled him to do, his preoccupation with the dynamo and the Virgin—all this was no mere dilettante dabbling in curious and recondite matters; nor can we suppose him, after life was fairly done, to have traversed the dreary wastes of scholastic philosophy as an idle stunt, or for the academic satisfaction of constructing a neat formula within which the vagrant facts of history might be comfortably and amicably enclosed. He is indeed whimsical enough about it, and besprinkles himself liberally with the light showers of wit and sarcasm and delicious humor that everywhere fall upon the just and the unjust. But all this is mostly protective coloring; he laughs at himself that no one may suppose his own withers wrung, and forestalls sympathy in others by having none on his own account. At bottom he is engaged in a desperate endeavor to unravel the riddle of his own failure, to search out the heart of that mysterious force that made all his reasoned purposes futile and all his achievements vain. He never succeeded; and in the end he regarded the *Education* itself as a fragment, unfinished, avowedly incomplete, which might well remain unpublished and so be forgotten. And this too was part of the general failure. Not only had he failed to impress himself upon the life of his time; he had not even redeemed that failure by solving the mystery of it.

If this interpretation is in any measure true (one can never be sure), there was an element of tragedy in the life of Henry Adams. But in any case it is well concealed in the *Education* as it was in life. It is not likely that many readers will see the tragedy of a failure that looks like success, or miss the philosophy-clothes that were never found. And indeed we may all be well content with the doings of this manikin that turns out to be so lively an ego. Henry Adams was worth a wilderness of philosophies. Perhaps we should have liked the book better if he could have taken himself more frankly, as a matter of course, for what he was—a man of wide experience, of altogether uncommon attainments, of extraordinarily incisive mental power; and if, resting on this assumption, he had told us more directly, as something we should like to know, what he had done, what people he had met and known, what events he had shared in or observed, and what he thought about it all. This he does do of course, in his own enigmatic way, in the process of explaining where and how he sought education and failed to find it; and fortunately, in the course of the leisurely journey, he takes us into many by-paths and shows us, by the easy play of his illuminating intelligence, much strange country, and many people whom we have never known, or have never known so intimately. When this happens, when the manikin forgets itself and its education-clothes, and merely describes people or types of mind or social customs, the result is wholly admirable. There are inimitable passages, and the number is large, which one cannot forget. One will not soon forget the young men of the Harvard class of '58, who were "*negative to a degree that in the end became positive and triumphant;*" or the exquisitely drawn portrait of "Madame President," all things considered the finest passage in the book; or the picture of old John Quincy Adams coming slowly downstairs one hot summer morning and with massive and silent solemnity leading the rebellious little Henry to school against his will; or yet the reflections of the little Henry himself (or was it the reflection of an older Henry?), who recognized on this occasion "that the President, though a tool of tyranny, had done his disreputable work with a certain intelligence. He had shown no temper, no irritation, no personal feeling, and had made no display of force. Above all, he had held his tongue."

Those who have read the *Autobiography* of Charles Francis Adams will note with interest that Henry had a much higher opinion of his father than his elder brother had, which may have been due to the fact that he knew him much better. The elder Charles Francis, he says,

possessed the only perfectly balanced mind that ever existed in the name. For a hundred years, every newspaper scribbler had, with more or less obvious excuse, derided or abused the older Adamses for want of judgment. They abused Charles Francis for his judgment. . . . Charles Francis Adams was singular for mental poise— absence of self-assertion or self-consciousness—the faculty of standing apart without seeming aware that he was alone—a balance of mind and temper that neither challenged nor avoided notice, nor admitted question of superiority or inferiority, of jealousy, of personal motives, from any source, even under great pressure. This unusual poise of judgment and temper, ripened by age, became the more striking to his son Henry as he learned to measure the mental faculties themselves, which were in no way exceptional either for depth or range. Charles Francis Adams's memory was hardly above the average; his mind was not bold like his grandfather's or restless like his father's, or imaginative or oratorical—still less mathematical; but it worked with singular perfection, admirable self-restraint, and instinctive mastery of form. Within its range it was a model. . . . He stood alone. He had no master—hardly even his father. He had no scholars—hardly even his sons.

The estimate is just, the analysis penetrating. For analysis, Henry Adams had indeed a master's talent; and we are especially grateful for his dissection of the senatorial mind in general, and of the minds of such particular senators as Seward and Sumner and Lodge. But he was equally good at surprising the secret of the group mind, and of all groups the one that interested him most was the English. For studying the English he had ample opportunity; and although, according to custom, he professes never to have fathomed that peculiar people, his observations are always interesting and often profound. Even where his opportunity was limited he made the most of it. The picture of a whole judicial generation is made vivid in the chance statement that he "never set eyes on a judge except when his father took him to call on old Lord Lyndhurst, where they found old Lord Campbell, *both abusing old Lord Brougham.*" Nothing interested him more than English "society." What it was, he never knew—"one wandered about in it like a maggot in cheese; it was not a hansom cab, to be got into, or out of, at dinner time." He was much perplexed by Motley's remark that the London dinner and the English country house were "the perfection of human society." But after having studied carefully and practised painfully what seemed to be the favorite accomplishment, he came to the conclusion that

the perfection of human society required that a man should enter a drawing-room where he was a total stranger, and place himself on the hearth-rug, his back to the fire, with an air of expectant benevolence, without curiosity, much as though he had dropped in at a charity concert, kindly disposed to applaud the performers and overlook mistakes. This ideal rarely succeeded in youth, and towards thirty it took a form of modified insolence and offensive patronage; but about sixty it mellowed into courtesy, kindliness, and even deference to the young which had extraordinary charm both in women and in men.

Upon mature reflection I cannot resist the temptation to quote the passage on being called a "begonia" by a United States senator, since it reveals Adams's genial irony at its best, as well as his opinion of senators—not by any means at its worst. Returning home from England on one occasion, he found that his article in the *North American* reviewing the last session of Congress, had been widely circulated by the Democrats as a campaign document. The inevitable reply was made by Senator Timothy Howe, of Wisconsin, who, besides refuting Adams's opinions,

did him the honor—most unusual and picturesque in a Senator's rhetoric—of likening him to a begonia. The begonia is, or then was, a plant of such senatorial qualities as to make the simile, in intention, most flattering. Far from charming in its refinement, the begonia was remarkable for curious and showy foliage; it was conspicuous; it seemed to have no useful purpose; it insisted on standing always in the most prominent positions. Adams would have greatly liked to be a begonia in Washington, for this was rather his ideal of the successful statesman, and he thought about it still more when the *Westminster Review* for October brought him his article on the Gold Conspiracy, which was also instantly

pirated on a great scale. Piratical he was himself henceforth driven
to be, and he asked only to be pirated, for he was sure not to be
paid; but the honors of piracy resemble the colors of the begonia;
they are showy but not useful. Here was a *tour de force* he had never
dreamed himself equal to performing: two long, dry, quarterly,
thirty or forty page articles, appearing in quick succession, and
pirated for audiences running well into the hundred thousands;
and not one person, man or woman, offering him so much as a
congratulation, except to call him a begonia.

The number of passages one would wish to quote is
legion; but one must be content to say that the book is
fascinating throughout—particularly perhaps in those
parts which are not concerned with the education of Henry
Adams. Where this recondite and cosmic problem is touched
upon, there are often qualifications to be made. The perpetual profession of ignorance and incapacity seems at times
a bit disingenuous; and we have to do for the most part,
not with the way things struck Adams at the time, but
with the way it seemed to him, as an old man looking back
upon the "broken arch," they should have struck him.
Besides, in the later chapters, in which he deals with the
dynamic theory of history, the problem was so vague, even
to himself, that we too often do not know what he wishes
to convey. Apropos of the Chicago Fair, which like everything else in his later years linked itself to the business of
the dynamo and the Virgin, he says: "Did he himself quite
know what he meant? Certainly not! If he had known
enough to state his problem, his education would have
been completed at once." Is this the statement of a fact,
or only the reflection of a perversity? We do not know.
Most readers, at all events, having reached page 343, will
not be inclined to dispute the assertion. Yet we must after
all be grateful for this meaningless philosophy of history

(the more so perhaps since it is meaningless); for without it we should never have had either the *Mont-Saint-Michel* or *The Education of Henry Adams*—"books which no gentleman's library" need contain, but which will long be read by the curious inquirer into the nature of the human heart.

Henry Adams lies buried in Rock Creek Cemetery, in Washington. The casual visitor might perhaps notice, on a slight elevation, a group of shrubs and small trees making a circular enclosure. If he should step up into this concealed spot, he would see on the opposite side a polished marble seat; and placing himself there he would find himself facing a seated figure, done in bronze, loosely wrapped in a mantle which, covering the body and the head, throws into strong relief a face of singular fascination. Whether man or woman, it would puzzle the observer to say. The eyes are half closed, in reverie rather than in sleep. The figure seems not to convey the sense either of life or death, of joy or sorrow, of hope or despair. It has lived, but life is done; it has experienced all things, but is now oblivious of all; it has questioned, but questions no more. The casual visitor will perhaps approach the figure, looking for a symbol, a name, a date—some revelation. There is none. The level ground, carpeted with pine spills, gives no indication of a grave beneath. It may be that the puzzled visitor will step outside, walk around the enclosure, examine the marble shaft against which the figure is placed; and, finding nothing there, return to the seat and look long at the strange face. What does he make of it—this level spot, these shrubs, this figure that speaks and yet is silent? Nothing—or what he will. Such was life to Henry Adams, who lived long, and questioned seriously, and would not be content with the dishonest or the facile answer.

1919.

Henry Adams Once More[1]

IT was said of Thiers that he concealed his opinion of
Napoleon in twenty volumes; it might be said of Henry
Adams that he wrote thirty volumes to provide posterity with a psychological puzzle. The puzzle is to find out
why, having written all these admirable books, he believed, or professed to believe, that his life was a failure.
Several explanations were offered on the occasion of the
publication of his *The Education of Henry Adams*—that extraordinary book which leaves the reader certain of nothing
except that Henry Adams, by his own account of it, never
had an education. Unable to accept this palpable absurdity,
I have long wished that someone would write a full length
life of this most fascinating and perverse of the Adamses—a
biography that would explain the autobiography, that
would, in short, reveal the secret of Henry Adams. The
announcement of a life by James Truslow Adams led me to
hope that my wish had come true.

It turns out that Mr. Adams has not done quite what I
had hoped, for the adequate reason that his book was
"originally written for a collected edition of [Henry
Adams's] Works," and is now published separately only
because that enterprise had to be temporarily abandoned.
Regarded in this light, his short sketch is admirable, a
model of what an introduction to an edition of collected

[1] *Henry Adams*. By James Truslow Adams. New York: A. & C. Boni. 1933.

works should be. It is not too long. It gives, in chronological order, all the essential known facts about Henry Adams's life and activities, with just the sort of explanatory comment needed by one who might be using his collected works. In addition there emerges, from this running comment, a portrait of the man Henry Adams. The portrait is not, so to speak, painted and set up before us in any one chapter of the book; but the preliminary sketches from which we may compose it are to be found, scattered here and there, in the author's estimates of Adams's writings, the notation of his characteristic traits, and in many pertinent suggestions as to the motives that may have determined his less obvious actions, the frustrations that may in part explain his whimsical paradoxes, his obviously exaggerated self-depreciation. I find myself disagreeing with Mr. Adams's critical judgment only in two instances. I think he estimates too highly Henry Adams's disquisitions on history as a science, and I think he admires the *Mont-Saint-Michel and Chartres* for the wrong reasons. Unique and fascinating as the *Saint Michel* is, I cannot think it throws the "clearest and most concentrated light to be turned on the medieval period by any single volume in perhaps any language." Say rather that it throws a highly diffused, stained-glass light on the mind of Henry Adams.

Excellent as the book is for its original purpose, it is not as comprehensive a treatment as the subject deserves, or as Mr. Adams would no doubt have given it had he set out to write a biography in the usual sense. One would like, for example, a more detailed analysis of Henry Adams's *History of the United States*, and a more searching criticism of those interesting works, *A Letter to Teachers of History*, and *The Rule of Phase Applied to History*. One would like, above all, a less fragmentary and casual, a more reso-

lute attempt to formulate a closely integrated psychological interpretation of the life and personality of Henry
Adams. Mr. Adams will perhaps shy off at the words "psychological interpretation." Call it what you will, the
thing itself is in his book, despite his disclaimers. "I shall
not attempt," he says, "any biological inferences as to
Henry Adams's inheritance nor any Freudian guesses as to
his childhood." Again: "When one has to delineate a human
soul from fragmentary documents, it is merely insolent
egotism to claim that one has plumbed the depths." Surely
no biographer can rightly claim, no sensible critic expect,
so much. But after all a biographer, if he aims to "delineate
a human soul," must somehow get beneath the surface
meaning of the documents, fragmentary though they may
be, and indeed always are. Mr. Adams does himself endeavor,
neither inexpertly nor unsuccessfully, to do so. I suspect
he is merely raising his voice a little as a warning to
critics not to class him with the "debunkers." I don't ask
him, or any one, to debunk Henry Adams, the less so since
Henry Adams has, far better than any one else could do it,
debunked himself.

Why should Henry Adams have felt it necessary to
debunk himself? Why should he have employed all the
resources of his sardonic humor, all his talent for paradox
and allusive innuendo and recessive ironic overstatement,
to make himself small? This is the very nub of the riddle;
and one need not claim to have plumbed the depths to
suggest, as a possible reading of it, that Henry Adams was
impelled to debunk himself a little because he had in some
sense "bunked" his life. Having resisted his genius and
partly renounced his true "inheritance" to run after a mess
of pottage, he felt it necessary to tell the world, somewhat
shamefacedly, why he never got the pottage. This I take

it is essentially Mr. Adams's own view of the matter, although of course he never falls to the level of such brutality of statement. It is at least his view that Henry Adams desired to "control power in some form which could be the only touchstone of success for an Adams." Power in almost any form that would impress the world; but preferably that sort of power that an Adams, who could, as boy in church, "sit behind a President grandfather, and . . . read over his head the tablet in memory of a President great-grandfather," ought of right to possess. In short, political power. In England, watching his father function effectively as a diplomat, "one began to dream the sensation of wielding unmeasured power. The sense came, and passed, leaving the brain a little dazed, doubtful, shy." But the brain a little dazed, doubtful, shy, was not at all the brain to exercise that sort of power. The true "inheritance" of Henry Adams was a brain suited to exercise power in another realm altogether—the realm of the scholar, the teacher, the writer, the thinker. His writings are sufficient proof of the fact, but Adams himself seems never to have been reconciled to it. He seems always resisting his genius, but never successfully, so that one has the impression that he wrote all his admirable works in spite of himself. He might have said, and did in effect say, that he had demonstrated in thirty volumes the futility of writing books. Was he unaware that his genius was at war with his ambition? Or, aware of it, was he merely unwilling to submit wholeheartedly to his genius?

He seems at least to have realized his unfitness for politics or diplomacy. But he tried journalism as the next best chance for an Adams, and it was only as a side issue to his editorship of the *North American* that he accepted an assistant professorship of history at Harvard. Afterwards,

browbeating the facts a little, he said that his family browbeat him into this job, and that it turned out as he expected
—no good. Seven years of brilliant teaching proved, to
everyone except himself, that it was the very career for
which he was fitted. Yet he resigned his position, but
only, in the years following, to demonstrate once more
(was it in spite of himself? His family didn't browbeat
him into this) that he had in his hand the sort of power
suited to his genius by writing, in nine volumes, a history
which for clarity, tight construction, and sheer intelligence
applied to the exposition of a great theme, had not then,
and has not since, been equaled by any American historian.
Nevertheless, having achieved this masterpiece, he turned
his back on it in order to watch, from 1603 H Street, the
political Zoo in Washington, in the intervals of running
about the world searching for an explanation of the universe that would explain why he never found an explanation of his inability to achieve "success."

Why did Henry Adams abandon a career in which he accomplished more in ten years than most men of that profession do in a lifetime? He says he liked the students, and
liked teaching them. But he did not like faculty meetings
(was it necessary to attend them?), and "socially he preferred Congressmen to professors" . . . in spite of the presence of "some of the liveliest and most agreeable of men—
James Russell Lowell, Francis J. Child, . . . William James,
and a dozen others, who would have made the joy of
London and Paris" had not society spoiled them by "dub-
bing them professor." So, there it is. No doubt it was
difficult for an Adams to think of himself as no more than
a professor grandson of a President grandfather, but it is
surely superfluous to suppose that those good chaps, Francis
J. Child and William James, were "spoiled by society."

Someone said that the only void in which Shelley "beat his luminous wings in vain" was a void in the mind of Matthew Arnold. I suggest that the only quality that could possibly have spoiled William James for Henry Adams was a certain lack of quality (I don't like to call it snobbishness) in the mind of Henry Adams.

Equally illuminating is Adams's reason for urging Lodge to go in for the writing of history. It seems that a successful history would set Lodge up in Boston "as a species of literary lion" and that with that position would come "social dignity, European reputation, *and a foreign mission to close.*" If, in writing his *History of the United States*, Adams was taking his own incredible, naïvely cynical advice, one can easily understand why he abandoned history writing. His history was not "successful." It neither made him a literary lion, nor gave him a European reputation, or any reputation at all—except, of course, among those "dubbed professor." After such an anticlimax what could the poor author do? Forget it, refuse to discuss it (it is referred to but not named in the *Education*), say that the whole of it, including maps and index, meant less to him than any single chapter in *Esther*. Was that the way a merely disillusioned historian would treat a history acclaimed by the world of scholars? Or was it only the proper way to treat a history that was likely, from the vantage point of 1603 H Street, to be regarded as "unsuccessful?" We know that at 1603 H Street Adams associated with men—Hay, Lodge, Cameron—who exercised "power" never dreamed of by John Fiske and James Russell Lowell. Must we suppose that such men as Lodge and Cameron, not having been spoiled by society, were better able than Francis J. Child and William James to make of existence something more refreshing than a "social desert" for Henry Adams? It's a strange thought.

Space is lacking to develop this hypothesis further. The hypothesis must stand or fall, I think, according to the answer one gives to the following question: Was Adams's search for "a historical formula that should satisfy the conditions of the stellar universe" the result of genuine intellectual curosity, or only another, last, forlorn bid for the favor of the bitch goddess success? At this point the real difficulties crop up; for while there are relevant points to be made on both sides, Adams has, in his later works, so concealed himself behind a barrage of paradox and whimsical humor that neither supposition is convincing. On first thought one is inclined to say that Adams's repeated assertion that his life was a failure must be disingenuous unless we are to suppose that for him nothing could count as "success" that did not, in some sense, make him the observed of all observers. But that is too simple. No simple black or white, or black and white, will represent Henry Adams correctly. An American who saw something of Adams in Paris in 1910-1911 tells me that "his habitual attitude" was that of a man who somehow feels that he has "missed out," but does not really *believe* that he *has* missed out, and at the same time cannot quite understand why he should have missed out or should feel that he has. This strikes me as a penetrating observation, and one which the *Education* confirms. Isn't this precisely the attitude one might expect of a man whose genius for reflection was always at war with his desire for "power," and who never knew it? Perhaps then the secret of Henry Adams was simply that he didn't know what was the matter with him. But then again perhaps he did know, but was too proud or perverse to admit it, even to himself.

Mr. Wells And The New History

WHEN the cynical mood is uppermost, one is likely to agree with Voltaire that "after all history is only a pack of tricks which we play on the dead." There is nothing you cannot find in the past—except the truth: a truth you can indeed find; any number of truths are there ready to be picked out, and perfectly indifferent to the process. Such facts as the mind is predisposed to select as interesting or important will come out and "speak for themselves." The trouble is, they don't care what they say; and with a little intelligent prompting they will speak, within reason, whatever they are commanded to speak. In an educational journal I learn apropos of the teaching of American history, that by "making William the Conqueror a starting point, for example, it is possible to show the steady progress of the people onward and upward from the period of enslavement to the present time." I do not doubt it: onward and upward to the Great War, and beyond—to the League of Nations, or the Peace of Versailles, or the ultimate establishment of the Soviet régime throughout the world. The past will provide humanity with any fate you like to imagine. O History, how many truths have been committed in thy name!

In more judicious moments the same idea may be expressed by saying that each age reinterprets the past to suit its own purposes. Leaving aside the vagaries that distin-

guish individuals, historians cannot wholly free themselves, however detached they may strive to be, from the
most general preconceptions of the age in which they live.
In quiescent times, when men are mostly well satisfied
with the present, or when they fear change and wish to sit
tight, they are likely to be satisfied with the past, are
likely to be grateful to it for having contributed to the
best of worlds; and at such times historians will easily
fall into the habit of just recording what happened, as in
itself sufficiently interesting and instructive. But in periods
of stress, when the times are thought to be out of joint,
those who are dissatisfied with the present are likely to
be dissatisfied with the past also. At such times historians,
those of the younger generation at least, catching the
spirit of unrest, will be disposed to cross-examine the past
in order to find out why it did not usher in a better state
of affairs, will be disposed, as it were, to sit in judgment on
what was formerly done, approving or disapproving in the
light of present discontents. The past is a kind of screen
upon which each generation projects its vision of the future,
and so long as hope springs in the human breast the "new
history" will be a recurring phenomenon.

About the middle of the eighteenth century (not to go
farther back) the *Philosophes* proclaimed a "new history."
"All the weight of our historians," said Grimm in 1755,
"consists in a stupid and pedantic discussion of facts which
are commonly as unimportant as they are uncertain and
disputed." What Grimm and his friends demanded was a
study of the past which would enable them to understand
not how the present had come to be what it was, but how
they might make it better. "I shall not undertake to prove
the utility of history," says Duclos; "it is a truth too generally recognized to need proof. . . . When we see the same

faults regularly followed by the same misfortunes, we may reasonably think that if we could have known the first we could have avoided the second. The past should enlighten us on the future; the knowledge of history is no more than an experience anticipated.'' The *Philosophes* were well aware of the importance of studying the past, but they studied it in the light of a certain general preconception: they wished to disengage from the past those ideas, those institutions, those striking events and heroic actions, which might be regarded as having a permanent and universal validity, which might for that reason be regarded as conforming to the essential nature of man, and which might therefore serve as guiding principles in the pressing task of social regeneration.

After the French Revolution had run its course, it was the common opinion for a long time that the regeneration of society had gone far enough. The main drift and pressure of thought was away from change; and the minds of men, fearing revolution and desiring peace and a return to normal conditions, looked to the past in order to find there, if possible, new foundations for a stable social order. The ''new history'' of the nineteenth century became in consequence the chief intellectual bulwark of conservatism. Historians for the most part studied the past as an inevitable process which must in any case be submitted to, but which, once rightly understood, might at least be submitted to intelligently. ''What is the use of rebelling against historical right?'' asked von Ranke; and having asked this question, he went imperturbably on revealing God's will by relating the devices of Sixtus V for increasing the papal revenue. To-day this mood is passing. The tyranny of historic right grows as burdensome as the tyranny of kings; and men who once knew Joseph are calling for a reinterpretation of the past in the service of social reform. Professor Robinson, quite in the spirit of Grimm, deplores the time spent by historians in determining "whether Charles the Fat was in Ingelheim or Lustnau on July 1, 887," and invites them for a change to contemplate the jaw of the Heidelberg Man. He is only one of many who are again calling for a "new history," a history which will not be content to relate the fact just as it happened, but which will, on the contrary, "exploit the past in the interest of advance." Mr. Wells's book is a notable attempt to write the history of the world from this new, and at the same time very old, point of view.

In a brief introduction Mr. Wells states his purpose:

This *Outline of History* is an attempt to tell, truly and clearly, in one continuous narrative, the whole history of life and mankind so far as it is known to-day. It is written plainly for the general reader, but its aim goes beyond its use as merely interesting reading matter. . . . The need for a common knowledge of the general facts of human history throughout the world has become very evident during the tragic happenings of the last few years. . . . There can be no peace now, we realize, but a common peace in all the world; no prosperity but a general prosperity. But *there can be no common peace and prosperity without common historical ideas*. Without such ideas to hold them together in harmonious coöperation, with nothing but narrow, selfish, and conflicting nationalist traditions, races and peoples are bound to drift towards conflict and destruction.. . . . A sense of history as the common adventure of all mankind is as necessary for peace within as it is for peace between the nations. Such are the views of history that this *Outline* seeks to realize. It is an attempt to tell how our present state of affairs, this distressed and multifarious human life about us, arose in the course of vast ages and out of the inanimate clash of matter, and to estimate the quality and amount and range of the hopes with which it now faces its destiny.

A more ambitious attempt could not well be imagined. That one man should have the courage to undertake it, still more that he should have the resolution to carry it through, fills one with amazement and admiration. It is well known that "fools rush in;" it is well known that Mr. Wells rushes in; but it is well known that Mr. Wells is no fool. We cordially welcome his extraordinary performance. It may well be that more people will read his book than ever read Voltaire or Macaulay or von Ranke. What will they find in this plain history of life and mankind?

They will find, for one thing, that Mr. Wells begins at the beginning—or very nearly so. He does not begin with electrons, but at least he begins with the physical universe. "The earth on which we live is a spinning globe"—such is the dramatic opening of the first book in which we learn of "The Making of Our World." What will strike the reader particularly, and doubtless was intended to, is that it was an incredibly long time in the making—80 or 800 million years, more or less, according to the best guesses. Book II treats of "The Making of Man." In the history of life on the globe, man is a relatively recent product; but there is still a great discrepancy between the date fixed by Mr. Wells for the appearance of the first man and the date fixed by Archbishop Ussher. Mr. Wells barely mentions Archbishop Ussher's contribution to the solution of this problem, but takes it for granted that an earlier date has now been established. Through 101 pages he discusses the character and *mores* of those remote and unamiable first Europeans—the Heidelberg Sub-Man (*circ.* 250,000 B.C.), the Neanderthal men of the early Palaeolithic (50,000 B.C), the first "true men" of the late Palaeolithic, and the Neolithic men who came in some ten or twelve thousand years ago. These last were "ancestral to the modern

Europeans," there being "no real break in culture from their time onward." In the Neolithic culture the beginnings of modern civilization must accordingly be found. Giving three admirably clear and interesting chapters to the origins of thought and religion, the differentiation of races, and the variations of language, Mr. Wells passes to the third book, "The Dawn of History," in which the general reader will find excellent accounts of such subjects as Aryan Speaking Peoples in Prehistoric Times, the First Civilizations in Assyria, Egypt, China, and India, the early Aegean civilization, the origin of writing, the beginning of kingship, priestcraft, castes and social classes. Book III closes with a "summary of 5,000 years." At page 274, with one-fifth of the *Outline* finished, we come at last to "Judaea, Greece, and India"—that is to say, the beginning of human history as it used, not so long ago, to be written.

In the story as Mr. Wells relates it from this point, we miss the traditional landmarks. The table of contents does not contain those familiar terms by which we save ourselves the trouble of taking thought—Ancient History, Medieval History, Modern History, Medieval Church, Medieval Empire, Protestant Reformation. In Book IV, "Judaea, Greece, and India," and Book V, "The Rise and Collapse of the Roman Empire," we are still in fairly familiar country; but in the following books, "Christianity and Islam," "Mongol Empires of the Land Ways and the New Empires of the Sea Ways," "Princes, Parliaments, and Powers," Mr. Wells employs names for his major subjects which leave the well-drilled student wondering whether he has not inadvertently abandoned history for something else. The well-drilled student should remember that Mr. Wells, aiming at the history of mankind, en-

deavors, and with some success, to put Europe in its
proper place. From this novel point of view it is possible
to regard the history of mankind since the "fall of Rome"
in a somewhat less restricted way; to regard it as perhaps
centering in three major series of events: (1) the conflict
of Islam and Christianity, with the consequent closing in
of Western Europe, and the development there, in comparative isolation, of a restricted and provincial way of life
and thought; (2) the gradual expansion of the peoples of
Western Europe from the twelfth century, resulting in renewed contact with Asia, the liberalization of the intelligence of the Western European peoples, and the transformation of their institutions; (3) the rise of military
and industrial states in Europe and America, gradually
extending their economic and political power throughout
the world, and contending among themselves for the spoils
of victory.

To get the full effect of this new grouping, and indeed
of Mr. Wells's performance in general, one must read the
work as a whole. It is distinctly not a book of reference,
but one of which a primary purpose is to convey a sense of
the unity and continuity of human history; and there is
probably no book, certainly none for the general reader,
that so effectively performs that service. Speaking for myself at least (and for most of human history I am no more
than a general reader), I arise from a fairly continuous reading of Mr. Wells's book much refreshed, and much enlightened on certain points. I was glad to learn, for example,
that Christianity originated in Judaea with the teachings
of a man called Jesus, and not in Rome during the reign of
the Emperor Nero. I now know that there were people
living in Persia between the days of Xerxes and Mr.
Shuster, and that the history of India did not begin with

Vasco da Gama or that of China with Genghis Khan. In general, Mr. Wells has dispelled a vague impression that History, having made a few half-hearted attempts to get things started in the valleys of the Nile and the Euphrates, abandoned the effort about the sixth century B.C., and migrated to Europe where she has since resided. I have a renewed sense of history as "the common adventure of all mankind," and more than ever before it seems to me likely that mankind may safely be taken to include the "backward" peoples of Asia as well as the forward peoples of Europe.

Some books have high value because, aiming to do a great thing, they at least show us what the great thing is, and so make us wish to have it greatly done. Mr. Wells's book has this high value. It should enable thousands of intelligent men and women throughout the world to see history in better perspective, giving them, however imperfectly, a new sense of humanity's slow and painful emergence from savagery, and in some measure bringing home to them a realization of the intimate and inescapable interrelation of the fortunes of all peoples.

Such is the scope of the work. What are its special qualities? It may seem that if a novelist can write the history of mankind a professor of history might venture to pronounce upon its merits in respect to scholarship and as a contribution to knowledge. Such is not the case. The man of letters may without reproach acquire a knowledge of general history; but the professor of history is not thus free. It is understood that *his* knowledge is intensive to the point of exhaustion, but not sufficiently extensive to be of weight on questions with other than geographical or chronological limits. Upon Mr. Wells's scholarship and general accuracy I shall therefore pronounce no judgment. It will be sufficient to note that Mr. Wells is aware of his limitations in this respect, and that he has wisely sought the aid of many men, especially of Mr. Ernest Barker, Sir H. H. Johnston, Sir E. Ray Lankester, and Professor Gilbert Murray. These men, all competent scholars in their several fields, have doubtless saved Mr. Wells from serious errors in matters of fact; and it was open to them to make objection, in the form of signed footnotes, to whatever they found objectionable in matters of inference and opinion. It should, perhaps, be added that their objections are both more frequent and more pointed in the last five books than in the first four.

A contribution to knowledge the book does not of course pretend to be; but a contribution to the meaning which we may, and indeed ought, to attach to the knowledge we have, it does very particularly pretend to be. What chiefly concerns the critic, therefore, is not Mr. Wells's knowledge or technical competence, but his interpretation, his general philosophy of history. It may well be that he has not much thumbed the *Monumenta Germaniae* or the *Rolls Series*, that the *Wegweiser* has not been his *vade mecum;* perhaps he might with advantage have selected more or less or other facts; doubtless he has made erroneous statements. But the book does not stand or fall on these points. Mr. Wells has facts enough, and sufficiently accurate, for the main purpose. What is that purpose? In what frame of mind does the author approach his subject? Through what particular combination of present experience and knowledge of the past does the mind of Mr. Wells contrive to find a philosophy of history in which it can comfortably rest? Regarded from this point of view, what stands out most invitingly is that as Mr. Wells proceeds in his task his frame of mind changes; and this change is connected, whether as cause or effect I cannot tell, with his general conception of history, his particular theory of its meaning and purport.

In the earlier books Mr. Wells seems to be on good terms with his subject. He treats it with consideration, with friendliness, with a certain geniality. I have a strong impression that Mr. Wells found all these prehistoric questions intensely interesting, that he has gone into them probably for some years back, with all his wonderfully absorptive faculties working at top speed, that he has taken the time and the pains to read the best books and talk with the best scholars in each special field. The account strikes one as that of a man who has mastered the subject well enough to understand the evidence, to be aware of the difficulties, and to realize that the best he could do was to follow with caution and humility in the steps of better equipped men. It is in the spirit of the scientist, desiring only to know how it really was, with no special thesis to defend and no practical aims to further, that Mr. Wells approaches his subject in these first books.

In the later books this equable and objective attitude is more and more, and at last almost altogether, replaced by a different one. One may say that the genial, friendly mood, the mood of the intellectually interested mind, is in the ascendant whenever Mr. Wells is occupied with the descriptive setting forth of a religion, the advancement of science and learning, or some type of vanished civilization. But when he has to do with political history, with conquerors and kings and statesmen, or the narrative of events which concern them, especially if these events are relatively near our own time, the geniality is likely to give place to exasperation, the friendliness to dislike, and the clear flame of his intellectual interest is often obscured or quite put out

by the heavy atmosphere of a moral preoccupation. Much
of the later narrative has a perfunctory ring, as if written
by a man gone stale on a subject once interesting, who
nevertheless feels that he has to go through with it, and
who does go through with it as best he may from incomplete or incompletely assimilated knowledge. From the
seventeenth century especially, Mr. Wells pushes on,
hurriedly as we cannot but think; somewhat heedless of
the increasing, and increasingly pointed, protests of his
collaborators; of Mr. Ernest Barker particularly, who, as
it were, runs along the footnotes calling up to Mr. Wells
to take care what he is about. If we sometimes feel that
Mr. Wells doesn't know quite what he is about, we are
left in no doubt that he knows what he likes, and what he
dislikes. He dislikes many statesmen, almost all kings, and
all diplomats; he dislikes patriotism, nationalism, imperial-
ism; he dislikes Rousseau; he dislikes the classical education. In the eighth book, Mr. Wells leaves us with the
distinct impression that the last two centuries provide no
proper ending to the story of life and mankind; he seems,
as it were, disappointed that his characters, in the earlier
chapters all doing as well as could be expected, should be
so perversely going to the dogs at the close.

The gathering tide of Mr. Wells's exasperation reaches
the flood with Napoleon. To this central figure of modern
history he devotes a chapter of which the tone and temper
may be fairly judged by the following extract:

There lacked nothing to this great occasion but a noble imagination. And failing that, Napoleon could do no more than strut
upon the crest of this great mountain of opportunity like a cockerel upon a dunghill. The figure he makes in history is one of
almost incredible self-conceit, of vanity, greed, and cunning, of
callous contempt and disregard of all who trusted him, and of a

grandiose apeing of Caesar, Alexander, and Charlemagne which would be purely comic if it were not caked over with human blood. Until, as Victor Hugo said in his tremendous way, "God was bored by him," and he was kicked aside into a corner to end his days, explaining and explaining how very clever his worst blunders had been, prowling about his dismal hot island shooting birds and squabbling meanly with an underbred gaoler who failed to show him proper "respect."

The entire chapter is much like this—scarcely more than an angry tirade; often amusing, sometimes pat, but still a tirade. That Napoleon deserved the tirade, I do not deny; and if I note this chapter particularly it is only as a concrete instance of the effect of most of modern history upon Mr. Wells's peace of mind. Why is it that Mr. Wells maintains his equanimity so much better in dealing with certain aspects and certain periods of history than he does in dealing with other aspects and periods? Why is it that the Neanderthalers irritate him less than the Romans, the "Old Man" of the tribe than the pope of the Church, the Heidelberg Sub-Man than Napoleon?

Of course it is more difficult to maintain one's equanimity in respect to a man who has left thirty-six volumes of correspondence than it is in respect to a man who has left nothing but his jawbone. Or perhaps Mr. Wells finds his characters less interesting as he goes on because he has taken less time and pains to find out what they thought and did, and why it seemed reasonable to them thus to think and to do. Or it may be just that the telling of a story, of which the form is pretty rigidly determined by actions for the most part well known and often prosaic, enlists his interest and engages his powers less than the discussion of questions involving the nice use of odd bits of evidence, and giving freer play to the imaginative and constructive faculties. But fundamentally, I think, the temper which Mr. Wells brings to the consideration of different aspects and periods of history is no more than the emotional by-product of the motive which induced him to write the *Outline*, a normal expression of his interest in the past, a proper literary device, so to speak, for effectively expounding the meaning and purpose of history as he understands it.

It goes without saying that Mr. Wells is not, in the conventional sense, *objective*. (O thrice blessed anchorage of the academic mind!) He is biased. Alas yes! He has a very special, even a personal, interest in the past. He will not take that cosmic point of view which reduced Henry Adams to the cold comfort of a mechanical formula. But then, no historian does. We all agree with Mr. Wells that the last three thousand years of human history are more worthy of our attention than the preceding three hundred and forty-seven thousand, for the simple reason that they are *"more interesting to us."* We write history from the human rather than from the cosmic point of view because, however indifferent the doings of man may be to the cosmic force of which they are the result, they are vastly interesting *to us;* and vastly inportant, measured by the standard of human desires, purposes, and aspirations. If the historian is to write history at all, he must be interested in these desires, purposes, and aspirations, must regard them as important in some sense or other. The most disinterested historian in the world has at least one preconception, which is that he will at all hazards have none.

But still there are different kinds of bias, different methods of "exploiting the past," different conceptions of the way in which its value for us can best be appropriated. We may be interested in the activity of man in the past as something in itself worthy to be studied for no other immediate purpose than the increase of human knowledge. From this point of view, the motives and interests that have produced wars and permitted politicians to flourish may be contemptible, but it is important to know just how these motives and interests functioned, since they are part of the record without which we cannot understand what kind of a creature man is. The historian who takes this point of view will perhaps say that whether Napoleon strikes us as a cockerel strutting on a dunghill is beside the point; what is important is to understand how, so recently as a century ago, such a dunghill could exist on the earth, or such a cockerel so long strut on it and with so much and so loud crowing lord it over the barnyard. If we could once thoroughly understand this cockerel and this dunghill, I imagine the historian to say, perhaps we could understand our own cockerels and our own dunghills, and so get rid of them. There is something to be said for the view that we do little in the long run, to get rid of our dunghills by calling them nasty. But there is something to be said for the view that we do little to get rid of them by indulging a mere idle curiosity as to their chemical and bacteriological properties. It may be, especially in times of pressure like the present, that when the historian comes to a dunghill the best he can do is just indignantly and emphatically to call it a dunghill, just to make his readers intensely *feel* that so disgusting a thing must never again be permitted to accumulate. From this point of view, the historian is interested in the activity of man in the past, not primarily as something to be in itself intellectually apprehended, but rather as something to be practically appraised in the light of ends that are thought to be desirable and attainable in the future. This is clearly Mr. Wells's point of view.

He writes his history in order to estimate "the quality and amount and range of the hopes with which [humanity] now faces its destiny." He writes his history in the light of a definitely conceived theory of human progress.

The indispensable factor in progress, according to Mr. Wells, is intelligence—the expanding capacity of the human mind. In the prehistoric period the growth of intelligence is no more than the accidental result of the "inanimate clash of matter," or the striving of blind human instinct. In this stage, therefore, progress is just the concomitant of what man instinctively does. The Heidelberg Sub-Man contributes to progress no doubt, but without knowing it; and so Mr. Wells feels, and we do too, that it would be manifestly absurd to hold him responsible for actions done or omitted. The Heidelberg man is really too remote to arouse our ire, and we can easily contemplate his activities, we cannot but contemplate his activities, with the same detachment with which we contemplate the antics of the Triceratops. But Napoleon is not thus remote; he is sufficiently like ourselves to arouse our ire. For in the infinitely slow expansion of human intelligence there comes a time when it is a function of this intelligence to be aware of itself, to recall the past and to anticipate the future, to experience regret and to indulge in hope; in a word, to place a value on its purpose and decisions, distinguishing the better from the less good. This very awareness then becomes a factor in progress. Man not only knows that he may choose the better in place of the worse, but he forms a conception of what that better is. Progress can then be conceived as the anticipated result of deliberate human purpose; and so we find Mr. Wells, in so far as he deals with men whose actions and purposes can be determined, approving or disapproving, placing a value on the purpose or the activity, according as it is thought to have contributed to the desired and anticipated result. If Napoleon excites his ire more than others, it is because to him, more than to any other, "it was open to work out and consolidate the new order of things, to make a modern state that should become a beacon and inspiration to Europe and all the world."

You may say, of course, that it was impossible for Napoleon to do other than he did because he was the product of his time, the inevitable result of "all the conditions." Mr. Wells seems at times, rather reluctantly, to admit this. "Perhaps," he says in a kind of aside, "that amount of mischief had to be done by some agency; perhaps his career, or some such career, was a necessary consequence of the world's mental unpreparedness for the crisis of the revolution." If you should ask, why then grow so indignant about what had to be, if you should say that Napoleon like the Peace at Versailles, was "the best that could be had *under all the circumstances*" of this most impossible of all possible worlds, Mr. Wells would no doubt reply that the low aims and limited vision of Napoleon and his contemporaries were an essential part of the "circumstances," and that for his part he proposes to proclaim insistently to all the world that those aims were low and that vision limited, in order that higher aims and a broader vision may make part of the "circumstances" that are to condition, as inevitably as you please, the activities of men in the future. The answer is adequate enough. Mr. Wells's indignation is as much a part of the cosmic process as Napoleon's low aims; it would therefore be unfair, and contrary to the rules of the game, especially if the game is rigidly predetermined, to accept Napoleon's low aims as necessary while objecting to Mr. Wells's indignation as undesirable.

It comes to this, that Mr. Wells is too much aware of being himself a part of the cosmic process, is too intent upon shaping and improving that process, is too much in the game, to be willing to stand, aloofly wrapped in the blanket of intellectual curiosity, on the side lines, with no other purpose than to observe the intricacies of the play as it goes by. Interested primarily in the "may be's" rather than in the "has been's," the didactic instinct more and more overcomes the scientific instinct; so much so that in the end he seems not so much sitting at the feet of history in order to learn what she has to say, as to be holding the rod over her, and somewhat threateningly pronouncing her answers quite inadequate. Don't tell me what you have done, Mr. Wells seems to be saying; let me tell you what you ought to have done, and what, depend upon it, you have got to do before you are through. As the story draws to a close he conveys the impression of telling us less about Dame History than about what is "the trouble" with her; he lectures the perverse old lady, checks up her faults, notes her stupidities, and exposes all her worst blunders as if he took a warm paternal interest in the mending of her ways. Of her preposterous conduct between 1848 and 1878, Mr. Wells tells us roundly that:

all the diplomatic fussing, posturing, and scheming, all the intrigue and bloodshed of these years, all the monstrous turmoil and waste . . . all the wonderful attitudes, deeds, and schemes of the Cavours, Bismarks, Disraelis, Bonapartes, and the like great men, might very well have been avoided altogether had Europe but had the sense to instruct a small body of ordinarily honest ethnologists, geographers, and sociologists to draw out its proper boundaries and prescribe suitable forms of government in a reasonable manner.

Perhaps poor old History, being blinder than Justice, hasn't any sense. But Mr. Wells will accept no excuse; and the reason he is so inexorable is that he knows to a certainty what she ought to have been doing—he knows precisely what is *important* in history and what not. The importance of a man or an event is measured by what the man or event contributed to the "five-fold constructive effort" of the future. Men who contributed to this effort are the "real makers of the nineteenth century," in comparison with whom "the foreign ministers and 'statesmen' and politicians . . . were no more than a troublesome and occasionally incendiary lot of schoolboys . . . playing about and doing transitory mischief."

Obviously, the historian cannot estimate the importance of men and events in this manner, at least not with much security, unless he ventures to know what the future holds. Mr. Wells thus ventures. He has his idea of "the next stage in history," of the "world as it might be like, were men united in a common peace and justice." This idea is what inspired him to write the *Outline;* and it is this idea which gives him a standard of *values*, which enables him to say what history ought to have done and miserably failed to do; it is this idea which furnishes him with a philosophy. The Great Society of the future, in the light of which the value of all history is assessed, Mr. Wells sketches in the last book: a Federal World State, democratic in its political organization, without armies or navies, sustained by an educated consciously willing race, inspired by the religion of brotherhood, directed by critical and scientific knowledge, devoted to the exploitation of the material world for the benefit of mankind and to the joyous exploration of the unlimited possibilities of the human spirit.

Needless to say, it is not the study of history that has imposed this splendid ideal upon the mind of Mr. Wells. Like many another man he has created this refuge from despair to save his soul alive out of pessimism.

War is a horrible thing, and constantly more horrible and dreadful, so that unless it is ended it will certainly end human society; social injustice, and the sight of the limited and cramped human beings it produces, torment the soul; . . . Hitherto man has been living in a slum, amidst quarrels, revenges, vanities, shames and taints, hot desires, and urgent appetites. He has scarcely tasted sweet air yet and the great freedoms of the world that science has enlarged for him.

No, it is not the study of history, but present experience, which torments the soul and makes us all wish passionately to end war and suffering, that enables Mr. Wells to see the Promised Land. The Promised Land *must* be ahead, because—otherwise it would be too horrible! In the light of his ardent hope Mr. Wells looks back over the long past of the human race, and there, sure enough, he sees the substance of the thing hoped for. By the beginning of the third century, he can see already emerging the three great ideas of science, of a universal religion of righteousness, and of a world polity.

The rest of the history of mankind is largely the history of those three ideas . . . spreading out from the minds of the rare and exceptional persons and peoples in which they first originated, into the general consciousness of the race, and giving first a new color, then a new spirit, and then a new direction to human affairs.

Thus upon the screen of the past Mr. Wells projects his vision of the future: all the groping efforts of the human race, all its blood and tears, are seen to mean just this; that humanity has been moving, without knowing it perhaps, with many a tedious and discouraging return upon the path, toward the Great Society which *will* come because it *must* come.

Hitherto this forward movement has been mainly a blind striving, a blind leading of the blind. What is necessary is that men should become conscious of the goal and the way that leads to it. Now it is just the supreme value of history that, by revealing the way that leads to the goal, it enables us to proceed directly and consciously toward it. Whatever in the past has increased knowledge, or instilled into the human heart the spirit of brotherhood, or promoted the establishment of a polity based upon the allegiance of consciously willing subjects, has brought us forward; ignorance and egotism and blind obedience have held us back. Christianity gave us the ideal of the brotherhood of man, and by the thirteenth century there had dawned the "first intimation . . . of an ideal of government which is still making its way to realization.". Through ignorance and priestcraft this ideal unhappily failed. The modern world has banished priestcraft and acquired the means of knowledge that bid fair to banish ignorance. But in banishing priestcraft and acquiring knowledge it has lost its own soul, has lost sight both of the idea of a world polity and of a universal religion of righteousness. After the ideas of Roman Empire and Church lost their hold, while in "nearly every other field of human interest there was advance," in things political there was retrogression "towards merely personal monarchy and monarchist nationalism of the Macedonian type." Gradually, therefore,

men shifted the reference of their lives from the kingdom of God and the brotherhood of mankind to these apparently more living realities, France and England, Holy Russia, Spain, Prussia. . . . In the thirteenth and fourteenth centuries the general population of Europe was religious and only vaguely patriotic; by the nineteenth it had become wholly patriotic. In a crowded . . . railway carriage in the later nineteenth century it would have aroused far less hostility to have jeered at God than to have jeered at one of those strange beings, England or France or Germany. . . . They were the real and living gods of Europe.

But this relapse into a new egoism, in which we are still living, is only temporary; a thing only of the last few centuries, a "mere hour, an incidental phase, in the vast deliberate history of our kind." Sooner or later we shall pass out of it as men awake from a nightmare, and the conflicts of these days will seem to our posterity as insane as to us seem the feuds of the Blues and the Greens in the streets of Byzantium.

For a time men have relapsed upon these national or imperial gods of theirs; it is but for a time. The idea of the world state, the universal kingdom of righteousness of which every living soul shall be a citizen, was already in the world two thousand years ago never more to leave it. Men know that it is present even when they refuse to recognize it. . . . They still talk loudly of their "love" for France, of their "hatred" of Germany, of the "traditional ascendancy of Britain at sea," and so on and so on, like those who sing of their cups in spite of the steadfast onset of sobriety and a headache. These are dead gods they serve. By sea or land men want no Powers ascendant, but only law and service. That silent unavoidable challenge is in all our minds like dawn breaking slowly, shining through the shutters of a disordered room.

Well, what shall we say? Certainly the room is disordered; the dawn may be breaking, it has often come before, and gone; but those shutters—how with ineffectual fingers we still fumble at the unyielding clasps!

It may be that Mr. Wells has read the past too close to the desire of his heart. But there are worse things. We may hope at least that the future will be as he thinks. If it should turn out so, Mr. Wells's book will have been more than a history, even if it is not history; it will have been an action that has helped to make history. If it should turn out otherwise, still will the book have been a valiant deed. On November 28, 1760, Diderot wrote to Voltaire, apropos of the latter's *Essai sur les Moeurs:*

Other historians relate facts to inform us of facts. You relate them in order to excite in our hearts a profound hatred of lying, ignorance, hypocrisy, superstition, fanaticism, tyranny; and this anger remains, even after the memory of the facts has disappeared.

As much might be said of Mr. Wells's *Outline*. Mr. Wells is not Voltaire, but his *rôle* is much the same: like Voltaire he is a versatile man of letters, with warm human sympathies, interested in all the knowledge of his day; like Voltaire he is a man of faith, who believes that men may be made more enlightened and more humane; like Voltaire he is enlisted in the war on *l'Infâme*—on hypocrisy, superstition, fanatism, tyranny. Mr. Wells's history is a powerful weapon employed in that war. Like Voltaire's *Essai*, it is a criticism of the present in terms of the past; with all its imperfections, a notable effort to enlist the experience of mankind in the service of its destiny.

"Ah, but this is not *History!*" I hear someone exclaim. Very well, call it what you like. If you like not the term history for Mr. Wells's book, call it something else— for example, the adventures of a generous soul among catastrophes!

Frederick Jackson Turner

I WENT to the University of Wisconsin (in 1893 it was) for the same reason that many boys go to one college rather than another—because a high school friend of mine, whose cousin or something had "been at Madison," was going there. As youth will, I at once endowed the place, which I had never seen and had only recently heard of, with a romantic glamour. Was not Madison a distant and large city? (I am speaking now of a prairie country boy who had never ventured from his small town into the world so wide). And was it not located on a great body of water, a lake eight miles in diameter, no less? One other bit of knowledge contributed to the splendor that was Wisconsin. On the faculty of that University there was a man whom a young lawyer in my town had belauded and bragged about, and familiarly referred to as "old Freddie Turner."

"Is he old"? I asked, picturing the long gray locks of a Faust before the devil comes in the spotlight.

"Oh no, not *old*. We just called him that, I don't know why—just a rough way of showing boyish admiration without being sentimental about it, I suppose."

"What does he teach?"

"Well, he teaches American history. But it's not what he teaches, the subject I mean. The subject doesn't matter. It's what he is, the personality and all that sort of thing.

It's something he gives you, inspiration, new ideas, a fresh light on things in general. It's something he makes you want to do or be. I don't remember much American history, but I'll never forget that man Turner, old Freddie Turner."

So I went to the University of Wisconsin clear about one thing—I would take a course with old Freddie Turner. Unfortunately he taught history. The word held no blandishments for me. In high school I had studied (that isn't the word, but what word is there for it?) history, general history, Barnes' *General History*, or some such misdemeanor against youth; of which I remembered only one sentence: "*Egypt has been called the gift of the Nile.*" That alone of all the history of the world I remembered; and even that I hadn't learned the meaning of, hadn't indeed supposed or ever been told that it was expected to have a meaning. A dull subject, history. And yet there I was at the University of Wisconsin determined to take a course in history because, unfortunately, that was the only "subject offered" by old Freddie Turner.

I

I was not many days in Madison before the man was pointed out to me, on the campus, going somewhere in a hurry, loaded down with an immense leather portfolio bulging with books and notes; belatedly hurrying up the hill to class I dare say, probably perspiring but certainly unbowed. Of course he wasn't old—thirty-three or thereabouts at that time. To a youth of eighteen, men of thirty-three, professors at all events, might more often than not *seem* old; were at least likely to convey the impression of having settled all disturbing questions, of having as it were astutely encased themselves in a neat armor of fixed defensive habit warranted proof against the slings and arrows of whatever unusual experience or risky adventure the mischances of life, within cloistered academic walls, were likely to threaten them with. No such impression was conveyed by "that man Turner" beating it up the hill at 10:02 A.M. Even to a boy of eighteen there was something essentially youthful in the rounded lines of the short compact figure, in the free and unstudied swing of arms and legs; something gay and larky about the head ever so gallantly held, with ever so slight and so engaging a lifted backward tilt of valiant defiance to all the associated fates; something mischievously boyish even about the ruddy complexion, above all about the eyes and lips—eyes and lips that seemed always smiling even in repose, or always ready to smile, as if the world were so full of a number of things that odd chances and interesting episodes were to be momentarily expected. Expected and welcomed. Such was the impression. Serious indeed the man was, you never doubted that, but not solemn, above all not old, not professionally finished; just beginning rather, zestfully and buoyantly beginning, out for adventure, up to something, in the most casual friendly way inviting you to join in.

Inviting you to join in, yes. I don't mean (God forbid!) soliciting students to take his courses. Heaven knows he didn't need to make sly maneuvers to get you. Well I remember the opening day of the second year when I stood in line by his desk, waiting to ask him a question (totally unnecessary question, invented for the precise purpose of standing there and being spoken to). There I stood, and presently he turned to me with the quick upward flash of blue eyes that seemed to lift and throw over and through me a shaft of live light. I seemed, dumb shy youth that I was, to stand fully revealed in the light of those extraordinary eyes—cool, steady, challenging, yet friendly too, and hoping for the best. Haltingly I asked my foolish question, and was answered. The answer was nothing, the words were nothing, but the voice—the voice was everything: a voice not deep but full, rich, vibrant, and musically cadenced; such a voice as you would never grow weary of, so warm and intimate and human it was. I cannot describe the voice. I know only that it laid on me a kind of magic spell which I could never break, and have never wanted to. Well, there it was, the indefinable *charm*. An upward lift of the eyes, a few friendly words, and I, like I know not how many other lads of nineteen, was straightway a devoted disciple and questionless admirer of "old Freddie Turner." I didn't care *what* he offered. For him I would even study history.

Even then I didn't study history. I took courses in history, and in due time I took Turner's "junior course" in American history. But I didn't study history, not really; because I didn't know how to study it. Remembering what things happened at what times—that was what studying history meant to me then. Learning these things out of a book. Well, we had a book. To begin with Turner asked us to buy Thwaites' *Colonies*, and I bought it. I have it yet, with certain dates set down opposite the successive chapters in the table of contents; all these "assignments" having been given us once for all at the beginning of the term. Simple enough, I thought—each week I will learn a chapter. But after the second week we were behind the schedule, and after the fourth week we didn't know where we were, and never found out. Of course I read the book— I think I did; was expected to and, being an obedient boy, must have done so. But the book was like all history books, dull, filled with uninteresting facts which I couldn't remember; and so it happened that when Turner sometimes for ten minutes asked us questions,—"Mr. Becker, what were the provisions of the Tariff Bill of 1816?"—I never could answer, or almost never. During the second term I did answer one question, a question which had just gone its weary round without eliciting any response. I forget what the question was. The answer was "1811." "Precisely," said Turner, in a tone implying that he now recognized me as of that select company of scholars who would see at once the peculiar significance of 1811.

But if I didn't study history that year, I was infected with the desire to do so. This of course was Turner's fault, not mine (Haskins' fault too, by the way; and if I were writing chiefly about myself instead of Turner, which it may be thought I am doing if I don't watch out, there would be much to be said about Haskins). For it was true, as my lawyer friend said, that Turner had a singular capacity for making you want to do and be something—to do, in short, what he was doing, and to be, if possible, what he was. And what was he? And what was he doing? Fascinated by the man, I attended to his every gesture and expression, listened to everything he said, less at first for the content than for the voice, the intention, the implication. The implication of the whole performance was of something vital being under consideration, something that had in itself only incidentally to do with students "taking a course." The implication was that we (all of us together, if *we* chose—that was our affair) were searching for something, ferreting out hidden secrets. Facts there were, plenty of them, and as a matter of course to be known; but that wasn't the end. There was something concealed there, in and behind the facts, some problem that concerned humanity at large waiting to be solved. The implication was that we might, on our own account, turn over the dead facts once more, on the chance of finding something, something the others had missed.

Inconceivable that Thwaites had missed anything, I couldn't suppose it! Yet so it appeared. For here was a "teacher," who at one moment confessed his ignorance and the next modestly questioned the textbook. Inviting us one day to consider the problem of sovereignty, he quoted Austin's definition; said he couldn't understand it; admitted he wasn't blessed with the logical mind; and drew two (or was it three?) overlapping circles on the blackboard illustrating the theory of "divided sovereignty," which he said seemed to fit the facts of American history better, but even of that he wasn't certain either. Well, a "teacher" was supposed to know everything, yet there was Turner not able to explain sovereignty. Supposed to know everything, a teacher was, but of course not more than the textbook. Yet there another day stood Turner saying, as casually as ever you please, "I do not agree with Thwaites on this point." What to make of a teacher who knew more than the textbook, but was still ignorant of something? After I know not how long it dawned on me, and with what a joyous sense of emancipation, that Turner wasn't, that no university professor need be, merely a teacher. Turner obviously hadn't just learned his history out of a book. The rash sceptic had gone out of his way to get the "facts" somewhere else, had "investigated"—that was the word—the documents on his own account, had taken his own notes from the "sources," was in short an "authority" in his own right, and might if he wished write his own book of American history.

From the moment Turner ceased to figure in my mind as a teacher, I began to learn something from him. Not "teacher" but "historian" he was, better still "author,"

whose main occupation it was, not to teach us, but to be
deeply engaged in researches preliminary to the writing
of notable books. Obvious enough, once you got the idea.
For surely no professor, coming somewhat distraitly into
class at the last moment, ever spread about such a cheerful
happy air of having been interrupted in preparatory studies,
or ever more successfully conveyed the impression of going
cheerfully on, during the brief hour, for our benefit, with
the morning's labors. Material evidence of those labors
there was a plenty in the stacks of notes deposited on the
desk, notes on slips of paper 6 x 8, or some such size, filed
in labeled manilla envelopes; more enveloped notes every
day brought to class than could by any chance be looked
into; as if the preoccupied scholar, leaving his study on
the run, had hastily gathered together whatever he could
conveniently lay his hands on, hoping to be prepared with
illustrative material relevant to any one of a number of
interesting topics which might, happily, turn up during
the lecture.

The lecture itself, if that is the word for it, seemed
never "prepared," never studiously "got up" under the
lamp. It seemed rather the spontaneous result of prepara-
tions always going on and never finished. The lecture was
just informal, intimately conversational talk, beginning as
might happen with this interesting matter, and ending as
might happen with that; always serious without ever being solemn; enlivened with humor and wholesome infec-
tious laughter, yet never falling to the level of the sad
professorial joke; running off into revelant digressions
occasioned by some student query; coming back again to
the main point; coming now and again to the full stop
while "notes" were eagerly searched for and found (oh,
well, usually found), if not in one manilla envelope per-

haps in another, notes containing some desired quotation
from the documents, with exact reference given, illustrating a point, clinching an argument. No, lecture isn't the
word. Nothing *ex cathedra* here, no musty air of academic
infallibility clouding the room, no laying down of the law
and gospel according to Turner; but all compact of inquiry
and novel ideas carelessly thrown out with more questions
asked than were answered, more problems posed than
solved. The professor seemed not at all concerned to ladle
out the minimum dose of American history suitable to our
complaint. He was just talking to us as a man might talk
to men, about the problems that interested *him*, problems
which he had apparently been thinking about after break-
fast, and might very likely, one felt, think some more
about after luncheon.

Such was the impression. But where then did we, poor
dazed novices astray in the bright intellectual world, come
in on this business? No doubt the method, or lack of it,
was not well calculated to send the shining morning-faced
student away rejoicing with neatly wrapped and labeled
packets of "knowledge," to be held until called for, at
examination time, and then duly returned, unopened. No
doubt the student often felt like asking, as students will,
what precisely the "required work" was—"Professor,
what are we expected to know for examination?" Well,
one could trust to luck, would have to apparently. I at
least knew that something (something about the bank was
it?) happened in 1811. Curiously enough I didn't worry,
timid and cautious youth that I was, I didn't worry much
about the packets of useful information; for you see I was
getting, as failing students say, "a great deal out of the
course." I was getting a great deal out of Turner. I was
daily enjoying the inestimable privilege of watching an

original and penetrating intelligence at work, playing freely with facts and ideas, handling with discrimination the problems of history, problems which so often turned out to be the problems of life itself. Unorganized the course was certainly; but the resulting impression was nevertheless not one of confusion. The impression always was that of a brilliant light being thrown on dark places. For the talk, however desultory it may have been, was never merely rambling, but went always winding in and through and round about the matter in hand at the behest of some fresh idea, suggestion, or tentative hypothesis. Something vital and significant in the facts these flashed ideas and hypotheses seemed always revealing. An ordered body of information I could get, and did afterwards get, for myself; but from no other man did I ever get in quite the same measure that sense of watching a first-class mind at work on its own account, and not merely rehearsing for the benefit of others; the most delightful sense in the world of sitting there waiting for ideas to be born; expectantly waiting for secret meanings, convenient explanatory hypotheses to be discovered, lurking as like as not under the dullest mass of drab facts ever seen.

In this happy way I got a new idea of history. It was after all no convention agreed upon to be learned by rote, but just the infinitely varied action and thought of men who in past times had lived and struggled and died for means or great objects. It was in short an aspect of life itself, and as such something to be probed into, thought about, written about. Who would not like to study history as Turner studied it? And write about it as he would write about it? Not possible of course to do it with his brilliant competence, not a chance; but still there was something to try for, a standard set, an ideal. And so in this eventful

junior year I brought out my tiny little wagon and fum-
blingly hitched it to that bright particular star. Procuring
quantities of paper and manilla envelopes, I began "pen
in hand" to study history; with patient, plodding abandon
pouring over such fascinating works as *Niles Register* and
the *New York Colonial Documents*, or any other mouldy,
crumbling old tome, provided only it contained those "original sources" which Turner, by some species of white
magic, had invested with color and charm. What a joy
it was in those days merely to turn the yellow pages of
old books! With what a sense of solid work accomplished
one extracted the substance of no matter what official document, always, with reverent piety, noting the "exact reference"—*Niles*, XII, 749. Still preserved they are, those
stacks of notes in manilla envelopes, aging now undis-
turbed on upper shelves, long since covered with dust!

II

With the novitiate ended, one took the full vows. For
three years I pursued my researches in Turner's seminary, a
group of twelve or fifteen men, with a stray woman or two,
meeting in the Law Building, or, better still, in the state
Historical Society Library, then housed in the Capitol.
Here we did our work, each man having a table, or part of
one, in an alcove; and all of us assembling, on Mondays,
Wednesdays, and Fridays, round one of the larger tables,
with Turner in our midst. To be so commoded was to be in
the very center of the temple of learning; for we were here,
all of us, professor and pupils, daily boxed about with
walls of books, the books we needed and were currently
using, those very collections of "documents" which ex-
exhaled the mothy odors of scholarship; so that just to sit
motionless in the blest place breathing in the incensed

atmosphere of research at its thickest enabled one to anticipate the illusions of the fully erudite.

Informal to a degree this seminary was, more informal
even than the "junior course." Lectures there were none,
or almost none, unless one prefers to say there were always
lectures, or nearly always. For the engaging theory was
that we were all scholars together, surveying broadly the
field of American history, each man having his particular
subject—the colonization of Virginia, Internal Improve-
ments, or whatever—subjects large and unconfined, opening a career to talent. Each man was expected to master his
subject as well as might be; to be responsible for it; to be
ready like a cabinet minister to answer such questions,
bearing upon it, as might be asked by the opposition; above
all from time to time to make reports giving the matured
results of his investigation. In this way each of us, including the professor, would lecture in turn, and all of the
others, including the professor, would take notes. The professor, such was the theory, was just one of us, the principal one no doubt, organizing and directing the whole performance, but still not professing to know too much,
modestly deferring to any one of us where our particular
topics were concerned, and himself taking notes, when we
lectured, with an alert and convincing air of being instructed, of having old matter freshly examined and interpreted for him. I swear he did take notes, and he has
since assured me, with just a trace of asperity I thought,
that it was no frame-up, but that he did actually obtain
from us valuable ideas and information which afterwards
he sometimes made good use of. Well, I believe him. I do
believe he did sometimes get from us some or other odd
fact, such was his inordinate thirst for facts and his uncanny
instinct for finding them in the most unlikely places, such

his skill in disengaging what was significant from even the most confused jumble of the incompetent, the irrelevant, and the immaterial.

I took notes too, of course I did. It was part of the ritual, and I was nothing if not strong in the faith—in those old days. The notes I took are not such, I do confess, that one could reconstruct from them an adequate account of American history; but they had, and have had, for me at least, a high value nevertheless. Here before me, for example, are the notes, easily contained on one sheet of paper 6 x 8, of a two-days' report on the Mexican War.

Rogers' report—Mexican War. Polk. Taylor. Senate Bill. Biglow Papers frequently referred to. Turner asks: "By the way, Mr. Rogers, what exactly are the Biglow Papers?" Rogers says: "The Biglow Papers—" (Hesitates, seems a little dazed, has at last a happy inspiration) "Why, the Biglow Papers are—a well known work by—a famous author." Hilarious laughter, led by Turner, who then explains Biglow Papers. Don't myself know B. P. Remember look up and read B. P. Lowell, J. R.

Thus to my great regret I missed the significant points of the Mexican War, but at least I read the Biglow Papers, and have always remembered that the work is well known and by a famous author. Another sheet lies before me.

Turner asks, why the unusual literary activity in generation following 1815? Various suggestions. Becker says perhaps on account of feeling of relief and freedom after War of 1812 and Napoleonic wars. Turner says, perhaps. Is that a fact or only a plausible inference? What is an historical fact? Can you prove an inference? May historian be satisfied with inference? Have all great wars been followed by intellectual and literary activity? What in general is cause of changes in character of thought? Fifteen minute talk, mostly questions, a cascade of questions. No one answers these questions. Why doesn't Turner tell us the answers? Something to think about.

Something to think about, sure enough! Well, I have thought about it, off and on, for twenty-five years; but I don't now wonder why Turner didn't tell us the answers.

As time passed I was made aware indeed that Turner very often didn't answer questions. Heaven knows he asked enough, was always handing out some riddle to be solved, always giving us something to think about and then serenely leaving us to think about it. But there were questions he neglected either to ask or to answer. For example, did the colonies or the British government have the right of it in the War of Independence? Should one properly sympathize with Jefferson or Marshall? Was the tariff a wise policy? Was Jacksonian democracy a good or a bad thing? Were the slave states justified in seceding from the Union? Important questions these were surely; questions which a teacher who had given his life to the study of American history might be supposed to answer for students who came to college expecting to be furnished with right opinions and convictions. But I don't recall that Turner ever answered these questions, or the like of them; so that to this day I don't know what his convictions are on the great issues. Is he protectionist or free trader? Democrat or republican? Baptist or infidel, or member of that great church which Lord Melbourne commended for never meddling with either politics or religion? Above all is he a conservative, satisfied with the evils we have? Or a liberal, willing to substitute for them others which formerly existed? Or a radical, eager for the shock of new ones never yet tried? I don't know. Turner never gave us answers to these questions. He never told us what to think.

I hope I am not conveying the impression that Turner appeared to his students in the somber light of a "strong silent man." Somber is the last word in the world to describe him, and silent isn't the word either. He talked freely enough, and he answered questions freely enough, questions of a certain sort. After I don't know how many months or years I learned that the answers he commonly neglected to give were answers which would have enabled me to borrow his opinions and judgments, and so save myself the trouble of thinking. He would do what he could to help me think, but he wouldn't if he knew it tell me what to think. He was not much given to handing down final judgments.

This is important, and I wish to emphasize it a little. Turner didn't pronounce final judgments. In those days it sometimes troubled me that he didn't. But I have long since forgiven him, blessed him indeed, for it, having seen quite enough of those complacent people who go about recreating the world in their own image and expecting others to see that it is good. Turner might have said, with Mr. Justice Holmes, that one important article of his creed as a scholar was that he was *not* God. Like Margaret Fuller, he "accepted the universe," although, unlike that voluble lady, he did it silently. I am speaking now of Turner the scholar, not of Turner the man and citizen. As man and citizen he had, and always has had, convictions, knows what he thinks right and wise, and never leaves you in any doubt about it. As man and citizen he doesn't, I am sure, think this the best of conceivable worlds, or always find it a comfortable place to be in, as what intelligent or sensitive person does? He has indeed always met the reverses of life with serenity and high courage, no man I think ever more so; but I know not how many times he may in his heart have refreshingly damned the universe to extinction, as, on occasion, all good men do I hope. But I am now concerned with the scholar. As scholar, so it seems to me, Turner accepts men and things as given, the business of the scholar being not to *judge* but only to *understand* them.

To me at least it is a matter of no slight importance that he accepted us, graduate students, in that spirit. We, too, were apparently parts of the universe, to be accepted as given. He never made me feel that I was before the Judgement Seat. He was never the schoolmaster, standing behind me prodding, with sharp exclamation points pitchforking me up the steep path of learning. He criticized my work to be sure, but it was the work he criticized, and in the most honest friendly way, without leaving any aftertaste of personal depravity in the mouth. He appeared to take me as the associated fates had made me, more or less intelligent, and to assume that I would willingly do the best I could. Amazing, to me at least, was the casual friendly way he had of treating us as equals, as serious scholars with whom it was a pleasure to be associated in common tasks. Even our work he didn't criticize much, condemning it by silence mainly, commending it on rare occasions by a few hearty words of approval. How the rash man gambled on us to be sure, professing to see in us qualities and virtues marking us out for future *savants*. Perhaps there was some method in this madness. To get the best out of graduate students, or any students, it is perhaps just as well not to assume to begin with that there isn't any best there to be got out. Often enough there isn't, but then it doesn't greatly matter. If there was any best in me, I at least needed, in order to get it out, just the freedom and friendly confidence which Turner gave me, having until then been for the most part "criticized" and "trained" quite sufficiently; oh quite sufficiently told, by parents and uncles and aunts and teachers and pastors, what to do and what not to do; told in such an interesting variety of ways, and with such an implication of futility in the telling, as to leave me clutching the miserable little suspicion that I would probably never, all things considered, be much good at doing anything. Never having talked with my pastor, Turner didn't know this. He blandly assumed that I might amount to something, and at last one day told me that he thought I "had it in me" to become a scholar and a writer —seemed really to believe it. To be told by this admired master that I could probably do the very thing I most wanted to do released what little ability I had to do it. Released the ability, and intensified the desire to do it, because I then, and ever after, worked all the harder in order to justify Turner's faith in me.

This friendly method of dealing with graduate students (the honest ones, I mean; the occasional fakir got the full blaze of his hot scorn) might not have been the best method for another, but I am sure it was the best method for Turner. It was the best method precisely because there wasn't any method in it. When Turner came into class he didn't put on the teacher's manner because he didn't think of himself as a teacher. He thought of himself—or no, he didn't think of himself, that's just the point. He was just Turner, man and scholar, absorbed in his work, who met us because we were interested in the same thing he was; and who met us in the most casual democratic way in the world because it was perfectly natural for him to meet us in that way. The easy aristocratic grace and charm of this friendly democrat from Portage, Wisconsin, had about it neither a shade more nor less of any manner for his high placed colleagues than for the obscurest graduate student. It didn't, this unstudied friendly manner which at once put us at ease, seem to be even second nature. It seemed to be the instinctive expression of a lively and supple intelligence restrained and directed by some inexhaustible native fund of sincerity, integrity, and good will. This is after all one of the reasons, perhaps the chief reason, for his success with graduate students.

It is also, I think, one principal secret of his success as a scholar. For the scholar, the historian at all events, has to meet humanity in some fashion or other; and humanity will commonly reveal little to those who meet it with reticences and reservations and didactic motives. Even in those student days it seemed to me that Turner met humanity very much as he met us, graduate students; he didn't put on anything special for the occasion. Humanity, like graduate students, doubtless had virtues and qualities concealed somewhere about it, and might very well, such was the implication, stumble on, if you gave it rope enough, to some or other place worth going to. Best at all events to assume as much; for humanity is like graduate students in this too, that it will be more likely to do well if you trust it a little, if you have faith to gamble on its hidden capacities.

But who could tell us where poor old humanity is headed for, rope or no rope? I would not willingly charge a reputable historian with harboring a Philosophy of History. Yet I recall that one day Turner quoted Droysen, apparently with approval, to the effect that "history is the self-consciousness of humanity." And another day he said: "The question is not whether you have a Philosophy of History, but whether the philosophy you have is good for anything." In extenuation I feel moved to say that if Turner does indeed have a Philosophy of History, I can't imagine it taking the form of an answer. Much more likely to take the form of a question, thus: "If mankind could once really understand what it has done and thought in the past, is it not possible that it would stumble along now, and in the future, with more intelligence and a more conscious purpose?" I don't know whether this is a Philosophy of History or not. Whether, if it is, it is a good one, I know still less. But of one thing I feel quite sure: if Turner subscribes to it, whatever it is, it doesn't cost him much. It doesn't cost him anything in fact, for it doesn't burden him with any noticeable preoccupations or fixed ideas. He pursues his proper task, which is to find out what certain groups of men did and thought in past times, and to furnish the proximate explanation of their so acting and thinking; and this task he pursues as if he had no philosophy, as if it made no difference at all to him what they did and thought, or what the explanation might turn out to be. He pursues his task in short with detachment, with objectivity.

So at last we come to it, the inevitable word, objectivity. The word has many meanings. In those days I had myself got, or at least got up, chiefly out of books, a notion of objectivity scarcely distinguishable from complete indifference, a sort of stiff solemnity or *rigor mortis* of the spirit; so that I sometimes wondered if Turner really was "objective and disinterested," so lively and interested he always seemed. Certainly indifference, such as Renan's Man in the Moon might be supposed to exhibit, couldn't by any stretch of the imagination be attributed to Turner. Here then was a dilemma; and not being willing to abandon either Turner or the ideal of objectivity, I ended by seeing that Turner was objective in some other fashion than the Man in the Moon. The objectivity of Turner's mind, I found, was a quality he enjoyed in his own right, and not something acquired by training. It wasn't something he had painfully got up in college out of Bernheim—a set of arti-

ficially induced and cultivated repressions such as would
enable any careful historian to write, let us say, an account
of the Battle of Cold Harbor without revealing the fact
that his father was an ardent admirer of Grant. That kind
of objectivity is common enough, and often pernicious
enough, being the best substitute for ideas yet invented.
Turner at least didn't need it, having always more ideas
than he could perhaps well manage. The objectivity he had
seemed rather to spring from that intense and sustained
interest which an abundance of ideas can alone generate. A
hard truth for me to learn, this was, since I hadn't too
many ideas; but I couldn't help seeing that Turner was so
wholly absorbed in his work that he hadn't time to think
of anything else, not even of the necessity of being objective. He was "disinterested" because he was so interested
in the object before him that he forgot, for the time being,
to be interested in anything else; he was "objective" because he was so genuinely curious about that object, desired with such singleness of purpose to know it for the
sake of knowing it, that his mind was empty, for the time
being, of all other objects. This kind of objectivity doesn't
come by willing (not that any sane man, living in a world
of action, would will to have it); it is a quality of mind,
like the sense of absolute pitch, which one is or isn't born
with. No doubt it may, if one has it, be cultivated, but at
any rate it is inseparable from genuine *intellectual curiosity*,
the lively and irrepressible desire to know merely for the
sake of knowing. A rare quality indeed that is, but I think
Turner has it.

Another thing about Turner used in those days to strike
me as a little odd. I don't know just what to call it. "Independence" isn't quite the word. Of course he was an
independent scholar; but then most professors were inde-

pendent scholars in the ordinary sense of the term. His was a peculiar kind of independence which struck me then, and still strikes me, as relatively uncommon among professors. I might call it a certain obliviousness to professional convention, an almost complete freedom from academic provincialism. I first noticed it indeed because it seemed to me then not quite the thing. For I was then doing what many college boys do—emancipating myself from one form of provincialism by taking on another. Coming fresh, or almost fresh, from the farm into an academic community, the professor's world seemed to me the last word in sophistication. The most obvious form which this sophistication took was a certain smart awareness on the professor's part of belonging to a larger and freer society than the one in which, geographically speaking, he perforce lived. Comfortable enough his ivory tower in Madison was no doubt; but he was likely to be often looking out of it towards the more splendid towers of the east, over-anxiously concerned perhaps to know what the wise men there were thinking and doing. One gathered that there were decencies proper to the academic world, a minor one being that no professor should have too much confidence in himself until he received a call from Yale or Harvard, and even then a lively sense of the fitting, some hang over from colonial days perhaps, would keep him subtly servile and apologetic for being no more than an American scholar who must forever abandon hope of entering the sacred portals of Oxford, Paris, or Berlin. If all this was only a second provincialism worse than the first, I was not yet aware of the fact. It seemed to me then no more than the proper mark of those who had oriented themselves in the intellectual world, quite the attitude in short for a professor to have. Therefore it struck me as a little odd that my admired master Turner didn't have it.

For Turner didn't have it. There was no getting round the fact that he didn't have it at all. I got the distinct impression that he didn't mind living in Wisconsin, seemed to think Portage a jolly good place to come from, as if being born there, even if the fact became known, needn't seriously impair the quality of his scholarship. If he knew that Europe was infinitely richer than the United States in historic remains and traditions, I never heard him mention the fact, at least not with the appropriate air of regret for missed opportunities. He had, on the contrary, every appearance of being contented with his opportunities, seemed indeed to rejoice in his opportunities, quite as a man might who had just discovered a gold mine in his back yard. American history, he seemed to say, is a new lead, never yet properly uncovered, as rich and enticing a mine for the scholar as can anywhere be found, all the better for never having been worked by Waitz or von Ranke. It was as if some rank American flavor, some sturdy strain of backwoods independence, resisting every process of academic refinement, kept the man still proud to be an American citizen, contentedly dwelling in Madison, quite satisfied with the privilege of going every day to the State Historical Society Library where the Draper Manuscripts were.

Even in those days I felt, without quite understanding, this non-professional attitude on Turner's part. The time was to come when I found the professional attitude less engaging; and it was probably just because I saw Turner as "different" that these old student day impressions never faded, just because he was never quite the "professor" that his influence was more enduring than that of many professors. His influence was enduring I think because he himself

didn't "date." Above all his ideas about American history
didn't date, never struck one as being modeled upon any
established authority or cribbed from any school of historians. Something personal there always was in his "point
of view," in his "interpretations," as if the subject were
being freshly looked at by a mind washed clean of scholastic dust. Not that there was anything aggressive about
his independence. He never gave one the impression that,
having made up his mind to be original, he was somewhat
bellicosely making good. His independence wasn't an
achievement. And yet I wonder. Was there not about him
too (or did I just imagine it?) some indefinable but quite
jolly air of conscious insubordination, just a quick little
gesture of the mind impatiently dismissing the solemn
snobbery of all that is academically canonized and sacro-
sanct? I can't be sure, but I like to think so.

That is as it may be. But this I know, that three qualities of the man's mind made upon me a profound and indelible impression. These qualities were: a lively and irrepressible intellectual curiosity; a refreshing freedom from
personal preoccupations and didactic motives; a quite unusual ability to look out upon the wide world in a humane,
friendly way, in a fresh and strictly independent way, with
a vision unobscured by academic inhibitions. These are also
the qualities, I think, which have enabled him to make an
"original contribution" (not so common a performance as
is often supposed) to the study of American history. What
then is this original contribution?

III

A distinct achievement, I count it, to have written
twenty pages about Turner without having once mentioned
the word "frontier." But of course this sort of thing can't

be allowed to go on indefinitely. Impossible to tell the
story of Turner without mentioning the frontier—as impossible as it would be to tell the story of Jack Horner
without mentioning the plum. The "frontier" was a plum,
sure enough; but still there is the pie, and the pie is important too, a fact often forgotten. Therefore I wish first
of all to say something about the pie, in the hope that it
will help us to understand how the plum came to be discovered and pulled out.

The pie of this sad metaphor (very sad metaphor indeed
if it leads any one to picture Turner sitting in a corner
bragging of his plum) is of course American history, or
rather American history considered as an example of social
evolution.

I have no desire to make Turner out a sociologist; but
it must be said that narrating events was never his forte,
finding proximate explanations always has been. In his
first published work he raised straight off the question
which has occupied him ever since. "The exploitation of
the Indian is generally dismissed with the convenient explanatory phrase, 'The march of civilization.' But *how did
it march?*"[1] Well, there it is, the central question of all
Turner's work: How does civilization march? Not how did
civilization march from January to November, but how did
and does it march from simple to complex forms? This is no
doubt a question proper to the sociologist; and the pure
sociologist, if there be any such, might attempt an answer
based on the total experience of mankind up to date. What
saves Turner for history, if he can be saved, is that he attempts no universal answer. It is not given to all, as he
modestly says, to "bend the bow of Ulysses." He will at-

[1] "The Fur Trade in Wisconsin." *Proceedings of the State Historical Society of
Wisconsin.* 1889. p. 53.

tempt only a conditioned answer, since he deals only with a limited experience—the experience of the American people within definite space and time limits; and so, if he is concerned with the evolution of society, it is after all the evolution of a particular society. He studies American history as furnishing a concrete illustration, many times repeated and on a relatively grand scale, of the social process.

If Turner still lies under suspicion, one thing I will stoutly affirm in his defence; the social process which entices him is not the Transcendent Idea, or any of its many poor relations. His social process isn't something in the void working over the heads of men, rough hewing them to its own ends. His social process is something that emerges from the thought and action of men, something incidental to what people do for their own ends. It wasn't the "march of civilization" that chased the Indian, nor did the poor fellow die of deficient "cultural capacity." The poor fellow died of bullets fired from rifles in the hands of Daniel Boone, and men of his ilk; men who fired the bullets, not on behalf of civilization or the social process, but on their own behalf, because they wanted land for hunting purposes or for planting, in order to feed themselves and their families and have as good a time generally as circumstances permitted. Turner seems to take it for granted that commonplace people, acting in commonplace ways, somehow or other, unconsciously for the most part, determine the social process and shape the course of history. First of all, therefore, the historian would learn what people did and why they did it.

What people did was an old story with historians, why they did it had doubtless never occupied their thought unduly. This is of course an endless question forever discussed by philosophers; and one might easily push the explanation of action back to ultimate causes—to God, or to the electron revolving rapidly round the nucleus, or, more simply, to a "stress in the ether." But such ultimates are of little use to the historian. They exhaust their virtue in explaining everything in general, so that none is left for explaining anything in particular. This is perhaps why Turner, being especially interested in the particular, is willing to leave final causes to serve the only uses they can serve, to be, that is to say, *final*, signposts at the end of the road signifying "no thoroughfare." The explanations he seeks are proximate explanations, the causes he can make use of are causes operating above and immediately below the level of conscious purpose.

If, for example, the first settlers in New England established the "Town Meeting" that was doubtless because they consciously desired to establish it. But still one may reasonably ask what made them consciously desire to establish the Town Meeting? Perhaps it was an institution which they had, without knowing it, "brought over with them" from England, an institution which they had, in common with Englishmen and Teutonic folk generally, "inherited" from farther back, from the primitive Germans or elsewhere. Why didn't Turner accept this explanation? One naturally asks because the genetic explanation of institutions was going strong at Johns Hopkins when Turner studied there in the eighties; and Herbert B. Adams, the teacher under whom Turner studied, had himself published a monograph pointing out that the New England Town Meeting was a survival from early German custom. Turner must have been thoroughly indoctrinated with the theory of the "continuity of history" and the "inheritance of institutions," must have been given a full adult dose of that prolific institutional germ known as the Teutonic Mark.

Well, it was an overdose, I dare say. Turner couldn't stomach it. Still less to his taste was Adams' dictum that American institutions had already been "well done." This was really too much for the doughty American whose ancestors had preached and pioneered on every frontier from Massachusetts to Nebraska. He therefore left Johns Hopkins in an unsanctified state and returned to Wisconsin proclaiming that "the germ theory of politics has been sufficiently emphasized."[2]

Not that Turner would deny the influence of inheritance. The first settlers obviously brought with them their English, or Dutch, habits of thought and action. These would at first determine what institutions they would try to establish in the new world; and no doubt it would be possible to point out, in the Virginia Hundred or the New England Town Meeting, vestiges of early custom, similarities to the ancient German Mark (or what Nineteenth Century German historians, looking for political liberty somewhere outside of France, imagined the German Mark to be). But Turner would insist (and how clearly I recall his making the statement in class one day!) that "the *similarities* of institutions are less important than the *differences*." If the differences interested him more than the similarities, the reason, I dare say, is to be found in the man's deep-seated loyalty to America. If he has any fundamental preconception or bias it is this. He is a thoroughly good American with never the slightest gesture of apology. He has the rugged patriotism, seven times refined no doubt, of the middle west from which he comes. It was this deep-seated loyalty to America that made him "indignant" when Adams said that American institutions had been "well done." On the contrary, Turner thought, they had

[2] "Significance of the Frontier"; *The Frontier in American History*, p. 2.

not been done at all, not really; for America was important, not because it resembled Europe, but precisely because it was different. He would approve down to the ground Goethe's saying that "America has the best of it." America has the best of it not only, and not chiefly, because of her incomparable material resources, but because she has brought into the world something new, something original—"the ideal of a democracy developing under conditions unlike those of any other age or country."[3] This was what made American institutions really significant and worth studying—this "difference." Well, you could hardly inherit a difference. Where then did the difference come from? Certainly not from the German Mark. Not from the Black Forest but from the American wilderness. American democracy "was not carried in the *Susan Constant* to Virginia, or in the *Mayflower* to Plymouth. It came out of the American forest."[4] So Turner turned away from the theory of inheritance as an adequate explanation of American institutions and set himself to study the influences of the environment. Here if at all would be found the "conditions"—geographic, economic, social—which enabled America to make its peculiar contribution to human civilization.

As a point of vantage from which to observe the influence of environment in a new country, the town of Portage was after all no bad place to be born in. With his father, the boy Turner had poled in dugouts, with Indians from "Grandfather Bull Falls" as guides, on Radisson's old route down the Wisconsin, through virgin forests of balsam firs, startling the deer that came to gaze at them through the foliage with curious frightened eyes, past Indian

[3] *The Frontier in American History*, p. 335.
[4] *The Frontier in American History*, p. 293.

villages where the polesmen would sometimes stop to
palaver with the squaws standing sociably on the high
bank. In Portage, coming home from school, he had seen a
lynched man hanging from a tree. He had seen red-shirted
Irish raftsmen tie up and "take the town," and blanketed
Indians on their ponies file down the street to exchange
furs for baubles and paint. The town itself was a rough
frontier settlement—the meeting place of many nationali-
ties. It had its Irish ward into which boys of Turner's sort
ventured, with whatever tense bravado they could muster,
only in gangs; its Pomeranian ward where kerchiefed
women in wooden shoes still drove community cattle to
common pasture; and, in the country round about, there
were Scotch, Welsh and Swiss settlements. What doubtless
helped to make vivid the significance of such folk was the
fact that Turner's father, the editor of a local paper, was a
politician of sorts, who "sheparded all these new people,"
lectured them in his editorials on farming and politics, and
was wonderfully trusted and followed by them. Here it
was then, before his very eyes, the past and present curiously joined together; the frontier in many stages—virgin
forest, Indian villages, lawless raftsmen, fur trade, the
rough frontier town a simmering pot skillfully stirred by
the descendant of Connecticut Yankees who, in every
generation since the seventeenth century, had got on the
"wrong side of the hedge." Here it was to be observed by
one who had eyes to see, the very process which had been
making America, such as it was, so different from Europe—
and, for that matter, why shouldn't it be?

This youthful experience Turner didn't put aside in some
unused garret of the mind when, at the university, he came
to study history. The past seemed to him a dead thing except as he could see it still living in the present. Tenuous

and vanishing vestiges of ancient custom interested him but little, so that when his teacher, William F. Allen, suggested that he look into the faint remaining evidences of common lands in the region round about Prairie du Chien, he soon found that he "couldn't get very far with that." He didn't get anywhere with it in fact but presently turned up, in his rakish independent way, with an essay on "The Fur Trade in Wisconsin."[5] This fresh topic, redolent of Indians and balsam trees, he took with him to Johns Hopkins, afterwards presenting it there, with revision and enlargement, as a doctor's thesis. In due time it was published under a new title in the Johns Hopkins Studies,[6] where it may still be seen curiously hobnobbing with sedater monographs on local government and comparative institutions. In this essay one may find, dimly suggested, the ideas, or some of them, which shortly after were presented in the now famous paper, "The Significance of the Frontier in American History."[7]

The significance of the frontier in American history was just this, that America was itself the frontier, the march lands of western civilization, the meeting place of old and new, the place in the world where one could still observe the civilized man adjusting his habits to the rude conditions of life in a primitive environment. From the civilized man the frontier "strips off the garments of civilization

---

[5] *Proceedings of the State Historical Society of Wisconsin*, 1889.

[6] "The Character and Influence of the Indian Trade in Wisconsin": *Johns Hopkins University Studies*, 1891.

[7] The essential ideas of this paper were first presented in an article ("The Problems of American History") written for the student periodical, *The Aegis*, November 4, 1892. In its present form it was read before the American Historical Association at its meeting in Chicago, July 12, 1893. First printed in *Proceedings of the State Historical Society of Wisconsin*, December 14, 1893, and again in *Report of the American Historical Association*, 1893. Similar ideas were set forth by Woodrow Wilson in his review (*Forum*, December, 1893) of Goldwin Smith's *History of the United States*. But Turner had, in his house at Madison, read his paper to Wilson before the latter wrote his review.

and arrays him in the hunting shirt and the moccasin." It
drags him out of his coach-and-four and throws him into a
birch-bark canoe, deprives him of his panelled halls and
gives him a log cabin. A rude shock this to the civilized
man, who finds that his traditional habits and ideas serve
him but inadequately in the new world; and so, the environment proving at first too strong for the man, he
temporarily reverts to the primitive, to something half
savage. But little by little he masters his environment, by
ingenious devices fashions rude comforts, falls into a rough
routine of life, imposes crude laws and a ready-made justice, snatches at such amusements and amenities as are to
be had for the taking—in short, painfully builds up once
more a "civilization," a civilization all compact of memories and experience. The memories are old, but the experience is new. And the experience modifies the tradition, so
that in the end the "outcome is not the old Europe, not
simply the development of Germanic germs. . . . The fact
is that here is a new product that is America."[8]

Here then was a fresh field for the historian. Not that
American history had more importance than European,
but certainly it had not less importance. The point was that
it had a *peculiar* importance, and this peculiar importance
was that it presented an unrivalled opportunity for studying the general in the particular. "Loria, the Italian econo-
mist, has urged the study of colonial life as an aid to understanding the stages of European development. . . .
'America,' he says, 'has the key to the historical enigma
which Europe has sought for in vain, and the land which
has no history reveals luminously the course of universal
history.' There is much truth in this. The United States
lies like a huge page in the history of society. Line by line

[8] "The Significance of the Frontier": *The Frontier in American History*, p. 4.

as we read this continental page from west to east we find the record of social evolution." [9] Complex it was, this social evolution, because of the vast extent of the country. "All peoples show development. . . . In the case of most nations, however, the development has occurred in a limited area. . . . But in the case of the United States we have a different phenomenon. Limiting ourselves to the Atlantic coast we have the familiar phenomenon of the evolution of institutions in a limited area, such as the rise of representative government; the differentiation of simple colonial governments into complex organs, progress from primitive conditions of society, without division of labor, up to manufacturing civilization. But we have in addition to this a recurrence of the process of evolution in each western area reached in the process of expansion. Thus American development has exhibited not merely advance along a single line, but a return to primitive conditions on a continually advancing frontier line, and a new development for that area. American social development has been continually beginning over again on the frontier. This perennial rebirth, this fluidity of American life, this expansion westward with its new opportunities, its continuous touch with the simplicity of primitive society, furnish the forces dominating American character." [10]

All this might mean but little to those for whom "history is past politics." But those who wished to look behind institutions might find much in it. A quite unrivalled opportunity they would find, in this perennial rebirth on different frontiers, for studying the evolution of a society from simple to complex forms under conditions generally similar but differing in point of detail; an unparalleled

[9] *The Frontier in American History*, p. 11.
[10] *The Frontier in American History*, pp. 2, 3.

opportunity to note the interaction of all the "influences" (geographic, economic, social, and whatever others might be found) that shape the thought and action of men. Regarding history in this novel way, the historian would of necessity be less concerned with the "what" than with the "how," less with the result than with the process; less concerned with chronicle, the narrating of events from decade to decade, than with the description and comparison of regional and sectional societies, and with the complex of influences creating, in each of these regional societies, certain economic interests and political activities. Chronology, being treated with scant respect, would inevitably lose something of its commanding position and high repute, since the historian would be continually throwing past and present, as warp and woof, back and forth to make the woven fabric of a living civilization. "Continuity" there would be, certainly so, but the continuity would be found, not in the sequence of little event following on little event, but in the persistence of certain general conditions, in the recurrence of certain psychological reactions determined by the conditions, above all perhaps in the emergence (the evolution if you like), out of the interaction and conflict of regional societies ranging from the relatively primitive to the relatively complex, of a distinctively American society with its peculiar traditions and ideals.

Regarded thus, not as a sequence of events, but as a social evolution, American history up to the present could be regarded as a single phrase of universal history; could be regarded as the history of the frontier, which is not so much a region as a process. "The West, at bottom, is a state society rather than an area. It is the term applied to the region whose social conditions result from the application of older institutions and ideas to the transforming influence of free land."[11] Up to the present, or the very recent past, it is above all the abundance of free land, underlying and equalizing the diverse influences of regional geography, that has made America a frontier society, that has made possible the "perennial rebirth," that has kept society always in touch with the primitive. These are the conditions that explain the essential traits of American character— "that coarseness and strength combined with acuteness and inquisitiveness; that practical, inventive turn of mind, quick to find expedients; that masterful grasp of material things, lacking in the artistic but powerful to effect great ends; that restless, nervous energy; that dominant individualism, working for good and for evil, and withal that buoyancy and exuberance which come with freedom."[12] And these also are the conditions that explain American institutions, American "democracy"—the questionless faith in "liberty" and "equality" and the right and the capacity of the people to govern themselves; not by the "glorious constitution" are these ideals to be explained, but by the conditions peculiar to our situation—our situation on the frontier of western civilization. "The larger part of what has been distinctive and vaulable in America's contribution to the history of the human spirit has been due to this nation's peculiar experience in extending its type of frontier into new regions; and in creating peaceful societies with new ideals in the successive vast and differing geographic provinces which together make up the United States."[13]

This first phase, the phase of the frontier, is obviously passing. For a quarter of a century now there has been, relatively speaking, no free land. Westward expansion has

[11] *The Frontier in American History*, p. 205.
[12] *The Frontier in American History*, p. 37.
[13] Preface to *The Frontier in American History*.

ceased, and with it the "perennial rebirth," the continual return to primitive conditions. The country becomes increasingly urban, increasingly industrial. Classes tend to become fixed. Parties show signs of dividing on economic and social issues. Accumulated capital, seeking investment throughout the world, proves more powerful than senatorial oratory, and the old isolation gives way to imperial entanglements and conflicts. The United States is ceasing to be a country on the frontier of European civilization in which the cardinal fact is the steady expansion of population into the unoccupied areas of free land. It too is now becoming "old," "eastern," a settled community, a federation of sections, varying greatly in point of geographic and economic conditions, but approaching uniformity in point of social evolution. [14]

The first phase is passing; and Turner, always occupied primarily with the present, and with the past as illuminating the present, has in recent years turned his attention to the fascinating problem of the United States as a federation of sections. In two of his most brilliant essays [15] he has developed this idea. Underlying the formal federation of states, he points out, is the real federation of great geographic and economic areas, each one comparable, in extent and variety, to the most important of the European nations; so that the problems of American political history are in a measure comparable to those of European history. There are striking differences surely. We have not the racial and religious antagonisms of Europe. We lie less uneasy

[14] In his presidential address before the Historical Association in 1910, Turner took occasion to emphasize the passing of the first phase of American history, and to suggest ways in which present problems might be illuminated by a study of the past. "Social Forces in 1911"; *American Historical Review*, January, 1911. Reprinted in *The Frontier in American History*, p. 311.

[15] "Sections and Nation"; *Yale Review*, Oct. 1922. "The Significance of the Section in American History"; *Wisconsin Magazine of History*, March, 1925.

under the heavy weight of tradition. Nevertheless the great sections of our country have their deep-seated differences of interest, they have their differences of temperament and ideals. Their antagonisms are such that, if fortune had separated them into independent states, they would, like the European nations, be engaged in a new-world struggle for the balance of power. Happily we have a federal government which holds us together in a league of sections; so that while the European nations employ diplomatic negotiations, conference, and war for the settlement of their conflicts, the American sections manage to get on amicably by peaceful bargains and compromises legally negotiated through the national party system and the Federal government.

And what of the future, since the first phase is passing? Since the peculiar conditions under which American institutions have hitherto developed no longer exist, what is to be the fate of American "democracy," of American "ideals," such as we have known them? "Can these ideals of democracy and invididualism be applied and reconciled to the twentieth century type of civilization?"[16] It is Turner himself who asks this question, and it is perhaps with a certain note of apprehension that he asks it. In recent addresses he has asked it repeatedly, and, one feels, with a somewhat diminished zest and optimism. The answer would seem to be obvious. If American institutions and ideals, such as we have known them, have been the result of primitive frontier conditions, it would seem that they must, with the passing of those conditions, be transformed into something different—perhaps into something altogether different. At least this is so unless there is more efficacy in the "inheritance" of institutions

[16] *The Frontier in American History*, p. 203.

and ideals than Turner has led us to suppose. Turner the
scholar sees that this is so; but Turner the frontier democrat
from Portage, Wisconsin, addressing students at commencement time, and wishing (rightly enough!) to say something appropriately hopeful for the occasion, regrets it—
I was about to say, for the moment seems almost to forget
it. But no, that cannot be, since it is precisely Turner's
contribution to the study of American history that makes
it impossible to forget it. For his contribution, from the
point of view of a general interpretation, is just this, that
American institutions and ideals are the result of a primitive, and therefore surely a passing stage of social evolution.

IV

Turner's contribution to history and the social sciences
has been set forth in monographic studies, essays, occasional addresses, and the volume which he contributed to
the American Nation Series. [17] In addition, so he assures
me, he is now "finishing up a book on the period 1830-
1850," a book in which he endeavors "to sketch the
characteristics and development of the leading sections
during those decades, and briefly to indicate . . . the inter-
sectional aspect of political history." Even with this book
completed, Turner's collected works will not fill much
space, would doubtless leave much of a five-foot shelf open
to the collection of dust; and many devoted, if not always
discriminating, disciples and publishers have grown gray
expectantly waiting for the "great work" which does not
appear. Seven volumes at the very least they seem to demand, stately leather-backed tomes for preference, something they may point to with pride as an achievement, a

[17] For a full list of Turner's publications, see *American Masters of Social Science*.
Howard W. Odum. Henry Holt and Company, p. 310.

life work, one of those "comprehensive" and "definitive" histories no doubt which posterity may be expected to label "standard," and straightway shelve with Gibbon and Grote behind glass doors, rarely opened.

Such expectations, I think, will not be fulfilled, for many reasons no doubt, but at least for one very good one, which is that history, as Turner conceives it, is not well adapted to quantity production. The easiest kind of history to write is the kind that lends itself to narrative—history conceived as a succession of events in a time series. The factual substance is there, inexhaustible, lying conveniently under the hand, needing not to be invented or imagined, needing only to be carefully searched out and verified. The problem of the correlation of ideas scarcely presents itself, since, strictly speaking, none but rudimentary ideas are essential. Even the problem of arrangement lays no great strain on the intelligence, being already half solved by the accidents of time and space. With industry and patience, therefore, the manuscript runs to seven volumes (or even, unless cruel and unusual precautions are taken, to ten) by the simple process of narration, the process of telling concretely what happened in such abundance of circumstantial detail that, as Leslie Stephen says, "an event takes longer to describe than to occur."

In this sort of history, history conceived as a succession of events in a time series, Turner is but little interested. If in all his published work there are five pages of straight narrative I do not know where to find them. His writing is all essentially descriptive, explicative, expository. Heaven knows he doesn't lack "material." Always on the still hunt for "data," he has facts enough; quantities of facts and events, but all wrenched loose from their natural setting in time and place by his curious inquiring mind in order to be assembled again in support of some idea that has occurred to him, or for the illumination of some problem that he has found interesting. This is the chief reason why he goes his own way, heedless of voices in the wilderness calling for the "comprehensive history." Left to his own devices, he gives us work suited to his objectives and his methods of approach—he gives us monographs and essays; and even when, on one happy occasion, he was caught by his friends and set the task of writing ten years of history for the American Nation Series, he produced a book that fits but oddly into the scheduled plan. In place of telling us what happened by narrating the succession of events, he endeavored to make intelligible what happened by describing the economic, social, and cultural conditions which, in each of the great geographic sections of the country, determined the political interests and conflicts of the time.

Well, one point is that in this kind of history many volumes are not required for presenting the results of wide researches and much reflection. The detailed and orderly narrative gives place to the static description of environment; and for such description a hundred details (details relating to climate, geography, psychology, economic technique, social custom), which would fill ten pages if narrated for their own sakes, are enclosed in a few compact generalizations which may be set forth in a brief paragraph or two. The point is that the generalized description, by virtue of condensing and symbolizing the bulky concrete, does not easily run to many volumes. Consider the extended researches concealed beneath the modest surface of those admirable opening chapters in Turner's *Rise of the New West*. To raise the completed structure of American history on such solid foundations throughout would be a herculean task indeed. Men there have been no doubt who might have done it—a Gibbon, a Mommsen, a Sorel. But Turner at least has not the encyclopaedic or the systematizing mind for it.

The "comprehensive history" presents another difficulty to those who, like Turner, are primarily interested in the complex of influences that determine political events. This is a difficulty in what is called synthesis. It is true that historians, the "Newer Historians" at all events (and who would wish to be excluded from that ancient and honorable company!), have long since agreed that the business of the historian is to make a "synthesis of social forces," and at the same time to "trace the evolution of society" (or whatever you wish to call it). We even boast of it in a casual, off-hand way, as of a thing often done. But I suspect that all we have as yet done is to invent various methods of avoiding the difficulty. One method of avoiding the difficulty is triumphantly illustrated in the *Cambridge Modern History*. The difficulty is more resolutely faced, but not by any means overcome, in Lavisse's admirable *Histoire de France*. Lamprecht may really have solved the problem for all I know; but if so, then he has solved it, so far as I am concerned, at the heavy expense of rendering the experience of mankind thoroughly incomprehensible. The difficulty (well enough illustrated in Turner's *Rise of the New West*) is fundamental, and, I think, radically unsolvable. The point is that for the "synthesis of social forces" one must employ the method of generalized description; while for the "evolution of society" (in the chronological sense that is) one must narrate the forward march of events. Well, the generalization spreads out in space, but how to get the wretched thing to move forward in time! The generalization, being timeless, will not move forward; and so the harrassed historian, compelled to get on with the story, must return in some fashion to the individual, the concrete event, the "thin red line of heroes." Employing these two methods, the humane historian will do his best to prevent them from beating each other to death within the covers of his book. But the strain is great. And while any courageous historian may endure it for one volume, or even for two, few there are who can survive ten.

If these pages are expected to label Turner—to say whether he is historian, or sociologist, or historical sociologist, or sociological historian—there must inevitably be disappointment. For labels do not rightly describe any one. Certainly no label rightly describes Turner. He is, strictly speaking, neither historian nor sociologist. He is at all events not the academician, systematically preparing standard works according to scheduled plan. In his writings, as in his teaching, he is not quite the "professor," not quite what you look for in the "historian." He is just himself, a fresh and original mind that goes its own way, careless of the proprieties, inquiring into everybody's business, hobnobbing with cartographers, economists, sociologists, geographers, census compilers, editors of *Who's Who*. In his writings, as in his teaching, he is forever the inquirer, the questioner, the explorer; a kind of intellectual Gentleman Adventurer, fascinated by "this new world called America," fascinated above all by the American people and by their habits of thought and action, avid for "data" about them, wishing for his own peace of mind to understand them, to know what their "significance" may be. With this end in view he ranges far and wide through their history, past and present, in the ceaseless search for facts and for explanatory ideas; ranges far and wide on his own hook, poking into every sort of unlikely place, getting lost it may be, yet al-

ways finding himself again, and always buoyantly turning up
at last with a rich freightage of information and notions; a
rich freightage which he lays before us as best he can, in
collections of documents, heavily weighted monographs,
illuminating charts and graphs, dreadfully informing
statistical tables, or brilliant essays in which happy ideas
and analogies elbow one another for standing room. He
lays it before us, this rich freightage of information and
ideas, and asks us to take it, not as an exhaustive and
definitive contribution, but only as an accumulated capital
for new and larger ventures. And how many men, rummaging in this rich store, have carried away something useful
for their purpose? How many graduate students, colleagues,
scholars at home and abroad? And not historians only, but
geographers, sociologists, economists, lawyers and political scientists.

Yes, quite beside the mark to expect, or ever to have
expected, the ordered history in ten volumes from this
lively intelligence! We must take Turner as he is, must be
content with the qualities he has, with what he has given
us, and will give. Content? But content is not the word.
We must be grateful for these qualities, so rare they are,
and for this work which has proved so fruitful. Turner's
fame must rest, not upon the massed bulk of books published, but upon the virtue and vitality of the ideas he has
freely scattered about. For my part I do not ask of any
historian more than this, that he should have exerted in
his generation a notable influence upon many scholars in
many branches of humanistic study. This is enough; and
this, I think, must be accorded to Turner.

Not everyone, I find, can quite understand the influence
of Turner upon this generation of scholars. It is indeed not
easily understood by those who know only his published

work, by those who have not well known the man. But his friends and colleagues understand it. And his pupils understand it better than any others, because his pupils know, better than any others, that the man is more than his work. And so I end as I began—with "that man Turner," who laid and still lays upon us all the spell of his personality. Some indelible impression of him, some virtue communicated to us from the alert intelligence and the fine integrity of a high-minded gentleman, still shapes our lives and gives added substance to our work. I have said this before, and now I say it again. And yet, when all is said, something still escapes the crude phrase—some rare and moving quality in the man, some lifted light of the human spirit which no words of mine can adequately convey.

1927

Everyman His Own Historian[1]

I

ONCE upon a time, long long ago, I learned how to reduce a fraction to its lowest terms. Whether I could still perform that operation is uncertain; but the discipline involved in early training had its uses, since it taught me that in order to understand the essential nature of anything it is well to strip it of all superficial and irrelevant accretions—in short, to reduce it to its lowest terms. That operation I now venture, with some apprehension and all due apologies, to perform on the subject of history.

I ought first of all to explain that when I use the term history I mean knowledge of history. No doubt throughout all past time there actually occurred a series of events which, whether we know what it was or not, constitutes history in some utlimate sense. Nevertheless, much the greater part of these events we can know nothing about, not even that they occurred; many of them we can know only imperfectly; and even the few events that we think we know for sure we can never be absolutely certain of, since we can never revive them, never observe or test them directly. The event itself once occurred, but as an actual event it has disappeared; so that in dealing with it the only objective reality we can observe or test is some material trace which the event has left—usually a written document.

[1] Presidential Address delivered before the American Historical Association at Minneapolis, December 29, 1931.

With these traces of vanished events, these documents, we must be content since they are all we have; from them we infer what the event was, we affirm that it is a fact that the event was so and so. We do not say "Lincoln is assassinated"; we say "it is a fact that Lincoln was assassinated." The event *was*, but is no longer; it is only the affirmed fact about the event that *is*, that persists, and will persist until we discover that our affirmation is wrong or inadequate. Let us then admit that there are two histories: the actual series of events that once occurred; and the ideal series that we affirm and hold in memory. The first is absolute and unchanged—it was what it was whatever we do or say about it; the second is relative, always changing in response to the increase or refinement of knowledge. The two series correspond more or less, it is our aim to make the correspondence as exact as possible; but the actual series of events exists for us only in terms of the ideal series which we affirm and hold in memory. This is why I am forced to identify history with knowledge of history. For all practical purposes history is, for us and for the time being, what we know it to be.

It is history in this sense that I wish to reduce to its lowest terms. In order to do that I need a very simple definition. I once read that "History is the knowledge of events that have occurred in the past." That is a simple definition, but not simple enough. It contains three words that require examination. The first is knowledge. Knowledge is a formidable word. I always think of knowledge as something that is stored up in the *Encyclopaedia Britannica* or the *Summa Theologica;* something difficult to acquire, something at all events that I have not. Resenting a definition that denies me the title of historian, I therefore ask what is most essential to knowledge. Well, memory, I should think (and I mean memory in the broad sense, the memory of events inferred as well as the memory of events observed); other things are necessary too, but memory is fundamental: without memory no knowledge. So our definition becomes, "History is the memory of events that have occurred in the past." But events—the word carries an implication of something grand, like the taking of the Bastille or the Spanish-American War. An occurrence need not be spectacular to be an event. If I drive a motor car down the crooked streets of Ithaca, that is an event— something done; if the traffic cop bawls me out, that is an event—something said; if I have evil thoughts of him for so doing, that is an event—something thought. In truth anything done, said, or thought is an event, important or not as may turn out. But since we do not ordinarily speak without thinking, at least in some rudimentary way, and since the psychologists tell us that we cannot think without speaking, or at least not without having anticipatory vibrations in the larynx, we may well combine thought events and speech events under one term; and so our definition becomes, "History is the memory of things said and done in the past." But the past—the word is both misleading and unnecessary: misleading, because the past, used in connection with history, seems to imply the distant past, as if history ceased before we were born; unnecessary, because after all everything said or done is already in the past as soon as it is said or done. Therefore I will omit that word, and our definition becomes, "History is the memory of things said and done." This is a definition that reduces history to its lowest terms, and yet includes everything that is essential to understanding what it really is.

If the essence of history is the memory of things said and done, then it is obvious that every normal person, Mr.

Everyman, knows some history. Of course we do what we can to conceal this invidious truth. Assuming a professional manner, we say that so and so knows no history, when we mean no more than that he failed to pass the examinations set for a higher degree; and simple-minded persons, undergraduates and others, taken in by academic classifications of knowledge, think they know no history because they have never taken a course in history in college, or have never read Gibbon's *Decline and Fall of the Roman Empire*. No doubt the academic convention has its uses, but it is one of the superficial accretions that must be stripped off if we would understand history reduced to its lowest terms. Mr. Everyman, as well as you and I, remembers things said and done, and must do so at every waking moment. Suppose Mr. Everyman to have awakened this morning unable to remember anything said or done. He would be a lost soul indeed. This has happened, this sudden loss of all historical knowledge. But normally it does not happen. Normally the memory of Mr. Everyman, when he awakens in the morning, reaches out into the country of the past and of distant places and instantaneously recreates his little world of endeavor, pulls together as it were things said and done in his yesterdays, and coordinates them with his present perceptions and with things to be said and done in his to-morrows. Without this historical knowledge, this memory of things said and done, his to-day would be aimless and his to-morrow without significance.

Since we are concerned with history in its lowest terms, we will suppose that Mr. Everyman is not a professor of history, but just an ordinary citizen without excess knowledge. Not having a lecture to prepare, his memory of things said and done, when he awakened this morning, presumably did not drag into consciousness any events connected

with the Liman von Sanders mission or the Pseudo-Isidor-
ian Decretals; it presumably dragged into consciousness an
image of things said and done yesterday in the office, the
highly significant fact that General Motors had dropped
three points, a conference arranged for ten o'clock in the
morning, a promise to play nine holes at four-thirty in the
afternoon, and other historical events of similar import.
Mr. Everyman knows more history than this, but at the
moment of awakening this is sufficient: memory of things
said and done, history functioning, at seven-thirty in the
morning, in its very lowest terms, has effectively oriented
Mr. Everyman in his little world of endeavor.

Yet not quite effectively after all perhaps; for unaided
memory is notoriously fickle; and it may happen that Mr.
Everyman, as he drinks his coffee, is uneasily aware of
something said or done that he fails now to recall. A common enough occurrence, as we all know to our sorrow—
this remembering, not the historical event, but only that
there was an event which we ought to remember but cannot. This is Mr. Everyman's difficulty, a bit of history lies
dead and inert in the sources, unable to do any work for
Mr. Everyman because his memory refuses to bring it alive
in consciousness. What then does Mr. Everyman do? He
does what any historian would do: he does a bit of historical research in the sources. From his little Private
Record Office (I mean his vest pocket) he takes a book in
MS., volume XXXV it may be, and turns to page 23, and
there he reads: "December 29, pay Smith's coal bill, 20
tons, $1017.20." Instantaneously a series of historical
events comes to life in Mr. Everyman's mind. He has an
image of himself ordering twenty tons of coal from Smith
last summer, of Smith's wagons driving up to his house,
and of the precious coal sliding dustily through the cellar

window. Historical events, these are, not so important as
the forging of the Isidorian Decretals, but still important
to Mr. Everyman: historical events which he was not
present to observe, but which, by an artificial extension of
memory, he can form a clear picture of, because he has
done a little original research in the manuscripts preserved
in his Private Record Office.

The picture Mr. Everyman forms of Smith's wagons
delivering the coal at his house is a picture of things said
and done in the past. But it does not stand alone, it is not
a pure antiquarian image to be enjoyed for its own sake;
on the contrary, it is associated with a picture of things to
be said and done in the future; so that throughout the day
Mr. Everyman intermittently holds in mind, together with
a picture of Smith's coal wagons, a picture of himself going
at four o'clock in the afternoon to Smith's office in order to
pay his bill. At four o'clock Mr. Everyman is accordingly
at Smith's office. "I wish to pay that coal bill," he says.
Smith looks dubious and disappointed, takes down a
ledger (or a filing case), does a bit of original research in
his Private Record Office, and announces: "You don't owe
me any money, Mr. Everyman. You ordered the coal here
all right, but I didn't have the kind you wanted, and so
turned the order over to Brown. It was Brown delivered
your coal: he's the man you owe." Whereupon Mr. Everyman goes to Brown's office; and Brown takes down a
ledger, does a bit of original research in his Private Record
Office, which happily confirms the researches of Smith; and
Mr. Everyman pays his bill, and in the evening, after returning from the Country Club, makes a further search in another
collection of documents, where, sure enough, he finds a
bill from Brown, properly drawn, for twenty tons of stove
coal, $1017.20. The research is now completed. Since his

mind rests satisfied, Mr. Everyman has found the explanation of the series of events that concerned him.

Mr. Everyman would be astonished to learn that he is an historian, yet it is obvious, isn't it, that he has performed all the essential operations involved in historical research. Needing or wanting to do something (which happened to be, not to deliver a lecture or write a book, but to pay a bill; and this is what misleads him and us as to what he is really doing) the first step was to recall things said and done. Unaided memory proving inadequate, a further step was essential—the examination of certain documents in order to discover the necessary but as yet unknown facts. Unhappily the documents were found to give conflicting reports, so that a critical comparison of the texts had to be instituted in order to eliminate error. All this having been satisfactorily accomplished, Mr. Everyman is ready for the final operation—the formation in his mind, by an artificial extension of memory, of a picture, a definitive picture let us hope, of a selected series of historical events—of himself ordering coal from Smith, of Smith turning the order over to Brown, and of Brown delivering the coal at his house. In the light of this picture Mr. Everyman could, and did, pay his bill. If Mr. Everyman had undertaken these researches in order to write a book instead of to pay a bill, no one would think of denying that he was an historian.

II

I have tried to reduce history to its lowest terms, first by defining it as the memory of things said and done, second by showing concretely how the memory of things said and done is essential to the performance of the simplest acts of daily life. I wish now to note the more general implications of Mr. Everyman's activities. In the realm of affairs Mr. Everyman has been paying his coal bill; in the realm of consciousness he has been doing that fundamental thing which enables man alone to have, properly speaking, a history: he has been re-enforcing and enriching his immediate perceptions to the end that he may live in a world of semblance more spacious and satisfying than is to be found within the narrow confines of the fleeting present moment.

We are apt to think of the past as dead, the future as nonexistent, the present alone as real; and prematurely wise or disillusioned counselors have urged us to burn always with "a hard, gemlike flame" in order to give "the highest quality to the moments as they pass, and simply for those moments' sake." This no doubt is what the glow-worm does; but I think that man, who alone is properly aware that the present moment passes, can for that very reason make no good use of the present moment simply for its own sake. Strictly speaking, the present doesn't exist for us, or is at best no more than an infinitesimal point in time, gone before we can note it as present. Nevertheless, we must have a present; and so we create one by robbing the past, by holding on to the most recent events and pretending that they all belong to our immediate perceptions. If, for example, I raise my arm, the total event is a series of occurrences of which the first are past before the last have taken place; and yet you perceive it as a single movement executed in one present instant. This telescoping of successive events into a single instant philosophers call the "specious present." Doubtless they would assign rather narrow limits to the specious present; but I will willfully make a free use of it, and say that we can extend the specious present as much as we like. In common speech we do so: we speak of the "present hour," the "present year," the "present generation." Perhaps all living creatures have a specious present; but man has this superiority, as Pascal says, that he is aware of himself and the universe, can as it were hold himself at arm's length and with some measure of objectivity watch himself and his fellows functioning in the world during a brief span of allotted years. Of all the creatures, man alone has a specious present that may be deliberately and purposefully enlarged and diversified and enriched.

The extent to which the specious present may thus be enlarged and enriched will depend upon knowledge, the artificial extension of memory, the memory of things said and done in the past and distant places. But not upon knowledge alone; rather upon knowledge directed by purpose. The specious present is an unstable pattern of thought, incessantly changing in response to our immediate perceptions and the purposes that arise therefrom. At any given moment each one of us (professional historian no less than Mr. Everyman) weaves into this unstable pattern such actual or artificial memories as may be necessary to orient us in our little world of endeavor. But to be oriented in our little world of endeavor we must be prepared for what is coming to us (the payment of a coal bill, the delivery of a presidential address, the establishment of a League of Nations, or whatever); and to be prepared for what is coming to us it is necessary, not only to recall certain past events, but to anticipate (note I do not say predict) the future. Thus from the specious present, which always includes more or less of the past, the future refuses to be excluded; and the more of the past we drag into the specious present, the more an hypothetical, patterned future is likely to crowd into it also. Which comes first, which is cause and which effect, whether our memories construct a pattern of past events at the behest of our desires and hopes, or whether our desires and hopes spring from a pattern of past events imposed upon us by experience and knowledge, I shall not attempt to say. What I suspect is that memory of past and anticipation of future events work together, go hand in hand as it were in a friendly way, without disputing over priority and leadership.

At all events they go together, so that in a very real sense it is impossible to divorce history from life: Mr. Everyman cannot do what he needs or desires to do without recalling past events; he cannot recall past events without in some subtle fashion relating them to what he needs or desires to do. This is the natural function of history, of history reduced to its lowest terms, of history conceived as the memory of things said and done: memory of things said and done (whether in our immediate yesterdays or in the long past of mankind), running hand in hand with the anticipation of things to be said and done, enables us, each to the extent of his knowledge and imagination, to be intelligent, to push back the narrow confines of the fleeting present moment so that what we are doing may be judged in the light of what we have done and what we hope to do. In this sense all *living* history, as Croce says, is contemporaneous: in so far as we think the past (and otherwise the past, however fully related in documents, is nothing to us) it becomes an integral and living part of our present world of semblance.

It must then be obvious that living history, the ideal series of events that we affirm and hold in memory, since it is so intimately associated with what we are doing and with what we hope to do, cannot be precisely the same for all at any given time, or the same for one generation as for another. History in this sense cannot be reduced to a verifiable set of statistics or formulated in terms of universally valid mathematical formulas. It is rather an imaginative creation, a personal possession which each one of us, Mr. Everyman, fashions out of his individual experience, adapts to his practical or emotional needs, and adorns as well as may be to suit his aesthetic tastes. In thus creating his own history, there are, nevertheless, limits which Mr. Everyman may not overstep without incurring penalties. The limits are set by his fellows. If Mr. Everyman lived quite alone in an unconditioned world he would be free to affirm and hold in memory any ideal series of events that struck his fancy, and thus create a world of semblance quite in accord with the heart's desire. Unfortunately, Mr. Everyman has to live in a world of Browns and Smiths; a sad experience, which has taught him the expediency of recalling certain events with much exactness. In all the immediately practical affairs of life Mr. Everyman is a good historian, as expert, in conducting the researches necessary for paying his coal bill, as need be. His expertness comes partly from long practice, but chiefly from the circumstance that his researches are prescribed and guided by very definite and practical objects which concern him intimately. The problem of what documents to consult, what facts to select, troubles Mr. Everyman not at all. Since he is not writing a book on "Some Aspects of the Coal Industry Objectively Considered," it does not occur to him to collect all the facts and let them speak for themselves. Wishing merely to pay his coal bill, he selects only such facts as may be relevant; and not wishing to pay it twice, he is sufficiently aware, without ever having read Bernheim's *Lehrbuch*, that the relevant facts must be clearly established by the testimony of independent witnesses not self-deceived. He does not know, or need to know, that his

personal interest in the performance is a disturbing bias
which will prevent him from learning the whole truth or
arriving at ultimate causes. Mr. Everyman does not wish
to learn the whole truth or to arrive at ultimate causes. He
wishes to pay his coal bill. That is to say, he wishes to
adjust himself to a practical situation, and on that low
pragmatic level he is a good historian precisely because he
is not disinterested: he will solve his problems, if he does
solve them, by virtue of his intelligence and not by virtue
of his indifference.

Nevertheless, Mr. Everyman does not live by bread
alone; and on all proper occasions his memory of things
said and done, easily enlarging his specious present beyond
the narrow circle of daily affairs, will, must inevitably, in
mere compensation for the intolerable dullness and vexation of the fleeting present moment, fashion for him a more
spacious world than that of the immediately practical. He
can readily recall the days of his youth, the places he has
lived in, the ventures he has made, the adventures he has
had—all the crowded events of a lifetime; and beyond and
around this central pattern of personally experienced
events, there will be embroidered a more dimly seen pattern of artificial memories, memories of things reputed to
have been said and done in past times which he has not
known, in distant places which he has not seen. This outer
pattern of remembered events that encloses and completes
the central pattern of his personal experience, Mr. Everyman has woven, he could not tell you how, out of the most
diverse threads of information, picked up in the most
casual way, from the most unrelated sources—from things
learned at home and in school, from knowledge gained in
business or profession, from newspapers glanced at, from
books (yes, even history books) read or heard of, from

remembered scraps of newsreels or educational films or *ex cathedra* utterances of presidents and kings, from fifteen-minute discourses on the history of civilization broadcast by the courtesy (it may be) of Pepsodent, the Bulova Watch Company, or the Shepard Stores in Boston. Daily and hourly, from a thousand unnoted sources, there is lodged in Mr. Everyman's mind a mass of unrelated and related information and misinformation, of impressions and images, out of which he somehow manages, undeliberately for the most part, to fashion a history, a patterned picture of remembered things said and done in past times and distant places. It is not possible, it is not essential, that this picture should be complete or completely true: it is essential that it should be useful to Mr. Everyman; and that it may be useful to him he will hold in memory, of all the things he might hold in memory, those things only which can be related with some reasonable degree of relevance and harmony to his idea of himself and of what he is doing in the world and what he hopes to do.

In constructing this more remote and far-flung pattern of remembered things, Mr. Everyman works with something of the freedom of a creative artist; the history which he imaginatively recreates as an artificial extension of his personal experience will inevitably be an engaging blend of fact and fancy, a mythical adaptation of that which actually happened. In part it will be true, in part false; as a whole perhaps neither true nor false, but only the most convenient form of error. Not that Mr. Everyman wishes or intends to deceive himself or others. Mr. Everyman has a wholesome respect for cold, hard facts, never suspecting how malleable they are, how easy it is to coax and cajole them; but he necessarily takes the facts as they come to him, and is enamored of those that seem best suited to his interests or promise most in the way of emotional satisfaction. The exact truth of remembered events he has in any case no time, and no need, to curiously question or meticulously verify. No doubt he can, if he be an American, call up an image of the signing of the Declaration of Independence in 1776 as readily as he can call up an image of Smith's coal wagons creaking up the hill last summer. He suspects the one image no more than the other; but the signing of the Declaration, touching not his practical interests, calls for no careful historical research on his part. He may perhaps, without knowing why, affirm and hold in memory that the Declaration was signed by the members of the Continental Congress on the fourth of July. It is a vivid and sufficient image which Mr. Everyman may hold to the end of his days without incurring penalties. Neither Brown nor Smith has any interest in setting him right; nor will any court ever send him a summons for failing to recall that the Declaration, "being engrossed and compared at the table, was signed by the members" on the second of August. As an actual event, the signing of the Declaration was what it was; as a remembered event it will be, for Mr. Everyman, what Mr. Everyman contrives to make it: will have for him significance and magic, much or little or none at all, as it fits well or ill into his little world of interests and aspirations and emotional comforts.

III

What then of us, historians by profession? What have we to do with Mr. Everyman, or he with us? More, I venture to believe, than we are apt to think. For each of us is Mr. Everyman too. Each of us is subject to the limitations of time and place; and for each of us, no less than for the Browns and Smiths of the world, the pattern of remembered things said and done will be woven, safeguard the process how we may, at the behest of circumstance and purpose.

True it is that although each of us is Mr. Everyman, each is something more than his own historian. Mr. Everyman, being but an informal historian, is under no bond to remember what is irrelevant to his personal affairs. But we are historians by profession. Our profession, less intimately bound up with the practical activities, is to be directly concerned with the ideal series of events that is only of casual or occasional import to others; it is our business in life to be ever preoccupied with that far-flung pattern of artificial memories that encloses and completes the central pattern of individual experience. We are Mr. Everybody's historian as well as our own, since our histories serve the double purpose, which written histories have always served, of keeping alive the recollection of memorable men and events. We are thus of that ancient and honorable company of wise men of the tribe, of bards and story-tellers and minstrels, of soothsayers and priests, to whom in successive ages has been entrusted the keeping of the useful myths. Let not the harmless, necessary word "myth" put us out of countenance. In the history of history a myth is a once valid but now discarded version of the human story, as our now valid versions will in due course be relegated to the category of discarded myths. With our predecessors, the bards and story-tellers and priests, we have therefore this in common: that it is our function, as it was theirs, not to create, but to preserve and perpetuate the social tradition; to harmonize, as well as ignorance and prejudice permit, the actual and the remembered series of events; to enlarge and enrich the specious present common to us all to the end that "society" (the tribe, the nation, or all mankind) may judge of what it is doing in the light of what it has done and what it hopes to do.

History as the artificial extension of the social memory (and I willingly concede that there are other appropriate ways of apprehending human experience) is an art of long standing, necessarily so since it springs instinctively from the impulse to enlarge the range of immediate experience; and however camouflaged by the disfiguring jargon of science, it is still in essence what it has always been. History in this sense is story, in aim always a true story; a story that employs all the devices of literary art (statement and generalization, narration and description, comparison and comment and analogy) to present the succession of events in the life of man, and from the succession of events thus presented to derive a satisfactory meaning. The history written by historians, like the history informally fashioned by Mr. Everyman, is thus a convenient blend of truth and fancy, of what we commonly distinguished as "fact" and "interpretation." In primitive times, when tradition is orally transmitted, bards and story-tellers frankly embroider or improvise the facts to heighten the dramatic import of the story. With the use of written records, history, gradually differentiated from fiction, is understood as the story of events that actually occurred; and with the increase and refinement of knowledge the historian recognizes that his first duty is to be sure of his facts, let their meaning be what it may. Nevertheless, in every age history is taken to be a story of actual events from which a significant meaning may be derived; and in every age the illusion is that the present version is valid because the related facts are true, whereas former versions are invalid because based upon inaccurate or inadequate facts.

Never was this conviction more impressively displayed than in our own time—that age of erudition in which we live, or from which we are perhaps just emerging. Finding the course of history littered with the *debris* of exploded philosophies, the historians of the last century, unwilling to be forever duped, turned away (as they fondly hoped) from "interpretation" to the rigorous examination of the factual event, just as it occurred. Perfecting the technique of investigation, they laboriously collected and edited the sources of information, and with incredible persistence and ingenuity ran illusive error to earth, letting the significance of the Middle Ages wait until it was certainly known "whether Charles the Fat was at Ingelheim or Lustnau on July 1, 887," shedding their "life-blood," in many a hard fought battle, "for the sublime truths of Sac and Soc." I have no quarrel with this so great concern with hoti's business. One of the first duties of man is not to be duped, to be aware of his world; and to derive the significance of human experience from events that never occurred is surely an enterprise of doubtful value. To establish the facts is always in order, and is indeed the first duty of the historian; but to suppose that the facts, once established in all their fullness, will "speak for themselves" is an illusion. It was perhaps peculiarly the illusion of those historians of the last century who found some special magic in the word "scientific." The scientific historian, it seems, was one who set forth the facts without injecting any extraneous meaning into them. He was the objective man whom Nietzsche described—"a mirror: accustomed to prostration before something that wants to be known, . . . he waits until something comes, and then expands himself sensitively, so that even the light footsteps and gliding past of spiritual

things may not be lost in his surface and film."[1] "It is not I
who speak, but history which speaks through me," was
Fustel's reproof to applauding students. "If a certain
philosophy emerges from this scientific history, it must be
permitted to emerge naturally, of its own accord, all but
independently of the will of the historian."[2] Thus the
scientific historian deliberately renounced philosophy only
to submit to it without being aware. His philosophy was
just this, that by not taking thought a cubit would be
added to his stature. With no other preconception than the
will to know, the historian would reflect in his surface and
film the "order of events throughout past times in all
places"; so that, in the fullness of time, when innumerable
patient expert scholars, by "exhausting the sources,"
should have reflected without refracting the truth of all
the facts, the definitive and impregnable meaning of human
experience would emerge of its own accord to enlighten and
emancipate mankind. Hoping to find something without
looking for it, expecting to obtain final answers to life's
riddle by resolutely refusing to ask questions—it was
surely the most romantic species of realism yet invented,
the oddest attempt ever made to get something for nothing!

That mood is passing. The fullness of time is not yet,
over-much learning proves a weariness to the flesh, and a
younger generation that knows not Von Ranke is eager to
believe that Fustel's counsel, if one of perfection, is equally
one of futility. Even the most disinterested historian has at
least one preconception, which is the fixed idea that he has
none. The facts of history are already set forth, implicitly,
in the sources; and the historian who could restate without
reshaping them would, by submerging and suffocating the

---

[1] *Beyond Good and Evil*, p. 140.
[2] Quoted in *English Historical Review*, V. 1.

mind in diffuse existence, accomplish the superfluous task of depriving human experience of all significance. Left to themselves, the facts do not speak; left to themselves they do not exist, not really, since for all practical purposes there is no fact until some one affirms it. The least the historian can do with any historical fact is to select and affirm it. To select and affirm even the simplest complex of facts is to give them a certain place in a certain pattern of ideas, and this alone is sufficient to give them a special meaning. However "hard" or "cold" they may be, historical facts are after all not material substances which, like bricks or scantlings, possess definite shape and clear, persistent outline. To set forth historical facts is not comparable to dumping a barrow of bricks. A brick retains its form and pressure wherever placed; but the form and substance of historical facts, having a negotiable existence only in literary discourse, vary with the words employed to convey them. Since history is not part of the external material world, but an imaginative reconstruction of vanished events, its form and substance are inseparable: in the realm of literary discourse substance, being an idea, *is* form; and form, conveying the idea, *is* substance. It is thus not the undiscriminated fact, but the perceiving mind of the historian that speaks: the special meaning which the facts are made to convey emerges from the substance-form which the historian employs to recreate imaginatively a series of events not present to perception.

In constructing this substance-form of vanished events, the historian, like Mr. Everyman, like the bards and storytellers of an earlier time, will be conditioned by the specious present in which alone he can be aware of his world. Being neither omniscient nor omnipresent, the historian is not the same person always and everywhere; and for him, as for Mr. Everyman, the form and significance of remembered events, like the extension and velocity of physical objects, will vary with the time and place of the observer. After fifty years we can clearly see that it was not history which spoke through Fustel, but Fustel who spoke through history. We see less clearly perhaps that the voice of Fustel was the voice, amplified and freed from static as one may say, of Mr. Everyman; what the admiring students applauded on that famous occasion was neither history nor Fustel, but a deftly colored pattern of selected events which Fustel fashioned, all the more skillfully for not being aware of doing so, in the service of Mr. Everyman's emotional needs—the emotional satisfaction, so essential to Frenchmen at that time, of perceiving that French institutions were not of German origin. And so it must always be. Played upon by all the diverse, unnoted influences of his own time, the historian will elicit history out of documents by the same principle, however more consciously and expertly applied, that Mr. Everyman employs to breed legends out of remembered episodes and oral tradition.

Berate him as we will for not reading our books, Mr. Everyman is stronger than we are, and sooner or later we must adapt our knowledge to his necessities. Otherwise he will leave us to our own devices, leave us it may be to cultivate a species of dry professional arrogance growing out of the thin soil of antiquarian research. Such research, valuable not in itself but for some ulterior purpose, will be of little import except in so far as it is transmuted into common knowledge. The history that lies inert in unread books does no work in the world. The history that does work in the world, the history that influences the course of history, is living history, that pattern of remembered events, whether true or false, that enlarges and enriches the collective specious present, the specious present of Mr. Everyman. This is why the history of history is a record of the "new history" that in every age rises to confound and supplant the old. It should be a relief to us to renounce omniscience, to recognize that every generation, our own included, will, must inevitably, understand the past and anticipate the future in the light of its own restricted experience, must inevitably play on the dead whatever tricks it finds necessary for its own peace of mind. The appropriate trick for any age is not a malicious invention designed to take anyone in, but an unconscious and necessary effort on the part of "society" to understand what it is doing in the light of what it has done and what it hopes to do. We, historians by profession, share in this necessary effort. But we do not impose our version of the human story on Mr. Everyman; in the end it is rather Mr. Everyman who imposes his version on us—compelling us, in an age of political revolution, to see that history is past politics, in an age of social stress and conflict to search for the economic interpretation. If we remain too long recalcitrant Mr. Everyman will ignore us, shelving our recondite works behind glass doors rarely opened. Our proper function is not to repeat the past but to make use of it, to correct and rationalize for common use Mr. Everyman's mythological adaptation of what actually happened. We are surely under bond to be as honest and as intelligent as human frailty permits; but the secret of our success in the long run is in conforming to the temper of Mr. Everyman, which we seem to guide only because we are so sure, eventually, to follow it.

Neither the value nor the dignity of history need suffer by regarding it as a foreshortened and incomplete representation of the reality that once was, an unstable pattern of remembered things redesigned and newly colored to suit

the convenience of those who make use of it. Nor need our
labors be the less highly prized because our task is limited,
our contributions of incidental and temporary significance.
History is an indispensable even though not the highest
form of intellectual endeavor, since it makes, as Santayana
says, a gift of "great interests . . . to the heart. A barbarian is no less subject to the past than is the civic man
who knows what the past is and means to be loyal to it;
but the barbarian, for want of a transpersonal memory,
crawls among superstitions which he cannot understand or
revoke and among people whom he may hate or love, but
whom he can never think of raising to a higher plane, to
the level of a purer happiness. The whole dignity of human
endeavor is thus bound up with historic issues, and as
conscience needs to be controlled by experience if it is
to become rational, so personal experience itself needs to
be enlarged ideally if the failures and success it reports are
to touch impersonal interests."[3]

I do not present this view of history as one that is
stable and must prevail. Whatever validity it may claim, it
is certain, on its own premises, to be supplanted; for its
premises, imposed upon us by the climate of opinion in
which we live and think, predispose us to regard all
things, and all principles of things, as no more than "in-
constant modes or fashions," as but the "concurrence, renewed from moment to moment, of forces parting sooner or
later on their way." It is the limitation of the genetic
approach to human experience that it must be content to
transform problems since it can never solve them. However
accurately we may determine the "facts" of history, the
facts themselves and our interpretations of them, and our
interpretation of our own interpretations, will be seen in a

[4] *The Life of Reason*, V. 68.

different perspective or a less vivid light as mankind moves into the unknown future. Regarded historically, as a process of becoming, man and his world can obviously be understood only tentatively, since it is by definition something still in the making, something as yet unfinished. Unfortunately for the "permanent contribution" and the universally valid philosophy, time passes; time, the enemy of man as the Greeks thought; to-morrow and to-morrow and to-morrow creeps in this petty pace, and all our yesterdays diminish and grow dim: so that, in the lengthening perspective of the centuries, even the most striking events (the Declaration of Independence, the French Revolution, the Great War itself; like the Diet of Worms before them, like the signing of the Magna Carta and the coronation of Charlemagne and the crossing of the Rubicon and the battle of Marathon) must inevitably, for posterity, fade away into pale replicas of the original picture, for each succeeding generation losing, as they recede into a more distant past, some significance that once was noted in them, some quality of enchantment that once was theirs.

1932

Juliette Drouet and Victor Hugo[1]

IN 1833, Julienne Gauvain, formerly the model and the mistress of Pradier but then living with a Polish millionaire, was playing minor parts at the Porte-Saint-Martin under the stage name of Juliette Drouet. When *Lucrece Borgia* was put on she took the part of Princess Negroni. It was in connection with this event that Victor Hugo first saw her; and in no long time Mlle. Drouet had renounced her millionaire and her career to become the mistress, the life-long friend, the most worshipful adorer, of the great poet. Hugo was already married, and his friends were amazed, as Mr. Davidson says in his excellent life of Hugo, to find the model husband and father, the poet whose verses proclaimed the sacredness of hearth and home, running like any common mortal after an actress. "It is very seldom," writes one of them, "that one can find Hugo at home now; he goes there only at meal time. Poor Madame Hugo!"

The circumstance of a man's leaving his wife to run after an actress presents nothing that is novel, and but little that is interesting. Yet Hugo's state of mind on this occasion, so far from commonplace was it, is perhaps worth noting. He did not adopt the cynical tone of a man of the world, nor can it be discovered that he ever experienced any

[1] *The Love Letters of Juliette Drouet to Victor Hugo.* Edited by Louis Gimbaud. Translated by Lady Theodora Davidson. New York: McBride, Nast & Co.

feeling of remorse. To one of his friends, who uttered some protest or other, he replied:

> No one understands me, not even you, Pavie. . . . I have never committed more faults than this year, and I have never been a better man—far better now than in my time of innocence which you regret. Yes, formerly I was innocent; now I am indulgent. That is a great gain, God knows. I have beside me a dear friend, (his wife, he means) an angel whom you venerate as much as I do, who pardons me and loves me still. To love and to forgive—that is not of Man, it is of God or of Woman.

To one who is familiar with Hugo, even this is not novel; but it must be allowed to be rather interesting. I do not recall that Rousseau, who was very good at this sort of intellectual prestidigitation, ever proved himself a better master of the art. And perhaps Hugo never revealed himself more perfectly, or ever better exposed the peculiar quality of the romantic mind, than in just this phrase: "*I have never committed more faults than this year, and I have never been a better man.*" Hugo was of those who value experience rather by its intensity than its quality. Experience, if only it be of a penetrating sort, adds to the sum of emotional expression in the world,—a quite sufficient justification. Now, to betray your wife and to be forgiven is such an experience—all the more so in case your purpose is to go on betraying her and to be still forgiven: an experience which stimulates the sensibilities and, by multiplying these poignant memories that touch the source of tears, proves the presence of the good heart. Remorse! There could be no question of remorse, still less of cynicism. Hugo could only be thankful for faults which were the outward expression of an inward grace; they but intensified in him, as it were, that *elan vital* which is the measure of virtue.

Poor Madame Hugo! Yes, but poor Mlle. Drouet also. Her connection with Hugo lasted fifty years—until the lady's death in 1883. After she left the excitement of the theater for the somewhat cloistered existence which Hugo provided for her, time hung heavy on her hands, and she complained of it. "Write to me," said Hugo. "Write me everything that comes into your head, everything that causes your heart to beat." And so she did. Day after day, for fifty years, she produced these notes, left in the room to be picked up by her lover,—"scribbles," as she called them, twenty thousand of them still preserved, from which M. Gimbaud has selected a few as worthy to be printed. As letters, it can hardly be said they were worth printing at all. Their value is in displaying the behavior of Hugo's really sublime egoism in a relation the most intimate in the world, in revealing the effect of it, day by day and year by year, upon the woman who was bound to him as with wainropes by an overmastering and singularly enduring attachment.

It is well known that few people found it possible to associate on terms of equality with Hugo. If he had possessed a sense of humor he might have defined his friends as those who were willing to take him at his own valuation. And Mlle. Drouet's taking him so sincerely and so unreservedly at his own valuation was doubtless one secret of her persistent hold upon him. But even Hugo must soon have grown weary of a woman who could flatter him in no more delicate way than by repeatedly calling him the greatest man in the world; and in fact there was, in his relation with Mlle. Drouet, or in their manner of regarding it, something which ministered to his vanity in a way quite out of the ordinary. Their relation, from the beginning, they transformed, in true romantic fashion, into something other than it was, into a religious rite if you please, a sacrifice or atonement that was to work a kind of redemption of the lady's unregenerate nature. Such, at least, was her own understanding of the matter. "I see you as you are," she writes, "that is to say, a God-made man to redeem and rescue me from the infamous life to which I had so long been enslaved." This is an idea to which we can imagine Hugo assenting without reluctance, and without a smile. The rôle was one for which he was well fitted; and it had this singular advantage, that it enabled him to say at any time, and with a clear conscience: "I have never committed more faults than this year, and I have never been a better man." Surely, the redemption of one poor woman provided a treasury of good works upon which one could safely draw for indulgence to persist in very human faults.

It would be interesting to follow in some detail the fortunes of this idealized conception of their affair, to disengage, as it were, from the commonplace events of their lives the process of redemption. In the early years, the prospect of achieving an object so intangible seemed slight enough. For Mlle. Drouet was no docile penitent. She was often in passionate revolt, protesting against Hugo's insane jealousy, complaining bitterly of his self-absorption, resenting his brutal reminders of her fallen days, mad with jealous rage at his betrayals. She threatens to leave him, often thinks on suicide, or darkly hints at dire misfortunes coming to pass when he is least prepared. But the impulse to action seems always spent in the frenzy of disclosing the reasons for it; and we can well imagine the exhausted lady, whenever her lover crosses her threshold again, gladly sinking into his reconciling embrace. Her state of mind during these early years she has herself not inaptly portrayed in a graphic sentence. Having distinguished, apropos of nothing in particular, her varied ways of loving her "great little man," she says: "That is why, my glorious Victor, at one and the same moment I can rage, weep, crawl or stand erect: I bow my head and venerate you!"

Rage, weep, crawl, or stand erect as she might, Mlle. Drouet always ended by bowing her head in veneration. That is the main point: the idea that Hugo was the God-made man to redeem and rescue her never lost its power; and curiously enough this ideal, preposterous in itself no doubt, was in a manner realized; a kind of spiritual regeneration did in fact come to pass, such is the strange power of ideals, even the most unpromising. The poor lady learned the meaning of Faust's "Entbehren sollst du, sollst entbehren!" And we may contrast with the sentence just quoted words which she set down one evening in 1853, during the exile on the island of Jersey, as an evidence of the transformation that had been effected:

I come to tell you that I love you without regret for the past or fear for the future. I come with a smile on my lips and a blessing in my bosom, with my hand upon my mutilated heart and my eyes full of pardon, with my purity restored and my soul redeemed by twenty years of fidelity and love, with my delusions swept away and my faith shining. . . . I constitute you the supreme arbiter of my fate. Do with me what you will in this life so long as you take me with you in the next. I sacrifice my feelings to the virtue of your wife and the innocence of your daughter, as a homage and as a safeguard, and I reserve my prayers and tears for poor fallen women like myself.

For restoring the purity of fallen women, there are more conventional ways, and perhaps better ones, than that of bestowing twenty years of fidelity and love upon another woman's husband. Nevertheless, in Mlle. Drouet's case, a life of devotion and service, winning at last the recognition of Hugo's family and the respect of his friends, did invest the declining days of the white-haired lady with a certain nobility at least, if not perhaps with that "majestic dignity" which Jules Claretie attributed to her at the time of her death.

1914

The Dilemma of Diderot[1]

I

MRENE DOUMIC, in a critical essay entitled "Who is the Author of the Works of Diderot?", has thrown out, as a kind of provocative aside, a question of curious interest in itself and of which the answer takes one rather farther than might at first be supposed. "Another question," he says, "has to do with a kind of mystery which surrounds the last years of Diderot. Whereas, for a dozen years he had published book after book: the *Pensees philosophiques*, the *Bijoux*, the *Lettre sur les aveugles*, essays on dramatic art; suddenly he ceased to publish, and, for more than twenty years, the only work which he gave to the public was the dull and tedious *Essai sur les regnes de Claude et Neron*. What could have been the cause of this sort of retirement?" Of no other great writer of the century is this true. And the question becomes almost an enigma if we remember that "the moment when he ceased to publish was precisely that which saw the completion of the *Encyclopedie*": it was the moment too when Diderot, thanks to Catherine II, became financially independent; the moment, therefore, to which he had looked forward all his life for seriously attempting the creative work which vexatious responsibilities and grinding toil had hitherto made impossible.

[1] *La litterature francaise*, V, p. 87.

The plausible, surface answers to this question are all alluded to by M. Doumic and easily disposed of as inadequate; and it seems to him that a satisfactory answer, at the present moment, is not to be had. Yet he proposes an "hypothesis, for what it is worth." The hypothesis is that Diderot, who possessed the qualities and the defects of the bourgeois, "had also the supreme ambition of the clerk who for forty years has worked faithfully at his desk, or of the man of affairs who has, during his whole life, been up at six o'clock in the morning: the desire, namely, to be one's own master, to be dependent on no one, to follow one's fancy, to enjoy life from day to day, and take the hours as they come." And in support of this hypothesis we are presented with the letter, often quoted, which Diderot wrote to Mlle. Volland, September 10, 1768. "I do nothing, absolutely nothing, not even this *salon*. It is true that at night when I go to bed my head is full of the finest projects for the morrow. But in the morning, upon rising, there is a disgust, a torpor, an aversion from pen, ink, and paper, which is an indication either of laziness or declining powers. It is much pleasanter, with legs crossed and hands folded, to remain two or three hours with Madame and Mademoiselle, bantering them about everything they say and everything they do. When at last they grow weary of me, I find it is too late to begin any work, so I dress and go out. Where? In faith, I know not: sometimes to the house of Naigeon, or Damilaville."[2]

For this hypothesis there is doubtless something to be said. The correspondence of Diderot in 1765, about the time of finishing the *Encyclopedie*, reveals the pleasure with which he looked forward to his vacation, to a life of solitude, to days free of care spent with his books and his

[2] *Oeuvres complètes*, XIX, p. 272.

friends. But the letter which M. Doumic quotes proves rather too much, if it proves anything; the inference from it being that Diderot ceased to publish because he ceased to write. Now, it cannot be maintained that Diderot had ceased to write. The letter just quoted must not be taken for more than it is worth,—the expression of a passing fit of depression and disillusionment. In the letters of this period Diderot does not often profess to be idle; more often his tale is of some work going on; and over against the letter in which he says that he does absolutely nothing, one might set many others in which he complains of working day and night. "I think I have never worked harder in my life," he writes to Mlle. Volland, July 4, 1769. "I retire at an early hour; arise at break of day; and as long as the day lasts I stick to my study. . . . My publishers wish to print two volumes at a time."[3]

It is quite true that much of what he wrote during these years was written for others,—for Grimm, or Galiani; that much of it took the form of rough notes scribbled on the fly leaves of the books he read,—notes not written for publication so much as to satisfy an insistent demand for self-expression. But it has generally been supposed that much of Diderot's most original and characteristic work was produced after 1765; and the elaborate edition of his works, prepared by Assézat and published in 1876, confirms this supposition. Yet it is precisely in connection with this supposition that the essay of M. Doumic raises an interesting question. It is well known that M. Dupuy, in a critical study of one of the minor works of Diderot, the *Paradoxe sur le comedien*, has shown that the "revision" of this work, which Assézat, along with every one else, attributed to Diderot himself, was in fact an astonishingly free recasting

[3] *Ibid.*, p. 309.

of Diderot's original sketch by Naigeon. And on the basis of this revelation, M. Doumic raises the larger question of whether the other posthumous works of Diderot were left by him in their present form, or whether they were not also "revised" by Naigeon; who, after all, it is the primary purpose of his essay to ask us, was the author of the works of Diderot? It is from the point of view of this larger query that M. Doumic looks at the fact that Diederot published almost nothing after 1765: was it perhaps because there was nothing to publish,—nothing but work for others, or rough sketches which were later elaborated by Naigeon, or another, after the manner of the *Paradoxe sur le comedien*.

That Naigeon revised rather freely many of the manuscripts which Diederot left with him is quite possible. He was the man to do that sort of thing, and Diderot gave him full authority to do it. Yet it is most likely that his activity in this respect was confined to the less important manuscripts, of which the *Paradoxe* is itself an example. That Diderot did not write the *Paradoxe* in the form in which it was published after his death, one can easily suppose; that he did not write *Rameau*, for example, or the *Physiologie*, or the *Entretien*, or the *Refutation*, one can less easily believe. If Diderot did not write these works, who else, one may well ask, could have written them? Certainly not Naigeon. These works, to mention no others, are in conception so original, or in substance so profound, so oddly fashioned in point of form, so unpremeditated in point of arrangement, that the completest criticism, it is safe to suppose, will never seriously deny that they are in fact the works of Denis Diderot.

And so the question remains, why did Diderot, who published many books when he was too busy, as he tells us, to do good work, publish none when he acquired the leisure to write, and did in fact write, some of the most profound and original works of the eighteenth century? It is quite right, in answering this question, to take M. Doumic's hypothesis for what it is worth. And it is worth a good deal. Diderot is surely the great writer of the century of whom it would be least safe to assume that publication would follow production. Expression, for Diderot, was a primary need, like breathing; a flow of talk satisfied this need best; lacking that, he wrote. Besides, some of his later works, such as the *Entretien*, were of such a nature that publication was not to be thought of. But these considerations scarcely explain why, having published almost everything that he wrote up to a certain date, he published, after that date, almost nothing, although he wrote more then than ever before; and this in spite of the fact that his publishers, as he tells us, "wish to print two books at a time." The explanation I think is partly to be found in what may be called the dilemma of Diderot; and the explanation is perhaps worth noting because the dilemma of Diderot brings into relief those social and intellectual conditions which gave to French thought in the latter part of the century a peculiar direction and a distinctive character.

II

Modern critics and biographers of Diderot have remarked the extraordinary versatility of the man. There was scarcely any field of knowledge wholly unfamiliar to him, scarcely any question interesting to the men of his day to which he had not given much thought, or about which he was unable to say something really worth while. This was also the opinion of his contemporaries. Voltaire thought him "perhaps the one man capable of writing the history of philosophy."[4] "In every branch of human knowledge," said Marmontel, "he is so much at home . . . that he seems always ready for what is said to him, and observations made on the spur of the moment strike one as the result of recent study and long meditation."[5] His published works tell the same story,—mathematics, natural science, philosophy, romance, poetry, the drama, literary and art criticism, political economy and political science, the psychological novel; and although he produced, with one possible exception, no masterpiece, nor scarcely anything systematically thought out in any of these fields, he threw the search light of his imaginative intelligence upon all of them. And Diderot's versatility was something more than familiarity with all fields of knowledge. It was the versatility which comes of the capacity to take in respect to every subject, for experimental purposes as it were, the most opposed points of view, to understand instinctively intellectual conceptions the most divergent, to experience with genuine sympathy the most antipathetic emotional states. Diderot was, as some one has said, the century itself: in him all the currents of that age, deep or shallow, crossed and went their separate ways.

And yet the mutiplicity of Diderot's interests is largely on the surface; the variety of subjects with which he was occupied has somewhat obscured the essential unity of purpose which guided his all-embracing intellectual curiosity. Although he professed a profound contempt for metaphysics and religion, it is not too much to say that the only things which interested him vitally,—and it is perhaps in this that he is most truly representative of the century,—were precisely metaphysics and religion. It was not

[4] *Oeuvres complètes*, XLIV, p. 190.
[5] *Mémoires*, I, p. 487.

after all metaphysics that he despised, but a particular type
of metaphysics,—the metaphysics that had been so largely
shaped by mediaeval Christian thought; nor religion that
he hated, but the Christian religion as embodied in the
Catholic Church; and his aversion from the prevailing type
of metaphysics and religion was tinged with contempt and
hatred just because he desired above all things to put in
their place a new metaphysics and a new religion, a metaphysics rationally defensible and a religion morally sound.

Of these two interests, the more fundamental was that
which centered in the theoretical and practical aspects of
conduct. The extraordinary enthusiasm of that age for
"virtue"—"ce fonds de rectitude et de bonté morale, qui
est la base de vertu," as Marmontel defined it[6]—is revealed
by the most cursory glance at its literature. A generous
action fired even those men like Voltaire about whom there
was something hard and metallic. The statement of
Fontenelle, that he had "relegated sentiment to the
eulogy," aroused in the cold and upright Grimm a feeling
very near aversion.[7] The little Abbé Galiani greatly dis-
pleased Diderot one day by "confessing that he had never
shed a tear in his life." Tears were thought to be the outward sign of an inward grace, and Diderot, whose tears
were never far from the surface, struck his contemporaries
precisely by those qualities which, by inclining them to
weep, were the sure evidence of his being a man of virtue:
much more than his penetrating intelligence, it was his
good heart that won their devotion. His friends, says
Madame d'Epinay, regard Diderot as more profound than
Voltaire, "but above all it is his character about which
they grow enthusiastic. Grimm says that he is the most

6 *Mémoires*, II, p. 195.
7 *Correspondance littéraire*, III, p. 345.

perfect moral man he knows."[8] And nothing could have pleased Diderot more than to feel that he deserved such a tribute. His devotion to virtue and morality was something more vital than the intellectual interest of a student of ethics; he wished not only to analyze virtue, but to practice it, and to induce others to practice it. He was always "preaching morality," as Sainte-Beuve says: always possessed of a profound faith in it as a reality, and as the most vital reality; always searching for an immovable basis for it in reason and nature; and although never able to find for it a quite satisfactory basis of that sort, still he preached it to the end of his life. "There is nothing in the world," he wrote about 1757, "to which virtue is not preferable."[9] Twenty years later he was of the same opinion. "I am convinced that even in a society as ill ordered as ours, where the vice which succeeds is often applauded, and the virtue which fails is almost always ridiculed, I am convinced, I say, that on the whole one can do nothing better for one's own happiness than to be a good man."[10]

It was this profound faith in the reality and value of true mortality that inspired the hatred which Diderot professed for false religions, of which Christianity, as embodied in the Catholic Church, was the chief; false, not primarily because they were based upon false premises, although that was true enough, but because they made bad men. "Wherever people believe in God, there is a cult; wherever there is a cult, the natural order of moral duties is reversed, and mortality becomes corrupted."[11] It should be possible to have a religion based "upon the primitive and evident notions which are found written upon the hearts of all

[8] *Mémoires*, I, p. 405.
[9] *Oeuvres complètes*, XIX, p. 449.
[10] *Op. cit.*, II, p. 435.
[11] *Oeuvres choisies*, V. p. 16.

men." Such a religion, he thought, would have no unbe-
lievers. Such a religion it was the business of philosophy to
establish; or rather, "philosophy," as Diderot understood it, *was* such a religion; a religion which would
approve itself, not primarily because it would have no un-
believers, but because it would make good men. The extraordinary lack of reserve exhibited by the writers of the
century, and especially by the greatest of them, the amazing frankness with which they laid their souls bare to the
public gaze has sometimes been noted as a curious phenomenon. In fact nothing could have been more in keeping:
"philosophy" was something infinitely more to them than
a body of correct inferences; it was a faith, to be justified,
if at all, only by the conduct and the motives, and particularly perhaps by the motives, of its devotees. Unbelief and
immortality were synonyms in the language of the Church,
and it was therefore essential that the man who published
his unbelief as the foundation of a new morality should
wear his heart on his sleeve for the world's inspection.
"Yes, I am an atheist; but look into my heart and examine
my conduct and you must admit that an atheist may be a
good man." Diderot has always the air of crying this
aloud. Rousseau's *Confessions* is only the most striking
example of the disposition, shared by most of the reformers
of the age, to disrobe in the market place in order to reveal
the shining beauties of the natural man. "It is not enough,"
said Diderot, referring to the theologians, "to know more
than they do: it is necessary to show them that we are better, and that philosophy makes more good men than
sufficient or efficacious grace."[12]

"It is not enough to know more than they do;" yet
that was necessary too: to know more than they do in

[12] *Oeuvres complètes*, XIX, p. 464.

order to undermine the intellectual foundation of their false system of morality; to know more theology than the theologians in order to refute their theology; to know more science in order to discredit their appeal to miracle; to know more history in order to disprove their claim to authority; to know more psychology in order to expose the viciousness of their moral regimen. This is the secret of Diderot's interest in science and philosophy. To discredit the old theology it was necessary to attack metaphysics; and although Diderot professed to be occupied only with scientific experiment, it is clear that in his philosophical and scientific works, from the *Pensées philosophiques* to the *Physiologie*, his primary interest is in questions of a metaphysical nature; scientific experiment was necessary only as a new means of approach. What interested him in the *Physiologie* was the ontological question: Is all mind, or is all matter? What interested him in the *Lettre sur les aveugles* was the bearing of a physiological experiment upon the question of the existence of a God. And Diderot inquired so intently into all the specific scientific activity of the day just because the new metaphysics, the new conception of the origin and nature of the universe, was necessarily to be based, as the old metaphysics had not been, upon positive knowledge derived from observation and experiment.

The solution of the metaphysical problem which commended itself most strongly to Diderot, which he set forth towards the close of his life in the *Entretien* and the *Physiologie*, was what may be termed vitalistic materialism. All is matter, said Diderot, because without matter nothing can be known or explained: "The soul is nothing without the body; I defy you to explain anything without the body."[13] To explain the soul in terms of matter he was quite

[13] *Op cit.*, IX, p. 377.

willing to think of matter, even inorganic matter, as sentient; and many suggestive things are said for the purpose of showing, after the manner of Hamlet, how marble dust might be transformed into thought. What matter might be in itself seemed to him a fruitless question. The world is as it behaves; so regarded, matter is the manifestation, infinitely varied, and continuously changing, of the energy that moves the universe: a vortex of moving forces,—to this the substance of the world reduced itself in the final analysis.

As to the origin of a world thus constituted, one may find different answers in the works of Diderot. The deistic explanation, which he first accepted, after the manner of the English deists, was soon renounced; it raised more difficulties than it disposed of; and he was left in the end with no more satisfactory solution than chance. But if the world originated in a mere fortuitous combination of forces, what of its purpose and end? It would be difficult to inject purpose into an accident. And yet the accident seemed rational in its form and operation: nature was intelligible, and Diderot seems often, in his reverent apostrophes, to conceive of it as therefore intelligent; in moments of enthusiasm he all but deifies nature, attributing to it something very near beneficent purpose. But most often, when the question is presented directly, he can find no sufficient evidence for believing that the continuous change of form, constant and uniform though it might be, was a change from "lower" to "higher," from worse to better; so far as reason went, it seemed quite as likely that the universe was returning to the dust heap from whence it came.

It would doubtless be a mistake to think of Diderot as having worked out a coherent philosophy, upon which he was ready to take his stand against all comers. If he sometimes ran his thought in the mould of logical categories, he never left it there to cool and harden. Diderot's mind was far too plastic, too continuously generative and creative, to formulate a rigidly consistent, a perfectly integrated explanation of things; far too curious and inquiring, having formulated such an explanation, to surrender to it past escape. In the very act of shaping a system essentially materialistic, we find him coquetting with notions which, if resolutely pursued, might have led him to the camp of Hume. "What do I perceive? Forms. And what besides? Forms. We walk among shadows, shadows to ourselves and others. If I look at a rainbow, I see it; but for one who looks from a different angle of vision, there is nothing."[14] Diderot has often the air of wishing to avoid the conclusions to which reason led him. But he had none of Rousseau's talent for ignoring difficulties; and the conclusions of the *Entretien* and the *Physiologie* are those which, had he thought it necessary to proclaim any, he would most probably have professed.

But then what was the bearing of such a philosophy upon the problem of morality and conduct? No question that it destroyed the intellectual basis of morality as taught by the Church; but it was one of the ironies of fate that the speculative thinking of Diderot, of which the principal purpose was to furnish a firm foundation for natural morality, ended by destroying the foundation of all morality as he understood it. This was the dilemma, that if the conclusions of Diderot the speculative philosopher were valid, the aspirations of Diderot the moral man, all' the vital purposes and sustaining hopes of his life, were but as the substance of a dream. For reason told him that man was after all but a speck of sentient dust, a chance

[14] *Oeuvres complètes*, IX, p. 428.

deposit on the surface of the world, the necessary product
of the same purposeless forces that build up crystal or dis-
solve granite. Aspiration, love and hope, sympathy, the
belief in virtue itself,—what were these but the refined
products of mechanical processes, spiritual perfumes, as it
were, arising from the alternate waste and repair of brain
tissue? Freedom was surely a chimera if the will could be
defined as "the last impulse of desire and aversion."[15]
And "if there is no such thing as liberty, there is no action
which merits either praise or blame: there is neither vice
nor virtue, nothing which can properly be rewarded or
punished. What is it then that distinguishes men? Good
action and bad action. The bad man is one whom it is
necessary to destroy rather than to punish: good action is
good fortune but no virtue."[16] Surely if philosophy, which
was to "make more good men than sufficient or efficacious
grace," could teach nothing more reassuring than that
vice is something for which the individual is not responsible, something to be avoided only in so far as it might be
found out, it could furnish little inspiration for the preaching of morality. In that case, the religion of philosophy,
Diderot was vaguely aware, must remain as vain a delusion
as the philosophy of religion.

The works of his later years reveal this conflict between
the two Diderots,—Diderot the speculative philosopher
unable to ignore reason, and Diderot the emotional preacher
of morality unable to renounce his conviction that good
action is a virtue. Turning, for example, from the *Refutation*, written in 1773, to the *Physiologie*, written in 1774, we
find there, as M. Caro says, "another Diderot revealed to
us."[17] But the most striking, the most artistic presenta-

[15] *Ibid.*, II, p. 175.
[16] *Op.cit.*, XIX, p. 436.
[17] *La fin du dix-huitième siècle*, I, p. 219.

tion of the dilemma of Diderot, and perhaps a conscious and deliberate presentation of it, is to be found in that little masterpiece, the *Neveu de Rameau*, written about 1762, probably in reply to Palissot's *Les philosophes*, but revised later and given the form in which we have it about 1772-1774.[18]

The real Jean Francois Rameau appears to have been an eccentric who amused his contemporaries by maintaining that the end of all effort was to "place something between the teeth," and so accomplish the laws of mastication. With this concise philosophy of life as a nucleus, Diderot has constructed a character compounded of pure intelligence, swelled and festering appetites, and an entire lack of feeling for any moral obligation. "He shows the good qualities that nature has bestowed upon him without ostentation, and the bad ones without the smallest shame," —so Diderot speaks of him. "I have," he is made to say of himself, "a mind as round as a ball, and a character as fresh as a water-willow":—a mind, that is, to which other men's experience has added nothing, a character shedding, as a water-willow sheds water, the effects of good and evil action. In no sense the product of society, unaffected by tradition or the pressure of conventional habit, Rameau is simply Diderot's materialism personified, a creature whose will is precisely nothing but "the last impulse of desire and aversion," a kind of Frankenstein's monster such as one might construct from the principles of Diderot's *Physiologie*, an example of the natural man, stripped of all "artificial" accretions, functioning in society as it existed, in Paris, about the year 1772.

With this creature, whose outward circumstances are those of a finished social parasite, Diderot the moral

---

[18] *Oeuvres complètes*, V. p. 361. There is a later edition by Monval, prepared for the *Bibliothèque Elzevirienne*. The essential parts of the dialogue have been translated by Lord Morley and printed as an appendix to his *Diderot*, II, p. 285.

philosopher enters into conversation; and the inimitable dialogue, touching upon many things, running hither and thither without apparent object other than to while away the hour, is in reality a searching inquiry into the basis of morality. Rameau is no straw man ingeniously constructed to fall over at the right moment. He is Diderot's other self, possessed of Diderot's powerful rationalizing imagination, and of his profoundly sensuous nature, looking out upon a corrupt society in the perfectly dry light of reason untouched by sentiment or any altruistic impulse.

Now reason tells Rameau that nature, that chance combination of purposeless forces, made him what he is, "sloth, madman, and good-for-naught"; and, not being responsible for what he is, he feels no obligation, and therefore no desire, to be better than he is, but only more happy. "Everything that lives, without exception, seeks its own well-being at the expense of any prey that is proper to its purposes." Therefore he, Rameau, will seek his well-being, his happiness, by the "vices that are natural" to him, and not (how could that be?) by the virtues that are natural to some one else. And this is his happiness, "to drink good wines, to cram one's self with dainty dishes, to rest on beds of down; except that, all is vanity and vexation of spirit." It is useless to appeal, as Diderot does, to the higher pleasures of self-sacrifice; these are not higher pleasures because, for Rameau, they are not pleasures at all; quite useless to appeal to the welfare of society, for happiness is individual, society is but an abstraction, and the conventional morality is only "what every one has in his mouth but what no one practices," a convenient mask which enables "men to keep the vices that are useful to them while avoiding their tone and appearance." A strange notion you philosophers have, says Rameau in effect, and all systems of morality are based upon the fallacy, that "the same kind of happiness was made for all the world." What is good for you, Diderot, may be bad for me, Rameau, and while you may suppress me I deny that you can know what makes me happy.

The dialogue ends, characteristically enough, without reaching any solution. "I see," says Diderot, speaking of the happiness to be derived from self-sacrifice and the performance of duty, "that you do not know what it is, and that you were not even made to understand it"; and Rameau replies, "so much the better." The basic thesis, which Hume thought axiomatic, that a thing is good because useful, not useful because good, was accepted without question by both Diderot and Rameau. But what is useful, and who is to judge? The dialogue turns on this. To be sure, the useful is what brings happiness; but the irresponsible creatures of a mechanical universe found that what made one happy made the other miserable; their standards of happiness were simply incommensurable, and the compact moral world dissolved under their feet in a conflict of wills.

It is worth noting again that Diderot was engaged upon the *Rameau* between the years 1763 and 1774, for these were probably the years when he first became fully aware of the dilemma of which it is so perfect an expression. These were the years, on the one hand, when his philosophy received its extreme and final formulation in the *Entretien* and the *Physiologie;* on the other hand, these were the years also when the question of practical morality was presented to him in the most intimate and disturbing form possible,—in connection with the education of his daughter. One consolation at least for the folly of a precipitate marriage Diderot found in the child who loved him, and the correspondence reveals to us how much he was concerned, as she came to maturity, to give her a good education, an education of which the chief part was to be, as he says in the *Rameau*, "a great deal of morality." It is true, he taught her some curious morality; but his principal aim seems to have been to demonstrate that "there is no virtue without two rewards: the pleasure of doing well, and that of obtaining the good will of others."[19] This was in 1769, and it was also in 1769 that the *Entretien* was written: so that one may picture Diderot the speculative philosopher, encased in his famous dressing gown, retiring, some morning of that year, to his study, and there engaged in explaining the soul in terms of matter and motion; but in the afternoon, transformed into the doting father, coming forth to teach his child a "great deal of morality," as he walks with her in the park. This very morning, perhaps, he committed to cold paper that desolating doctrine about the will,—"last impulse of desire and aversion." And what is the moral instruction which this philosophy inspires him to convey to his daughter in the afternoon? Something original surely, something profound, at the very least something unconventional? Not at all. Excellent bourgeois that he is, he tells her to be a good girl! So strangely remote sometimes, as Diderot found, is philosophy from life.

What use to preach "a great deal of morality" to a creature whose will is nothing but "the last impulse of desire and aversion?" This was the question which came to stare Diderot in the face about the year 1765; and about the year 1765 he ceased to publish. Diderot had no intention, indeed, of publishing works like the *Entretien*, as he told Mlle. Volland when it was written. Some great constructive work on morality, which should prove that "one can

19 *Oeuvres complètes*, XIX, p. 321.

do nothing better for one's own happiness than to be a good man," was, as he tells us, "the most important and the most interesting to be written"; and that was the work which he most wished to write,—"which I would recall with the most satisfaction in my last moments." But he never wrote such a work. "I have not even dared to take up the pen to write the first line. I say to myself: if I do not come out of the attempt victorious, I become the apologist of wickedness; I will have betrayed the cause of virtue, I will have encouraged men in the way of vice. No. I do not feel myself equal to this sublime work; I have uselessly consecrated my whole life to it."[20] Diderot never wrote such a work; but perhaps the "dull and tedious *Essai sur les regnes de Claude et Neron*" may be taken as a frantic, half-despairing effort, at the last moment, to thrust upon the world the fragmentary and ill-digested results of his thinking on the subject.

And why indeed should a man whose ambition was to contribute something towards the regeneration of a corrupt society publish philosophical works which taught nothing more reassuring than that "good action is good fortune but no virtue?" Or works on morality which had nothing more original to say than that virtue is good action? Under the circumstances, it would be as well perhaps to throw the manuscripts into the fire. Diderot did not, indeed, throw his manuscripts into the fire; but he gave them to Naigeon.

III

The dilemma of Diderot is chiefly interesting as a concrete example of the fundamental intellectual difficulty of the century,—fundamental at least for those who were primarily concerned for the social regeneration of France.

[20] *Op. cit.*, II, p. 345.

The empirical method, announced by Locke, and carried to its logical conclusion in one direction by Hume and in another by the French materialists, was thought to be an excellent instrument, so neatly did it shelve the Absolute, so effectively bring all values to the relative test, for undermining the theoretical foundations of the *ancien régime;* and, for this purpose, excellent it undoubtedly was: effective for purposes of criticism, but, for purposes of reconstruction, not so effective; and in truth Empiricism, so far from destroying the *ancien régime,* ended by intrenching it more firmly than ever. For the last word drawn from the premises of Locke in that century was that man and nature were one. But if man was only a part of nature, if all his action and all his thinking were determined by forces beyond his control, then "society" must be "natural" too; superstition was in that case as natural as enlightenment, the *ancien régime* in France no less a state of nature than primitive Gaul or second-century Rome. The identification of man and nature, and the conception of both as the necessary product of uniform natural law, had done nothing more after all than to put blind force in the place of God, and by eliminating purpose from the world leave men face to face with the *reductio ad absurdum* that "whatever is, is right."

A hopeless conclusion like this might satisfy a poet in search of resignation and an epigram; and in England, where most men, if not resigned, were fairly content with things as they found them, it was generally thought to be profound. In England, indeed, much keener men than Pope, if they were suspicious of the poet's epigram, were well satisfied with the philosopher's restatement of it in terms of relative utility, as Hume restated it: whatever is, is relatively good, because relatively useful, useful in relation to the conditions that produced it: a statement which in our day has been illumined, but not essentially changed, by the scientific law of survival and the results of historical research. This solution of the ethical problem was perhaps the only one possible from empirical premises; at least it is the one which would most naturally occur to one steeped in empirical philosophy of the time. But why, in that case, did it not occur to Diderot? One might almost say that it did. Diderot, curiously enough, was in some respects nearer the modern point of view than Hume. That utility was the test of virtue, he took for granted quite in the manner of Hume; he just failed of formulating the theory of evolution in terms of natural selection;[21] the idea of progress was ready to his hand; it remained only to combine these ideas, to interpret the philosophy of "perpetual flux" in the light of the resplendent theory of perfectibility, to have anticipated most of the characteristic political and ethical speculation of the nineteenth century. It may well be asked why after all there was any dilemma for Diderot? Since he was on the very frontier of the promised land, why did he not enter and possess it?

The answer must be sought in those social conditions which determine the drift of fruitful speculative thinking. In France men were not content with things as they found them. If the French "philosophers" were certain of anything, they were certain that the existing régime, so far from being best, was not even relatively good, but evil, and the parent of all evil. What they needed was a standard for judging society rather than a principle for explaining it. The overturning which men like Diderot dreamed of required some fixed and sure fulcrum not to be found in the shifting sands of relative utility. And so, in France, the

[21] Caro, *La fin du dix-huitième siècle*, I, p. 179.

Absolute, so contemptuously thrown out of the window early in the century, had to be brought in again, by some back stairs or other, at its close. To weigh the *ancien régime* in the balance and find it wanting, it was necessary to separate society from nature once more, to make a distinction between the natural and the artificial man, to disengage the abstract man, naturally good, from the tangled skein of temporary circumstance which made him bad.

It is well known that such a separation was effected by Rousseau: "man is born free, but is everywhere in chains," "naturally good, it is society which corrupts him,"—so ran the famous formula of the new dualism. But Rousseau cut the knot instead of untying it; and it is worth noting that many of those who denounced his methods were themselves seeking for some valid principle which would effect just this separation of the natural from the artificial man. It would be interesting to follow Diderot himself in the vain search for such a principle: his recurring interest in contrasting the sentiments of the savage with those of the civilized man; his attempt to find some instinct common to all men, such as pity, from which the social virtues might be derived; above all, perhaps, his desperate resolve, revealed in his correspondence with Falconet, to see in the lessons of history and in the judgments of posterity some standard, more or less absolute, by which the particular act, the concrete institution, might be judged:—what was all this but the effort to discover, as Kant said, "the constant elements in man's nature in order to understand what sort of perfection it is that befits him?"[22]

Few men, it is true, were philosophers enough to be troubled by the difficulty which Diderot never solved, and which Kant himself solved only with the aid of Rousseau.

[22] *Sämmtliche Werke*, II, p. 319. Quoted in Hoffding, *Hist. of Phil.*, II, p. 72.

To the unphilosophical person the difficulty presented itself in a less technical form. Many a "fervent soul," like Madame Roland, whose emotional nature had found abundant nourishment in the literature of Catholicism, renounced the harsh creed of the Church only to be chilled by the cold and barren rationalism of the very philosophers whose works had pointed the way to intellectual emancipation. "The atheist," said Madame Roland, "is seeking for a syllogism, while I am offering up my thanksgiving." "Helvetius hurt me," she says in another place. "He destroyed the most ravishing illusions, and showed me everywhere a mean and revolting self-interest. *I persuaded myself that he delineated mankind in the state to which it had been reduced by the corruption of society.*"[23] Here was a mind already attuned to the siren voice of the man whose over-topping egoism enabled him to credit himself with virtues which he regarded as natural, while charging his neighbors with vices which he felt had been thrust upon him by an artificial society. To direct Kant on the way to fruitful speculation in the rare upper regions of pure philosophy, and at the same time to inspire Madame Roland and her kind with an unquenchable faith in the fair destiny of humanity, required other talents than those which Diderot possessed.

1915

[23] *Works of Madame Roland*, II, pp. 108, 115.

John Jay and Peter Van Schaack

MAY 20, 1774, Gouverneur Morris wrote to John Penn a letter in which the following statement may be found:

Yesterday I was present at a grand division of the city, and there . . . my fellow citizens . . . fairly contended about the future forms of our government, whether it should be founded upon aristocratic or democratic principles. I stood in the balcony, and on my right hand were ranged all the people of property, with some few poor dependants, and on the other all the tradesmen. . . . The spirit of the English Constitution has yet a little influence left, and but a little. The remains of it, however, will give the wealthy people a superiority this time, but the mob begin to think and to reason. . . . The gentry begin to fear this. Their committee will be appointed, they will deceive the people, and again forfeit a share of their confidence. And if these instances of what with one side is policy, with the other perfidy, shall continue to increase, and become more frequent, farewell aristocracy.[1]

The reference is to the meeting at the Coffee House which confirmed the appointment of the committee known as the Committee of Fifty-one, of which the immediate occasion was the Boston Port Act, and of which the immediate effect was to place the direction of the popular movement largely in the hands of the conservative classes. Among the members of the Fifty-one were two young men who had not

[1] Jared Sparks, *Life of Gouverneur Morris*, I: 14-25.

hitherto taken any noticeable part in public affairs. These two men were John Jay and Peter Van Schaack.

Neither was of English descent, but both were thoroughly American. John Jay, descended from Huguenot ancestors exiled from France in the seventeenth century, was graduated from King's College in 1764 (upon which occasion he delivered a dissertation on the blessings of peace) and afterwards studied law with Benjamin Kissam, being admitted to the bar in 1768. In 1774 he was already known as a "hard reading" and successful lawyer, whose standing in the province is indicated by the fact that he had, in April, 1774, allied himself by marriage with the Livingston family. Peter Van Schaack was born at Kinderhook, of Dutch ancestry. He was also graduated from King's College. He also studied law, for some months with Peter Silvester at Albany but later with William Smith at New York, and in 1769 was admitted to the bar. While still at college he had married secretly the daughter of Henry Cruger, a wealthy merchant of New York. Frowned upon for some time by the irate father, he was afterwards forgiven; and in 1774, at the time of his appointment to the Committee of Fifty-one, he was, like Jay, a successful lawyer, and both by personal and professional ties associated with the "best families" of the province.

These two young men and intimate friends, whose careers were somewhat in the keeping of the colonial aristocracy, were well fitted both by temperament and conviction to represent the conservative interest. It was a favorite maxim of Jay's that "those who own the country ought to govern it."[2] From this safe principle, to which Van Schaack would doubtless have assented, it followed that, as the established government of the colony was

---

[2] Wm. Jay, *Life of John, Jay*, I: 70.

vested in the property-holders, the property-holders, and not the unfranchised mechanics and artisans who made the chief strength of the Sons of Liberty, should alone determine what steps it was right and expedient to take in opposition to the oppresive measures of the British Parliament. That these measures—Stamp Tax, Tea Act, Port Bill, and many others—were oppressive, destructive of that most fundamental of British rights, the right of property-owners to govern the country by representatives of their own choosing, both Jay and Van Schaack were profoundly convinced. They were fully prepared therefore to resist these measures in every way that was constitutional. But they were not willing to enter into any plan of resistance that was lawless, or that would tend to throw the control of the city into the hands of the mob, or that would be likely to lead to armed resistance or an irreparable breach with Great Britain. Neither political independence nor unquestioned submission to Parliamentary legislation made any part of their programme. If, on this 19th of May, 1774, they could have been required to choose, either unquestioned submission to Parliament or eight years of war with independence at the end of it, the chances are that they would have made the same choice and that that choice would have been for submission. Yet within three years Jay was classed as a British rebel, Van Schaack as a British loyalist; and in 1778 Jay was member of a committee that signed the decree of exile against his friend as a traitor to his country.

The conduct of these two young men makes an interesting study in political psychology and in historical interpretation. All the chances, seemingly, were in favor of their being found in the same camp. Van Schaack was as much attached to America (he returned after the war) as

Jay; Jay was no more opposed to the British measures than Van Schaack. The theory of economic self-interest as the basis of historical interpretation would neither lose nor gain in credibility if both men had sided with America or both with Britain; with equal complacence it would explain Jay as a loyalist or Van Schaack as a patriot. The difference cannot be explained on grounds of political or religious principles, because their principles were essentially the same, or on grounds of honesty, because both were men of the highest integrity. Something may be granted to the fact that by marriage Van Schaack was connected with the Delancey faction, while Jay was connected with the Livingston interest; something, but not much, for not all the Delanceys were loyalists nor all the Livingstons patriots. It is a case where the historian, seeking for causes, realizes that he must penetrate to those more subtle and impalpable influences, for the most part unconscious and emotional, which so largely determine motive and conduct. For such influences the sources are commonly slight; and this is peculiarly true in the present case. Neither Jay nor Van Schaack was much given to introspection; neither has left us precious letters or diaries, such, for example, as John Adams has, which by conscious or unconscious revelation enable us to observe those circumstances, often obscure and trivial, which are not infrequently of decisive importance.

Contemporaries may very well have noted obvious temperamental differences which are largely lost to us. It is likely that Jay was the more sanguine temperament. "I always endeavor," he writes to his wife, "to anticipate good instead of ill fortune, and find it turns to good account."[3] Van Schaack would doubtless have said the same of himself; but, if he possessed in a high degree, as his son tells us,

[3] H. P. Johnston, *ed.*, *Correspondence and Public Papers of John Jay*, I: 70.

the Christian virtues of charity and resignation, he may
well have been more disposed than Jay to anticipate good
fortune by "bearing the ills we have," and less disposed to
anticipate good fortune by "flying to others that we know
not of." We know at all events that Van Schaack was less
apt than Jay to attribute bad motives to the British government. As early as September, 1774, Jay spoke confidently of
England as having descended "to the ungrateful task of
forging chains for her friends and children"; while as late
as 1776 Van Schaack was affirming that the oppressive
measures "may have been passed without a preconcerted
plan of enslaving us, and it appears to me that the more
favorable construction ought ever to be put on the conduct
of our rulers."[4] Perhaps it was a slight difference in tem-
meramental bias, a difference in charitableness, a difference
in self-assertiveness, that led Van Schaack to give more
weight to the possible evils of war, that led Jay to give
more weight to the possible evils of submission.

One can imagine also that there was a certain preciseness
in Van Schaack, a certain awareness of small matters, a certain rigidity, that made it less easy for him than for Jay to
associate himself with others in a common cause, less easy
to ignore points of difference and to stress points of agreement for reasons of expediency. "Should the question be
asked, 'when are you going to Albany?' it would offend his
nice ear to receive for answer, 'I am going to Albany next
week,' when the two last words were all that was necessary
to give a complete answer to the question. Such an answer
unnecessarily repeating the question, he seemed to consider
disrespectful. He liked plain yes and no."[5] We are also told
that "his frequent criticisms of the inaccuracies of others

[4] *Ibid.*, I: 18; H. C. Van Schaack, *Life of Peter Van Schaack*, p. 56.
[5] H. C. Van Schaack, *Life of Peter Van Schaack*, pp. 455-56.

subjected him to the imputation of hypercriticism." A man possessed of so nice an ear, of a sensitiveness so easily offended, was not likely to breathe with the greatest comfort a revolutionary atmosphere. I can imagine him more often irritated than exhilarated after sitting through a session of the Committee of Fifty-one, and more likely, upon returning to his well-ordered and peaceful home, to meditate upon the irrelevance of his colleagues' speeches than upon the wisdom of subordinating his own carefully discriminated opinions to the practical necessity of "carrying on."

Jay was not, it is true, what one would call "hail fellow well met;" but he had, I should say, more than Van Schaack, what may be called the associating mind. He was probably more at home in a committee meeting, more likely to enjoy the process of reconciling conflicting opinions in order to reach an agreement in action, more disposed to accommodate his own opinions to the agreement thus reached. He had, like other men, his convictions and his principles, but there is little evidence in his early correspondence, much less than in the writings of Van Schaack, of their being the result of much careful thinking. The rounded and solemn commonplace is much in evidence in Jay's writings, such, for example, as the following: "The more the principles of government are investigated, the more it becomes apparent that those powers and those only should be annexed to each office and department, which properly belong to them."[6] I do not mean to say that Jay was in any sense a trimmer, but that he had the pragmatic mind, which easily shapes its thinking to the exigencies of action. "Promising theories," he says, "are not always confirmed by experience." He had

---

[6] *Speeches of the Different Governors of the State of New York*, (Albany, 1825), p. 49.

something of the practical man's contempt for theories, and much of the practical man's content with "the best that can be done under the circumstances."

Qualities such as these would mark Jay for leadership, especially in New York, where the situation called above all things for conciliation and compromise. For our purpose, in any case, it is important that, while the two men agreed in respect to the essential rights of America, Jay took a very active part, during the two critical years from 1774 to 1776, in determining what should be done, the part of Van Schaack being rather the passive acceptance of what was done. How Jay, like many another conservative, was carried on toward revolution by the complex pressure of events which he had himself helped to bring about, may be indicated by his attitude towards the famous Association of the first Continental Congress. The New York delegates, of whom Jay was one, were not pledged, as the radicals desired them to be, to work for non-intercourse measures.[7] It appears that at Philadelphia Jay was one of those who would have been satisfied to limit the action of Congress to protest and petition. It is known that he seconded the Galloway plan, and he must therefore have voted for it. But when the majority was found favorable to non-intercourse, Jay fell into line and signed the Association, probably not so much because he felt it to be altogether a wise measure as because he felt, like so many others, that any appearance of dissension would have a bad effect.

When the Congress adjourned, the practical question in New York, as elsewhere, was whether the Association should be put in operation. Not to execute it would clearly reveal to Britain a fatal lack of unity in the colonies; and

[7] Carl Becker, *Political Parties in the Province of New York*, p. 135.

what any man had to decide was whether the Association was so far unacceptable as to justify him in repudiating the Congress, and by so doing abandoning the conflict. Jay of course, having signed the Association, could not hesitate to approve its enforcement in New York; and most conservatives, including Van Schaack, felt that it ought to be enforced because they felt that Congress ought to be supported. But, having gone thus far, the conservatives were aware that, if the Association was to be carried into effect, it ought, precisely because it was a somewhat rash measure, to be carried into effect by moderate men. "I was surprised," Colden wrote[8] when he saw the list of the Committee of Sixty which was appointed to execute the Association, "to find such men joining with the committee. . . . I have at length discovered that they act with a view to protect the City from the ravages of the mob. For this purpose, they say, they are obliged to support the measures of the Congress; that if they did not the most dangerous men among us would take the lead: and under the pretense of executing the dictates of the Congress would ultimately throw the City into the most perilous situation."

There is little doubt that in supporting the Association, and in accepting positions on the Committee of Sixty, both Jay and Van Schaack were influenced by these motives. Whatever they thought of the Association in itself, they had now to regard it as an accomplished fact. But there was already this difference in the position of the two men: Jay, having been a delegate to the Congress and having signed the Association, was already responsible for the Association being an accomplished fact, while Van Schaack was not thus responsible. It was therefore much easier for the latter than for the former to view the whole situation

[8] Cadwallader Colden, *Letter Book*, II: 372.

objectively, as a judge, or as a spectator, of other men's decisions. Van Schaack was still, much more than Jay, in a position to consider the dispute between Great Britain and the colonies abstractly, as a question of what, precisely, were the rights of the colonies, of what, precisely, were the colonies legally justified in doing to maintain those rights. After all, the Association was not his doing. But Jay must have felt that the Association *was* his doing; and he was therefore every day much more under the pressure of justifying his own actions by seeing it through to a safe issue. His mind consequently could the less comfortably deal with the question of rights abstractly considered, but would rather be always seeking a reconciliation of the rights of his country with the measures he had himself pushed into the foreground for maintaining those rights.

This difference became more marked as time went on. In May, 1775, Jay went again to Philadelphia; and there, step by step, he found himself committed to all the vital decisions of the second Congress. Before the year was out, the man who had hesitated at adopting the Association was taking an active part in preparing the country to resist British measures by force of arms. Meantime, the position of Van Schaack was in the sharpest contrast to that of Jay. The month that Jay went to Philadelphia Van Schaack removed his family to Kinderhook, on account of ill health in his family, particularly perhaps on account of the illness of his eldest son, a promising lad of nine years who in fact died in July. A few days later the parents learned that their youngest son, whom, with his nurse, they were daily expecting from New York, had suddenly died and was already buried. Under these heavy afflictions Mrs. Van Schaack's health was further impaired and was the source of constant anxiety on the part of her husband until her death in 1778. As if to complete the measure of his troubles, Van Schaack had himself recently lost the use of one eye, and labored under the apprehension of total blindness.

For practising the Christian virtue of resignation, Van Schaack had in all this a sufficient opportunity. After the death of his two children, we find him seeking and finding consolation in religious faith. "We are incompetent judges of the ways of Providence," he writes.[9] "Not seeing the whole chain of things, we mistake good for evil, and evil for good;—the result of all which will be, that though we cannot unriddle, we shall learn to trust." Resignation to the will of God does not always lead to passive acceptance of the acts of men; but one can imagine that, sitting at Kinderhook under the shadow of many griefs, the wordy argumentation of Congress and the noisy demonstration of the Liberty Boys may well have struck Van Schaack as remote and somewhat irrelevant. The aspect of affairs at all events was not calculated to lift the depression that weighed down his spirits. "My mind is distressed with the gloomy prospect of my country," he writes.[10] "Such a spirit of anarchy . . . may prevail, as may prevent us from soon returning to the old channel, and that affection which is the bond of our common union with the mother country, may perhaps forever be destroyed." Naturally enough the distressed man longed to return to "the old channels." Apart from all other influences, his physical and spiritual isolation from the activities of his compatriots predisposed him to preserve that objectivity which was a native characteristic of his mind, and to assume that attitude of neutrality which determined his conduct throughout the war.

[9] H. C. Van Schaack, *Life of Peter Van Schaack*, p. 50.
[10] *Ibid.*, p. 38.

His detachment enabled him to look at the situation more and more as a spectator, and he judged it with remarkable penetration:

The article of *right* is almost out of the question, it turns altogether upon general *expedience*, and *policy;* for refined principles of government, applied to a case so peculiar, can have very little weight, when there is no common umpire to appeal to, when those who are to judge on both sides are parties, and when those parties are also the multitude. The opinion of the colonies is *fixed*. There are respectable individuals who think we ought to stipulate for a perpetual revenue, but the general current is the other way—and I think the better opinion is, that when the colonies are restored to their wonted good humor, they will occasionally contribute more largely than they would now (should they be compelled) stipulate for. It appears to me therefore, that this unhappy contest, so serious in its consequences, is maintained upon no better ground than a mere chimera—*vox et praeterea nihil.* . . . Upon the whole, there are doubtless errors on both sides; but a wise government will disarm itself of resentment and recrimination. A conflict between the different members of the same body politic, is too serious to be upheld for the sake of a punctilio.[11]

This was a way of saying that both parties had abandoned the test of reason, that each was prepared to impose its will upon the other by force. Van Schaack refused to abandon reason. He continued to be guided by what he regarded as the law and equity of the matter. He professed, as he had always professed, his allegiance to Great Britain; he claimed, as he had always claimed, that the British government had infringed certain clear rights of the colonies. He asserted, as he had always asserted: "Absolute *dependence* and *independence* are two extremes which I would avoid."[12] He therefore claimed the right to be neutral in

[11] *Ibid.*
[12] *Ibid.*, p. 57.

respect to the armed conflict, refusing to take the oath of allegiance to the Provincial Congress, yet refusing to give aid to Great Britain, nor ever putting any obstacle in the way of his countrymen in the prosecution of the war. He regarded himself as an American, politically subject to Great Britain. He admitted that Americans had serious grievances against the government. Some Americans, among them men of "the greatest ability and the soundest integrity," thought those grievances serious enough to justify armed resistance. That was their right, and Van Schaack agreed that "their measures should have a fair trial." What he refused to surrender was his own equal right to decide, for himself alone and for no other, whether it was his duty to take part in those measures.

For Jay, meanwhile, the "article of *right*" was indeed now largely out of the question. Sitting at Philadelphia in a responsible position, having by virtue of his own words and actions as it were given bail not to run away, sharing in great events and exhilarated by the sense of unselfish devotion to his country and of obstacles overcome in the service of human liberty, the situation could not well present itself to him otherwise than as a question of expedience, of policy. And the form in which this question presented itself most insistently was this: that, *if* the colonies should stand together as one man, and *if*, repudiating the idea of independence, they should nevertheless show themselves determined to defend, even by force of arms, their just rights, as those rights might be defined by Congress, why then Great Britain would surely back down in the end. In that case the great object, which every one desired, would be attained: they would turn out to have been, in the event, neither rebels nor slaves. In that case they would do precisely what Van Schaack wished to do—

they would avoid the two extremes of "absolute *dependence*
and *independence*."

But obviously the indispensable condition of this happy
event ever coming to pass was that Americans should all
stand together as one man; and this could not be unless
individuals were willing to give their opinions and conduct into the keeping of Congress. Men like Jay, every day
confronted with the immense difficulty of organizing a
united resistance, would instinctively thrust into the back-
ground of consciousness the question of what any individual might think the rights of his country to be, would
instinctively dwell upon the question of what it was the
duty of every individual to do for the welfare of his country.
Under the circumstances, it seemed clearly the duty of
every man to submit his will to the common will. For Jay
the situation no longer demanded of any man that he
should define his rights; it demanded of every man that
that he should declare his allegiance. "No one," he wrote
to Van Schaack some years later, "can serve two masters:
either Britain was right, and America wrong; or America
was right, and Britain wrong. They who thought Britain
right were bound to support her; and America had a just
claim to the services of those who approved her cause.
Hence it became our duty to take one side or the other."[13]
From the duty of the individual to support the state, it
was an easy step to the right of the state to compel obedience in the individual.

Van Schaack's reply to Jay is interesting. It was precisely his contention that neither Britain nor America was
wholly right or wholly wrong; precisely his contention
that he could therefore remain a good American and yet
refuse to support America in so far as he thought her wrong:

[13] Wm. Jay, *Life of John Jay*, I: 161.

I was actuated by no motive unfriendly to my country. . . . I can say, too, that my *wishes* were to have gone with you. The very appearance (and in my view of things it was appearance only) of taking part against my country distressed me in the extreme. Could it be for the sake of Great Britain that I could wish to sacrifice the welfare of my native country? My attachment to her (great indeed it was) was founded in the relation she stood in to America, and the happiness I conceived America derived from it: nor did it appear to me, from anything that had happened, that the connection was dissolved. Upon the whole, as ever in a doubtful case, I would rather be the patient sufferer, than run the risk of being the active aggressor; and as I should rather be even a figure for the hand of scorn to point its slow and moving finger at than to destroy the peace of my own mind, I concluded, rather than to support a cause I could not approve, to bear every distress that might result from the part I took; and if America is happier for the Revolution, I declare solemnly that I shall rejoice that the side I was on was the unsuccessful one.[14]

The phrase "the side I was on" is not strictly correct. Van Schaack was never, by his own will, on either side. The real issue between the two friends was indeed something more fundamental than the opposition of a man who supported Britain to a man who supported America. No personal antagonism divided them. Even during the war their fine friendship was preserved. It was no difference of opinion in respect to the rights of America, nor any difference in respect to love of native land, that put them asunder. The thing that came between them was an aspect of the venerable quarrel between "the One and the Many." Their case was a concrete example of the State versus the individual, of personal liberty versus social compulsion, of might versus right. "America is right," said Jay. But he identified "America" with the organized power wielded by govern-

---

[14] *Ibid.*, I: 163-64.

ment and affirmed the duty of the individual to bow in submission to this right which was might, or this might which was right. America is right, Van Schaack in substance replied, but only in so far as she can win the approval of Americans. I submit to the force which is the State, but I give my first allegiance to reason and conscience. He might have quoted Pascal: "It is necessary to follow that which is stronger; it is right to follow that which is just." In the end he was exiled, with Jay's approval, because he refused to place allegiance to the State above allegiance to his own conscience.

Whether, all things considered, Jay or Van Schaack was the better American, the better friend of mankind, who shall say?

1919

The Memoirs and the Letters of Madame Roland[1]

THE record of events, of what men have done, is relatively rich and informing. But a record of the state
of mind that conditioned those events, a record that
might enable us to analyze the complex of instincts and
emotions that lie behind the avowed purpose and the
formulated principle of action—such a record is largely
wanting. What one requires for such investigations are the
more personal writings—memoirs, and, above all, letters—
in which individuals consciously or unconsciously reveal
the hidden springs of conduct. In this kind of sources the
Revolution, otherwise so rich, is singularly poor. Memoirs
indeed there are, for the most part written years after the
event, to tell us what the author wished the world of that
day to regard him as having thought and felt in '93! But
if the memoirs, which are plentiful, are unreliable, the
letters, which might be reliable, scarcely exist. With one
exception, no person prominent in the Revolution has revealed the working of his mind in copious correspondence.
That one exception is Madame Roland.

I

The first extant letter of the precocious young girl,
Marie Jeanne Phlipon, was written in 1767 at the age of

[1] In this reprint all but a few of the references to the documents have been
omitted.

thirteen, but she did not begin to write regularly until three years later. Her first correspondents were the sisters Cannet of Amiens, whom she met, and with one of whom, Sophie, she formed an intimate girlhood friendship, during a brief retreat in the house of the Congregation of Notre Dame. In 1776 she met Roland, and after her marriage in 1780 the bulk of the letters are to her husband (he was much away from home until they moved to Paris), and to her friends Lanthenas, Bosc d'Antic, and Bancal des Issarts. The first published collection of Madame Roland's correspondence (the letters to Bancal) appeared in 1835. Two small volumes of the letters to the sisters Cannet appeared in 1841. Additional letters were published by Dauban in 1864 and 1867; and in 1896 Join-Lambert published a volume of the love-letters of Marie Phlipon and Roland. But the earlier collections have been largely superseded by the relatively complete and wholly admirable edition of the correspondence which Claude Perroud prepared for the *Collection de Documents Inedits*.[2] These four volumes, together with Perroud's edition of the love-letters,[3] contain practically all of the correspondence of Madame Roland—approximately one thousand letters, or an average of one letter each week (some of them very long indeed) for the twenty-three years from 1770 to 1793.

Madame Roland's famous *Mémoires*, written by stealth in prison, smuggled out *cahier* by *cahier* and deposited with friends, were first gathered and hastily published in 1795 by Bosc d'Antic.[4] Many subsequent editions of this popular

[2] *Lettres de Madame Roland*, 1780-1793, ed. Claude Perroud, 2 vols. (Paris, 1900-1902). *Lettres de Madame Roland*, nouvelle série, 1767-1780, ed. Claude Perroud (Paris, 1913-1915).

[3] *Roland et Marie Phlipon, Lettres d'Amour, 1777 à 1780* (Paris, 1900).

[4] *Appel à l'Impartiale Postérité, par la Citoyenne Roland, Femme du Ministre de l'Intérieur, ou Recueil des Écrits qu'elle a rédigés pendant sa Détention aux Prisons de l'Abbaye et de Sainte-Pélagie, imprimé au Profit de sa Fille Unique, privée de la Fortune de ses Père et Mère, dont les Biens sont toujours Séquestrés* (Paris, 1795).

work appeared during the nineteenth century; but, as in case of the letters, it was reserved to Perroud to prepare the definitive edition.[5] In one sense the memoirs are but a continuation of the letters, being themselves no more than a series of farewell epistles addressed to mankind—*appel à l'impartiale postérité*, as the author conceived them. They form thus a fitting close to a life chiefly devoted to self-revelation by means of correspondence. Besides the letters and the *Mémoires* Madame Roland wrote but little, and the outward events of her life, apart from the last brief months of furious adventure in revolution, were commonplace enough. Her career, her real career, was after all just this, to tell us copiously, day by day, what she did, what she thought and felt, above all what dreams she cherished in that imagined world of noble endeavor that she created as a compensation for the mean satisfactions which, to her thinking, were all that the real world commonly afforded. Neither the memoirs nor the letters are chiefly valuable as a record of outward events; but they are invaluable as a record of the working of a mind that was at once representative in quality and far above the average in power. It is rare indeed that the historian finds an intelligence so well documented as that of Madame Roland, rare that he comes upon so excellent an opportunity to study a mind in the making.

It can hardly be said that the most has been made of this rare opportunity, although critics and historians first and last have had a good deal, and a good deal that is admirable, to say about Madame Roland. The various editions of her memoirs and letters naturally called for more or less elaborate introductions by the editors, and furnished the occasion for some brilliant estimates by French critics.

[5] *Mémoires de Madame Roland*, ed. Claude Perroud, 2 vols. (Paris, 1905).

Sainte-Beuve contributed five essays, one of which served as an introduction to the volume of letters published in 1835.[6] The appearance of Dauban's edition of the memoirs in 1864 called forth a brilliant critique by Edmond Schérer,[7] and in 1896 René Doumic wrote a brief article in review of Join-Lambert's edition of the love-letters.[8] To this edition Join-Lambert himself contributed an introduction which is perhaps the most penetrating analysis of the personality of Madame Roland that exists. The innumerable works on the Revolution have of course all something to say about her; and there are works on certain subjects, such as Goncourt's *La Femme au XVIIIe Siècle*, and Gaudet's *Les Girondins*, which contain brief accounts of her life. The most notable biographies are Madeleine Clemenceau-Jaquemaire's *Madame Roland*, Ida Tarbell's *Madame Roland*, and Mrs. Pope-Hennessy's *Madame Roland: a Study in Revolution*.

These writers—editors, critics, and biographers—have had at their disposal the memoirs and at least some of the letters; but they have relied more upon the memoirs than upon the letters, and of the letters the earlier ones are those that have been most neglected. Yet the letters which Marie Phlipon wrote to Sophie Cannet (two volumes were in print as early as 1841) are of the highest value in two respects: they reveal, at least indirectly and with sufficient fullness, the emotional and instinctive influences that conditioned the rational thought of the young girl in her formative years; and they enable us to place Madame Roland's contemporary account of her life side by side with her recollection of it as she sat in prison under the

---

[6] *Portraits de Femmes*, pp. 165. 194; *Nouveaux Lundis*, VIII. 190.
[7] *Études sur la Littérature Contemporaine*, II.
[8] *Études sur la Littérature Française*, II.

shadow of the guillotine. The critics and biographers of Madame Roland have commonly taken the early letters at their face value, content with such factual information, slight indeed, as they yield. They have compared the letters and the memoirs, they have even noted certain slight inconsistencies; but finding that the letters and the memoirs commonly agree in their report of names, dates, and events, they have not thought it worth while to inquire further. This is well enough so far as the external events of Madame Roland's life are concerned; but in so far as Madame Roland is interesting for the way in which she thought rather than for what she thought, for the unconscious motives which determined her acts rather than for the acts themselves, a more careful comparison of the letters and the memoirs is the essential preliminary step.

II

Madame Roland said she had a good memory, and it is true. Considering that the memoirs must have been written without the aid of memoranda of any sort, one might expect them to be filled with inaccurate statements of fact relating to her early life. Such is not the case. A few trivial errors have been noted by Perroud; and H. Glagau, making a minute comparison of the memoirs and the letters in respect to Madame Roland's relations with Gerdane, discovered no more than a certain number of divergences of negligible importance.[10] But let it be said again (it will bear repeating) that neither the memoirs nor the letters are primarily concerned with events, since Madame Roland was not herself primarily interested in events. She was primarily interested in herself, in what she thought and felt, in justifying her thought and feeling to herself and to

[10] *Die Moderne Selbstbiographie* (1903), pp. 87-97.

posterity. She wrote the letters and the memoirs not so much to convey information as to satisfy a craving for self-expression, to let the world know that she would revenge herself by deserving a happiness which had been unjustly denied to her—"*Je me vengerai, à mériter le bonheur, de l'injustice qui m'en tiendrait privée.*[11] The memoirs and the letters are primarily concerned with Madame Roland's state of mind. It is accordingly in respect to their report of this state of mind that they need to be compared and collated.

The state of mind of the young Marie Jeanne Phlipon, dreaming of the great things she might do if she had not been born a woman, was naturally different from that of Madame Roland in prison, sitting by her window weeping. Yet it is not the sound of weeping that we hear in the memoirs. The note of self-pity is rarely present. There are indeed passages of splendid denunciation against the Jacobins, those scoundrels who had perverted the Revolution to base ends. But the prevailing note in the memoirs is one of sadness, of regret for what might have been. The memoirs are the expression of profound disillusionment, written by a woman condemned to watch the sacred Revolution fall away, as it seemed to her, into some incomprehensible *Walpurgisnacht* of bestial saturnalia.

Nowhere is this disillusionment more frankly confessed than in the following passage:

O Brutus! whose courageous hand vainly freed the corrupt Romans, we have erred as you did. These pure men whose ardent souls aspired to liberty, whom philosophy had prepared for it in the calm of the study and the austerity of seclusion—these men flattered themselves as you did that the overthrow of tyranny would forthwith bring in the reign of justice and peace; it was

[11] *Mémoires*, II, 159.

only the signal for releasing the most hateful passions and the most hideous vices. You said, after the proscription of the Triumvirs, that you were more ashamed of that which caused the death of Cicero than grieved by the death itself; you blamed your Roman friends for this, that they were made slaves more by their own fault than by that of the tyrants, and that they had the baseness to see and to suffer things the mere recital of which should have horrified them past endurance. It is thus that I grow indignant in the depths of my prison; but the hour for anger is past, for it is evident that it useless longer to expect anything good or to be astonished at anything evil.[12]

Madame Roland's disillusionment seems not to have followed immediately upon her arrest; and there is an apparent connection between the progress of her disillusionment and the writing of her memoirs. The memoirs fall into two parts. In one part (*Notices Historiques, Premier Ministère du Roland*, etc.) Madame Roland writes of the Revolution; in the other part (*Mémoires Particuliers*) she writes of her early life. The personal memoirs (*Mémoires Particuliers*), coming first chronologically, are in some editions printed first; but Perroud has shown that the historical notes and the account of Roland's ministry were for the most part written before the *Mémoires Particuliers*. This seems to mean that during the first months Madame Roland still looked forward to the triumph of the Girondins, and accordingly occupied herself with the present; but that later, losing all hope, she sought relief from the bitterness of the present by recalling the happier days of her youth.

That this was her reason for writing the personal memoires, Madame Roland leaves us in no doubt. "I propose to employ the leisure of my captivity," she says, "in tracing my private life from earliest youth to the present moment.

[12] *Mémoires*, II. 63.

Thus to follow again the course of one's career is like living a second time, and what better can one do in prison than *to transport one's existence elsewhere by a happy fiction or by interesting memories?*"[13] Here we may note once for all the motive, in its most inclusive form, that gives color and character to the personal memoirs. It was not from fear of death that Madame Roland sat by the window weeping, nor did she ever attempt to escape from prison. What made her weep was the overwhelming sense of futility, the realization that for her all the fair visions of life were phantoms. From this prison of spiritual disenchantment she did indeed endeavor to escape, and not without success, by writing her memoirs—by transporting her existence elsewhere, as she so happily expressed it, by renewing, as she says in another connection, "the tranquil moments of my sweet adolescence."

No doubt the moments of her youth, thus recalled, seemed to Madame Roland sweeter and more tranquil than they really were. This is nothing to marvel at, since distance lends enchantment to the view, particularly perhaps when the point of view is a prison cell. It is more important to note that in recalling her youth Madame Roland subtly reshaped her early opinions and sentiments. This she did, all unconsciously, because in writing the memoirs she sought, not only relief from the present, but support for the future. Now for Madame Roland sitting in prison the future, the future regarded as reality, was a very brief span ending in death. The fact that stared her in the face was that her brief revolutionary career would lead to the guillotine. Under the pressure of that fact it was necessary for the heroic woman to fortify her mind that she might make a good end. Madame Roland fortified her mind by

[13] *Ibid.*, II. 2.

idealizing that end, by regarding her death on the scaffold in the light of a supreme sacrifice on the altar of human liberty.

Since it would obviously be intolerable to think of this sacrifice as meaningless, Madame Roland endeavored to set it in the perspective of the centuries. She projected her expiation into history, where she could regard it as an event of more than personal or local significance, an event that coming generations might be disposed to record in humanity's great book of martyrdoms. Posterity, she was persuaded, would so regard it; posterity, that "other world of the philosopher" as Diderot said, would revenge her death by cherishing her memory. "Roland . . . ne mourra point dans la postérité; . . . et *moi aussi* j'aurai quelque existence dans la génération future."[14] She conceived of the memoirs themselves as an appeal to impartial posterity; under that significant title they were first published; and Bosc, in the preface to that edition, tells us that the "citoyenne Roland endeavored to find in the esteem of posterity the means of consoling herself for the injustice of contemporaries, and in future glory a compensation for her anticipated death." Thus Madame Roland transported her existence elsewhere, into the future—not, as it turned out, altogether in vain.

Yet into the past also it was necessary to transport her existence. Posterity would not be inclined to celebrate an accident; nor could Madame Roland herself see an adequate meaning in her expiation without regarding it as in some sense the work of a higher power—God, or the associated fates, or whatever beneficent moving forces might be supposed to concern themselves with human destiny. Then was not she also, like the martyrs of the past, an instrument of

[14] *Ibid.*, II, 141.

the universal purpose which in some inexplicable way had shaped her life to its predestined end? It was consoling to think so. "From the age of nine," she says, "I was aware of a destiny which I must prepare myself to fulfill." She even put this feeling in the form of an invocation, which from about the age of twenty, so at least she seemed to remember, was her only prayer: "O toi! qui m'as placée sur la terre, fais que j'y remplisse ma destination de la manière la plus conforme à ta volonté sainte et la plus convenable·au bien de mes frères!" At the time she did not indeed know what this destiny was to be; but when, as she sat in prison, it was revealed to her, her whole life unrolled before her, in recollection, as a kind of miraculous preparation for it. "Dans le siècle corrompu où je devais vivre et la Révolution que j'étais loin de prévoir, j'apportai de longue main tout ce qui devait me rendre capable de grands sacrifices et m'exposer à de grands malheurs. La mort ne sera plus pour moi que le terme des uns et des autres."

Thus Madame Roland, raising her expiation to the level of a cosmic event, became in her own eyes an instrument in the hands of God, a woman born to die for the liberation of mankind. Under the influence of this idea she wrote her memoirs. Inevitably, in recalling her past life, it seemed to her that she had always been a disciple of the faith for which she was about to suffer martyrdom; and all of the essential differences between the memoirs and the letters, with few exceptions, spring from this consoling illusion. In the memoirs we are led to suppose that from an early age Madame Roland was preoccupied with politics, that she had always been essentially, what she was in 1793, a pure republican soul, hating kings, despising *ces pitoyables anoblis*, instinctively preparing herself, perhaps even without knowing it, for her destiny, that Revolution which she could not foresee. The letters reveal to us, on the contrary, a woman who accepted the existing régime as a matter of course; a woman whose dissatisfaction with the world was the conventional one of desiring for herself a better place in it; a woman whose interest in politics, prior to 1789, was purely perfunctory, except indeed on the one occasion when she endured humiliations from the servants of the servants of royalty in order to obtain for her husband a title of nobility.

The parallel passages in the memoirs and the letters which reveal this contrast may be readily brought together and compared.

III

The impression that from an early age Madame Roland was politically minded is conveyed in the memoirs quite as much by subtle suggestions as by positive assertion. It not infrequently happens that an event or an incident, remembered correctly enough in itself, is recalled and related in a particular connection, a connection that gives to the event or incident a political significance which the letters do not lead us to suppose it had at the time.

An instance in point is the brief mention of Delolme. In a letter to Sophie Cannet, December 24, 1776, we read: "J'ai fait un petit extrait de l'ouvrage intéressant d'un Genevois sur la constitution d'Angleterre, monument curieux pour de yeux observateurs. Je pourrais t'en parler dans cette lettre; mais il faut à ce moment que je suive le goût libertin qui me porte à écrire sans suite," etc. In the memoirs the mention of Delolme plays a part in a quite different preoccupation. There she says that the dissoluteness of the court of Louis XV led her to ask whether such things could continue without a revolution. In contrast with the French she found the English less frivolous; and therefore: "je m'attachais à ces voisins; l'ouvrage de *Delolme* m'avait familiarisée avec leur constitution; je cherchais à connaitre leurs écrivains, et j'étudiais leur littérature." The contrast is illuminating, not for any difference in the statements of fact, but for the different implications. The young girl, Marie Phlipon, reading everything, came upon Delolme; and making extracts of everything, she made a brief extract of Delolme. But in the memoirs the reading of Delolme takes its appropriate place in a political preoccupation, and becomes, by implication, an act inspired by her interest in politics and the British constitution, instead of an act inspired by her interest in books and the making of extracts from them.

Another case in point has to do with the impression, which the memoirs convey, that Madame Roland was a republican long before the Revolution. The impression is indeed conveyed chiefly by numerous if unobtrusive phrases which imply more than they say. I do not find in the memoirs any passages in which Madame Roland says explicitly that she was a republican before 1789; what I do find are the following passages which contrive to convey the impression that she was. "It was from this time [the reading of Plutarch at the age of nine] that I received those impressions and ideas which were to make me a republican without my dreaming of becoming one." "I was enthusiastic for those republics where I encountered the greatest virtues to arouse my admiration, and men worthy of my esteem." "Everything united to inspire me with republican enthusiasm." "Plutarch had inclined me to become a republican." This same characteristic is well illustrated in the account of her visit to Madame de Boismorel, a passage often quoted to show Madame Roland's hatred of social distinctions. Witnessing the condescension with which

Madame de Boismorel treated her own *bonne maman* Rotisset on this occasion, she did not then ask herself why Madame de Boismorel should be superior, but "I had the sentiment which led to this reflection."

Instances such as these might be multiplied. Let us turn to the more important passages—those parallel passages in the memoirs and the letters which upon comparison yield a flagrant contradiction (at least superficially) in the sentiments and ideas expressed. There are not more than four or five, and they may all be given.

Take those first that relate to the exile and recall of the Parlements. In the memoirs we read: "From the beginning of the conflict between the Court and the Parlements my character and opinions led me to take the side of the latter; I procured all their remonstrances, and those pleased me most which expressed in the most vigorous form the most extreme opinions." From the point of view of 1793, that was no doubt what the young Manon should have done in 1771. But in fact the young Manon, in all her copious correspondence, mentions the exile of the Parlements only once, quite casually, at the end of a long letter to Sophie, September 15, 1771: "I have no news for you, at least unless you are still ignorant of the suppression of the Parlement of Toulouse—and its recreation, composed of some of the old members." Through two hundred pages we read on without finding further mention of the Parlements until their recall in 1774. Even then it was apparently only in response to Sophie's request for information that Manon deigned to give some account of the event. Her own comment on the affair is illuminating—the more so since it shows her to be in fact a disinterested defender of the king. A Prince ascending the throne under such critical circumstances could not well avoid this necessary and desired establishment.

Besides, what has he to fear from it? The Parlements are like old ruins which we still venerate, but they are no longer a barrier to royal authority; it is a cherished but impotent idol which must be restored to its adorers, since its presence consoles them.

This comment on the Parlements is really penetrating, far too just to have been made by a strong partisan who had read all the remonstrances and was most pleased by those which expressed the most extreme views. To be sure Manon rejoices—"As for me, I rejoice much." But the reasons for her joy are curiously unpolitical. "I rejoice much. Every universal sentiment affects me; and that which is a pleasure for the public seems to me should be a joy for the individual who finds his felicity in that of others and his happiness in that of his country." Evidently Manon was not much interested in the Parlements; she was interested in expressing opinions about them which seemed to her appropriate to a person of enlightened mind and lofty sentiment.

Much the same contrast appears in the passages which touch upon the state of French society at the close of the reign of Louis XV. In the memoirs we read:

The education which I had received, . . . the ideas acquired by study or social intercourse, all united to inspire me with republican enthusiasm, by making me see the absurdity or feel the injustice of innumerable preeminences and distinctions. Likewise, in my reading I sided passionately with the reformers of inequality; I was Agis and Cleomenes at Sparta, I was Gracchus at Rome. . . . When I witnessed those spectacles which the capital so often presented upon the entrance of the queen or the princes, . . . I sadly compared this Asiatic luxury, this insolent pomp, with the misery and servility of a brutalized people.

In the letters, apropos of distinctions, we read: "As for me, I think that, in a monarchy, it is essential to have authority and intermediate ranks, as well as a corporation to guard the laws." Manon had perhaps not thought much about the matter, but she had read Montesquieu. As to the quality of her republican enthusiasm, one may judge by the following passage:

The news of his (the king's) illness impressed me. . . . Although the obscurity of my birth, of my name, of my estate, seems to excuse me from interesting myself in the ruler, I feel, in spite of myself, that the general good touches me. My country is something to me. . . . How could it be indifferent to me? Nothing is so. I feel that my soul is a bit cosmopolitan; humanity and sentiment unite me to all that breathes; a Caribbean interests me, the fate of a Kafir touches me. Alexander sighed for new worlds to conquer; I would sigh for others to love, if I did not know of an Infinite Being capable of absorbing all my sentiments.

What can one say about this, except that it is a young girl's exercise in the expression of sentiments *à la philosophe?*

One other passage bears on the matter in hand. Late in September, 1774, Manon was taken by her mother and Mlle. d'Hannaches to Versailles, where they remained eight days to divert themselves, according to custom, with the spectacle of the court. In the memoirs, after describing the malodorous quarters in which they were lodged, Madame Roland recalls her impressions of this visit as follows:

I was not at all insensible to the effect of a great show, but it made me indignant to think that it had for its object to exalt a few individuals in no way remarkable in themselves and already too powerful. I liked better to look at the statues in the gardens than at the people in the chateau, and when my mother asked if I were content with our journey—"Yes," I replied, "provided it soon ends; a few more days and I shall detest the people I see to the point of not being able to contain my annoyance."—"But what harm do they do you?"—"At every moment they make me feel injustice and contemplate absurdity." I sighed to think of Athens,

where I could have equally enjoyed the fine arts without being
wounded with the spectacle of despotism; in imagination I walked
in Greece, I assisted at the Olympic games, and I grieved to find
myself a Frenchwoman. Impressed with everything which the
great age of the republics had presented to me, I overlooked the
troubles that disturbed them; I forgot the death of Socrates, the
exile of Aristides, the condemnation of Phocion. I did not know
that Heaven had destined me to be a witness of crimes similar to
those of which they were the victims, and to participate in the
glory of a persecution of the same kind, after having professed
their principles.

Such was the effect, as it seemed to the Girondin republican of 1793, which the spectacle of Versailles had
upon her mind at the age of twenty. The actual effect, if
we are to judge by a contemporary letter, was different:

I greatly enjoyed my stay at Versailles; it was a journey undertaken out of curiosity and for pleasure, and I, for my part, fully
realized those objects. With a little imagination and taste, it is
impossible not to be moved by the masterpieces of art. . . . And
when one is affected by the general welfare, one necessarily interests oneself in the persons who have so much influence upon it. If
I could have written to you from that place, I should have adopted
spontaneously the pleasant style which amuses you; the circumstances gave me the proper mood for it. . . . I cannot tell you how
what I saw makes me value my position and bless Heaven for
having given me obscure rank. You perhaps think this sentiment
founded upon the slight value I attribute to popularity and the
disadvantages that accompany high station? Not at all; it is
founded only on my character, which would be a nuisance to me
and to the state if I were placed close to the throne, because I
should be shocked by the extreme inequality which puts a barrier
between one individual and millions of people of the same species.
In my position I love my Prince because I do not much feel my
dependence; if I were too close to him I should hate his grandeur.

This disposition is not praiseworthy in a monarchy; when it appears in a person of rank and influence it is dangerous. With me it is of no importance, because the education of one in my station teaches me what I owe to the powerful, and makes me respect and cherish from a sense of duty and from reflection what I would not love naturally. . . . A beneficent king seems to me a being almost adorable, but if before being born I had been given my choice of a government, my character would have made me decide in favor of a republic; it is true I should have wished it constituted like none that now exists in Europe. I am very hard to please? It would then be necessary to change also the moment of my birth? The one would cost no more than the other. I think I see you laugh and count on your fingers the number of follies which this one makes when added to the others. But apropos of laughing, etc.

One does not gather from this passage that the spectacle of despotism disturbed Manon much. Nothing could be more conventional than the remark about "my Prince," or more in keeping with the spirit of the age than the expression of an academic preference for a republic.

But it is impossible, by the quotation of two or three extracts, to convey an adequate sense of Marie Phlipon's indifference to *res publica*. To comprehend this fully one must read *in extenso* these long and intimate letters. Veritable dissertations on life they are: literary exercises for the most part modelled on Rousseau or Madame de Sévigné; filled with the titles of books and with extracts from them; discussing with unflagging zest everything to be met with in literature, all the universal problems—man and nature, free will and determinism, the existence of the Supreme Being, the immortality of the soul, the wonders of the starry heavens above and of the human soul within us, the meaning of history, the uses of posterity, and the perfectibility of the human race. These interminable letters that touch upon everything in heaven and earth, *except* the deplorable state of French society; one must read them in order to realize that nothing was more remote from the interests of Marie Jeanne Phlipon than contemporary politics, that nothing disturbed her less than the absolutism of the reigning king or the inequity of existing social distinctions.

It would be odd perhaps were it not so, at the age of twenty. But Madame Roland retained this conventional point of view until the eve of the Revolution. After her marriage her indifference to politics could not indeed be quite complete, since her husband, as inspector of manufactures, was a government official; but, for that very reason doubtless, she was even less republican than before. From 1780 to 1789, if we may judge from the letters, Madame Roland was indeed the conventional good wife: less concerned than formerly with the universal problems posed in literature, more concerned with food and clothes and baby's milk; most of all concerned with her husband's success in his chosen career, very ambitious indeed for his advancement in a worldly way, quite prepared to believe that the king could do much to justify the existing régime by recognizing the undoubted merits of his inspectors of manufactures. In 1784 Roland had served faithfully for many years in this capacity. He had published monographs. His family in times past had borne titles of nobility which subsequently lapsed. Nothing seemed more obvious to his good wife than that he had earned retirement, a pension, and the restoration of his family to its former rank among the privileged.

Accordingly, in March of 1784, equipped with documentary evidence and with signed and sealed recommendations from the nobles of Beaujolais, Madame Roland went to Paris to solicit from Calonne, "le charmant roué," a title of nobility for her husband. There she remained until May; and the letters give us a vivid and humorous picture of the persistent and resourceful lady running about from office to office, waiting in antechambers, employing her graces upon lackeys and *femmes de chambre*, suffering herself to be bullied by minor officials, holding herself in while they sourly criticized her husband. And all for nothing so far as the title was concerned! But it presently appeared that a lucrative promotion might be obtained if—*if* Roland could be induced to accommodate his inflexible spirit to the humors of those intriguers, *Messieurs les Intendants*. "Above everything," Madame Roland implored her husband, "do not get angry in your letters, or else let me see them before you send them. You must not offend these people any more. Your pride is sufficiently well known, now show them your good nature. . . . My dear, these people are not so bad. They were ruffled, and the dryness of your style has done all the harm in making them think that you have a terrible disposition and intolerable pretensions. I assure you they can be managed."

The character of Madame Roland's interest in politics in 1784 may be judged from this episode. She was as yet far from the pure republican soul that penned the famous letter to Louis XVI in 1792. In 1793, inevitably, the enemies of Roland charged him with the crime of having aspired to a title of nobility; and Madame Roland, writing her memoirs in prison, felt that it was necessary to defend him. Her defense must have sounded feeble in her own ears, although for us it is adequate enough: "I do not know any one who, at that time and in his situation, would have thought it imprudent to act as he did." This is indeed the exact truth. In 1784 it did not occur to Roland, still less to

Madame Roland, that there was anything in their situation
or in their political opinions which made it incongruous
for them to solicit a title of nobility from a despotic
government. And in fact there was nothing.

The transformation of Madame Roland the conventional
philosophe into Madame Roland the militant *politique* was,
apparently, accomplished within the brief period of a few
months. One can not pronounce too confidently on this
point because she wrote relatively few letters during the
crucial years 1788-1789, or at least relatively few letters
have been preserved. Such as we have indicate that she
was only mildly excited by the pamphlet controversy between Calonne and Necker, or by the struggle between
Brienne and the Parlements. She sided with the Parlements
and regarded their recall as desirable; and, like most
friends of liberty, she was disappointed when the Parlements demanded the calling of the States General, organized according to the forms of 1614. And yet between
November, 1788, and June, 1789, Madame Roland wrote
nine letters to Bosc at Paris, in none of which, so far as
they have been preserved, is there any mention of the exciting events of the time—the calling of the Estates, the
elections, the opening of the Estates, the quarrel of the
orders over the verification of credentials.

Was it then during the famous days of July 12-17 that
Madame Roland the revolutionist first appears? It is impossible to say for sure, since there are no letters at all between June 9 and July 26. But at all events in the letter of
July 26, the first letter after the taking of the Bastille, we
recognize clearly, and for the first time, the Madame
Roland of the Revolution, the Girondin republican whom
we know so well.

No, you are not free; no one is yet. Public confidence is betrayed; letters are intercepted. You complain of my silence, I write you by every post. It is true that I no longer write of our personal affairs: where is the traitor who to-day has other affairs than those of the nation? It is true that I have written you more vigorously than you have acted; if you are not careful you will have made nothing but a vain gesture. . . . You are only children; your enthusiasm is only a flash in the pan; and if the National Assembly does not bring to trial two illustrious personages . . . you are all done for. If this letter does not reach you, let the poltroons who read it blush to recall that it was written by a woman, and tremble to think that she can make a hundred enthusiasts, who in turn will make millions more.

This is indeed a new manner—the temper and the language of '93.

Madame Roland was now thirty-five years old. Up to this time she had been the typical *philosophe*, loving her prince and knowing what was due to those in high station, the conventional good wife, ambitious for her husband's advancement in his chosen career. What was it that so quickly, within a few months at the most, transformed her into the passionate *politique*, the uncompromising revolutionist?

IV

This question could not be adequately answered without sketching the mental history of Madame Roland as it is revealed, or perhaps one should say concealed, in her correspondence. Such an enterprise would carry us too far afield and is in any case not essential to the present enquiry, which is concerned with the letters and the memoirs as historical sources. On that theme something remains to be said—something which, although it is not intended to supply an explanation of Madame Roland's sudden political conversion, may perhaps suggest the point of departure which would lead to one.

Hitherto, in comparing the memoirs and the letters, I have been concerned to point out certain differences between them. The differences are not unimportant; but the points in which the memoirs and the letters differ are more superficial and less important than the points in which they are alike. The memoirs and the letters differ in this, that they give us inconsistent reports of what Madame Roland thought at a given time about a given matter; but the characteristic mental process which enables us to understand how she came to give these inconsistent reports is the same in both cases. It is in this characteristic mental process, which so largely determined the ideas and the activities of Madame Roland, rather than in the ideas and the activities themselves, that the essential integrity of her personality is to be found.

Madame Roland possessed, in a quite unusual degree, an instinct which all men have in some measure—the disposition to withdraw from a real world which offers no adequate opportunity for action into an imagined world molded closer to the heart's desire. It was thus, as we have seen, that she effected an escape from prison—by "transporting existence elsewhere through a happy fiction or interesting memories." But it was not in prison alone that Madame Roland was engaged in transporting her existence elsewhere by a happy fiction. On the contrary, she was so constantly engaged in doing this throughout her life that it may be said to have been her chief occupation. She was a dramatist who created one great character, designed to play a noble part on a great stage. The character was Madame Roland, the stage was the world as it should have been. It

is in the memoirs and the letters alike that we meet this
character and follow this play.

The young Marie Phlipon, who at nine years of age
carried Plutarch to church in place of a prayer book and
before she was eighteen had read and assimilated the best
ancient and modern writers, must inevitably have possessed, from an early age, a lively sense of her own superiority to the lower-middle-class station in which she was
born. The stuffy apartment of an engraver doing a small
business near the Pont Neuf was obviously no adequate
theatre for displaying the talents of a young woman who
communed familiarly with the saints and sages of the
world, and who never read of "a single act of courage or
virtue" without feeling herself capable of imitating it
under similar circumstances. Had she been Regulus, she too
would have returned to Carthage; had she been Socrates,
she would have drunk the hemlock. Neither opportunity
was likely to come to her on the Pont Neuf. "More than
once," she said (and she said it more than once), "I wept
in vexation at not being born a Spartan or a Roman." What
she really wanted no doubt was not especially to be a
Spartan or a Roman, but to be somebody, anybody. What
she wanted was an adequate opportunity for the real exercise of her irrepressible energies, the real employment of
her extraordinary intelligence, the real expression of her
profoundly egoistic and ambitious nature. Since the real
world did not offer this opportunity, she constructed an
imaginary world in which she could play her part, and
that not a sad or ignoble one.

In an illuminating letter, written at the age of twenty-
one, the young girl revealed her secret in a pregnant sentence. "*Placed in a situation in which I can think more than I can
act, I persuade myself that I ought to busy myself in perfecting my*

being, not being able to do much for others." To perfect her being
was indeed Madame Roland's occupation. But where could
this perfected being move and speak and act the part?
Where could she converse with those who would understand her, where do heroic deeds or make sacrifices that
would not go unregarded or unacclaimed? Not, apparently,
in the real world of Paris. But in the world of history and
romance, in the world of Plutarch and Jean Jacques, in the
over-world of the imagination—there was a world where
others might see her as she saw herself. "I confess," she
wrote to Roland, "that in reading a romance or a play I
have never been much attracted by the minor parts. . . .
In studying history I am far from having for fine traits and
great actions that pure and cold admiration which I perceive most people have. The description of good acts performed by my fellows touched me, penetrated me with
tenderness and pleasure; it made me feel better in my own
eyes, because it awakened in me a confidence that I could
do as much, and regret at not being in the same situation
as those who have thus acted." Madame Roland could
never take the second place. But in the real world there was
no other place for her to take, a circumstance which constrained her to be ever engaged in idealizing the brute fact,
reshaping the outward world in decent conformity to an
imagined world in which she need never be condemned to
assume a minor rôle.

It is in exhibiting this characteristic mental process
that the memoirs and the letters are alike, and alike valuable. If one asks, therefore, which is the true Madame
Roland, the Madame Roland of the letters or the Madame
Roland of the memoirs, the answer is both and neither:
neither, in the sense that the letters no less than the memoirs give us the portrait of Madame Roland as she wished

to appear, an idealized portrait; both, in the sense that by virtue of always thinking of herself as that idealized person, by resolutely and persistently living up to it, she ends by becoming in no small measure that person.

The point may be conveniently illustrated by taking an incident already noted—the visit to Versailles. In the memoirs Madame Roland tells us that on that occasion she was wounded by the spectacle of despotism, shocked by the corruption of the court, indignant at the thought of the inequity of social distinctions. In the letters she tells us that she was amused by the spectacle, which led her to reflect that she loved her prince, knew what was owing to those in high place, and that whereas if the choice had been offered her she would have chosen to live in a republic, she nevertheless regarded a beneficent king as almost adorable. Which are the real sentiments and ideas of the real Marie Jeanne, those recorded in the letters or those recorded in the memoirs?

Those recorded in the letters undoubtedly, one is disposed on first thought to answer. But when I consider more curiously (I hope it will not be thought too curiously), I confess that such an answer seems inadequate, not indeed because the statements in the letters are unsupported "by the testimony of two independent witnesses not self-deceived," but because it is extremely difficult to disengage the real Marie Jeanne, if there was such a person, from the ideal Marie Jeanne, of whose existence there can be no reasonable doubt. It is of course possible, even probable, that the real Marie Jeanne was, as she says in the letters, thoroughly amused by the spectacle at Versailles. Yet is it not possible that the real Marie Jeanne was, as she says in the memoirs, profoundly shocked by the spectacle at Versailles—shocked, that is, until she reflected that when she

wrote to her friend Sophie about her visit the ideal Marie
Jeanne would certainly wish to write about it in the light
and witty and sophisticated tone of Madame de Sévigné?
The result of this reflection may well have been that the
real Marie Jeanne forthwith ceased to be shocked and became amused; or it may be only that, as a result of this
reflection, the real Marie Jeanne was forthwith transformed
into the ideal Marie Jeanne. I cannot say. Nor can I say
whether all of those ingenious reflections about republics
and princes, which we find set down in the letters and attributed to the real Marie Jeanne, were directly inspired in
the real Marie Jeanne by the spectacle at Versailles, or
whether they were inspired by the *idea* that these were the
kind of reflections that such a spectacle should properly
give rise to in the mind of the ideal Marie Jeanne—that is
to say, in the mind of a young woman whose soul was
"a bit cosmopolitan," a woman of taste and sentiment who
had read the best authors and who would naturally be inclined, by virtue of having emancipated herself from provincial prejudices, to look down upon the human scene
with the detached and amused curiosity of a true *philosophe*.

In any case what of all this is nature and what art? Is it
possible to separate the spectacle of Versailles from the
idea of it in the mind of the observer? Above all where does
the real Marie Jeanne end and the ideal Marie Jeanne begin? Difficult to say. If Madame Roland had been able on
occasion to stand off and take an objective survey of what
was going on at the moment in her own mind it would
have helped much. This she never, or very rarely, did. She
was too intent on "perfecting her own being," too much
concerned, when confronted with men and things, to note
the effect which they should properly have on the character
she was engaged in creating, ever to tell us quite, if indeed

she ever knew, how the men and things really struck her, or might have struck her if she had been content to be herself. Between Madame Roland and the outward world there was commonly interposed a carefully created character, an ideal self which intercepted and transformed first impressions, and which again intercepted, and as it were relayed, the resulting impulse to action. Neither the ideas nor the conduct of Madame Roland (as, for example, her sudden espousal of the Revolution in 1789) can be well understood without taking careful account of this created character, this very real if somewhat intangible ideal self. It may indeed very well be that this created ideal character became, as time passed, more and more, and at last altogether, the real Madame Roland. We shall be apt to think so on November 8, 1793, as we follow her slow-moving tumbril to the Place de la Révolution and note the courage with which she mounts the scaffold, the high disdain with which she looks down upon the wolfish mob below or lifts unflinching eyes to the poised and relentless knife.

1928.

QUADRANGLE PAPERBACKS

History

Frederick Lewis Allen. *The Lords of Creation.* QP35
Lewis Atherton. *Main Street on the Middle Border.* QP36
Thomas A. Bailey. *Woodrow Wilson and the Lost Peace.* QP1
Thomas A. Bailey. *Woodrow Wilson and the Great Betrayal.* QP2
Charles A. Beard. *The Idea of National Interest.* QP27
Carl L. Becker. *Everyman His Own Historian.* QP33
Ray A. Billington. *The Protestant Crusade.* QP12
John Chamberlain. *Farewell to Reform.* QP19
Chester McArthur Destler. *American Radicalism, 1865-1901.* QP30
Elisha P. Douglass. *Rebels and Democrats.* QP26
Herman Finer. *Road to Reaction.* QP5
Felix Frankfurter. *The Commerce Clause.* QP16
Lloyd C. Gardner. *A Different Frontier.* QP32
Ray Ginger. *Altgeld's America.* QP21
Louis Joughin and Edmund M. Morgan. *The Legacy of Sacco and Vanzetti.* QP7
Edward Chase Kirkland. *Dream and Thought in the Business Community, 1860-1900.* QP11
Adrienne Koch. *The Philosophy of Thomas Jefferson.* QP17
Walter LaFeber. *John Quincy Adams and American Continental Empire.* QP23
David E. Lilienthal. *TVA: Democracy on the March.* QP28
Arthur S. Link. *Wilson the Diplomatist.* QP18
Huey P. Long. *Every Man a King.* QP8
Gene M. Lyons. *America: Purpose and Power.* QP24
Jackson Turner Main. *The Antifederalists.* QP14
Ernest R. May. *The World War and American Isolation, 1914-1917.* QP29
Henry F. May. *The End of American Innocence.* QP9
George E. Mowry. *The California Progressives.* QP6
Frank L. Owsley. *Plain Folk of the Old South.* QP22
David Graham Phillips. *The Treason of the Senate.* QP20
Julius W. Pratt. *Expansionists of 1898.* QP15
Richard W. Van Alstyne. *The Rising American Empire.* QP25
Willard M. Wallace. *Appeal to Arms.* QP10
Norman Ware. *The Industrial Worker, 1840-1860.* QP13
Albert K. Weinberg. *Manifest Destiny.* QP3
Bernard A. Weisberger. *They Gathered at the River.* QP37
Bell I. Wiley. *The Plain People of the Confederacy.* QP4
William Appleman Williams. *The Contours of American History.* QP34
Esmond Wright. *Causes and Consequences of the American Revolution.* QP31

Philosophy

James M. Edie. *An Invitation to Phenomenology.* QP103
George L. Kline. *European Philosophy Today.* QP102
Pierre Thévenaz. *What Is Phenomenology?* QP101

Social Science

George and Eunice Grier. *Equality and Beyond.* QP204
David Mitrany. *A Working Peace System.* QP205
Martin Oppenheimer and George Lakey. *A Manual for Direct Action.* QP202
Erwin A. Salk. *A Layman's Guide to Negro History.* QP206
Egon Schwelb. *Human Rights and the International Community.* QP203
Clarence Senior. *The Puerto Ricans.* QP201

Carl L. Becker

EVERYMAN HIS OWN HISTORIAN

Essays on History and Politics

The seasoned essays of one of the most important historians of our times, including the famous pieces on "Kansas," "The Spirit of '76," and "Frederick Jackson Turner."

"As an historian of ideas, Professor Becker not only deals with his materials in an important way, but also writes with a charm that cannot fail to delight his readers."—*American Political Science Review*

"In these . . . essays, so full of tolerance and warm, human sympathies, essays characterized by penetrating logic that somehow never binds his mind, Mr. Becker has taken a stand for definite human values as well as for a definite attitude toward our craft . . . No reflecting mind can put it lightly aside."—MERLE CURTI, *American Historical Review*

"Professor Becker is one of the most readable, as well as one of the most scholarly, of historians."—*Christian Century*

COVER DESIGN BY STU GROSS

A QUADRANGLE PAPERBACK published by Quadrangle Books/Chicago

Sewn-bound for durability